BULLETS, BOMBS AND FAST TALK

Related Titles from Potomac Books

BULLETS, BOMBS AND FAST TALK

TWENTY-FIVE YEARS OF FBI WAR STORIES

James Botting

Potomac Books, Inc.
Washington, DC

Power grows out of the barrel of a gun.
- Mao Tse-Tung

Library of Congress Cataloging-in-Publication Data
Botting, James.
  Bullets, bombs, and fast talk : twenty-five years of FBI war stories / James
Botting. — 1st ed.
      p. cm.
  Includes bibliographical references.
  ISBN 978-1-59797-244-4 (hardcover : alk. paper)
  1. Botting, James. 2. United States. Federal Bureau of Investigation—
Biography. 3. Hostage negotiations—United States. 4. Police—United
States—Biography. I. Title.
  HV7911.B68A3 2009
  363.25092—dc22
  [B]
                              2008023619

(alk. paper)

Printed in the United States of America on acid-free paper that meets the
American National Standards Institute Z39-48 Standard.

Potomac Books, Inc.
22841 Quicksilver Drive
Dulles, Virginia 20166

First Edition

10 9 8 7 6 5 4 3 2 1

CONTENTS

ACKNOWLEGMENTS

Without the unwavering encouragement, support, and understanding of my wife, Robbin, this project would never have been finished. She has remained my loyal supporter and loving partner through all the challenges we've faced together over the years. This project started as something to leave for my children, Jason, Erin, and Christine, as some kind of explanation of what their father did when he disappeared in the middle of the night and left without an explanation or apology. I hope that they will forgive me for all the school plays, and the baseball, football, and soccer games that I missed and someday understand the call of the FBI. I love you all more than you know.

I am also extremely grateful to those in the FBI who gave me the opportunity to experience the challenges, the excitement, and the satisfaction of being a Special Agent, especially my former partner and mentor, Joe Alston, who saw something in me worth cultivating and who gave me a chance to learn from the best the FBI had.

I am especially appreciative of the assistance of Potomac Books editors Kevin Cuddihy, Don McKeon, and Jennifer Waldrop, who guided me through this process with encouragement, experience, professionalism, and most of all patience.

I relied upon numerous Special Agents of the FBI for the details of various incidents, as well as their comments and suggestions. Among them are Nick Boone, Regis Boyle, Ralph DiFonzo, Bill Elwell, Scott Hanley, Ron Iden, Kevin Kelly, Fred Lanceley, Richard Noyes, Jan Wilhelm, Jim Wilkins, and Mark Wilson.

Without the optimism and encouragement of Karl Pohrt, Stuart Abraham, and my brother Dennis Botting, who saw the potential for me to share these stories with others, this book would never have found its way to a publisher.

Lastly, this book is dedicated to all the hostage negotiators out there who are committed to the nonviolent resolution of the many human conflicts that too often require our intervention. You have saved thousands of lives. Keep on doing so.

A portion of the proceeds of this book will be donated to the Foundation of the Society of Former Special Agents of the FBI for distribution to the families and children of those agents who have lost their lives in the performance of duty.

AUTHOR'S NOTE

Many of the facts, dates, times, and direct quotations of dialogue are from official reports, personal notes, memos, and conversations as I recall them or as they were conveyed to me by those present. At all times, the re-creation of events was done as accurately as possible. Hopefully, those depicted in this book will find their portrayals to be fair.

The opinions, observations, and comments expressed in this book are those of the author only and do not necessarily reflect those of the Federal Bureau of Investigation. Furthermore, they may not reflect those of the editors, endorsers, publisher, FBI Special Agents, and other persons who are described in this book.

PROLOGUE

FBI profiler Ken Lanning and I stood outside Al's Market on Florence Avenue in Inglewood witnessing a West Coast version of *Dog Day Afternoon*. Al Pacino had nothing on these two mopes. A couple of local stickup guys had held up the market in a strip mall in the south LA suburb and got jammed inside when the cops who got the call were right around the corner. One look at the black-and-white skidding into the driveway as they tried to flee out the front door and they put on the brakes. They backed into the market and grabbed three employees hostage. That was about 11 PM last night.

Now it was about 8:30 AM and the cops that had been there all night were real tired of playing this game. Hypoglycemia had begun to set in and fur was starting to grow on their teeth. Lanning and I were fresh faces and the cops looked at us in desperation. We'd come down to offer any assistance the federal government could give. The locals always thought the feds had deep pockets. In truth, we were often just as pinched for funds as they were. But it was mostly just moral support they needed.

Shortly after our arrival one of the robbers, his confidence fueled by the bottle of Popov he held in one hand and the large chrome-plated semi-automatic pistol in the other, walked to the front door of the market. Ken and I watched as he paraded in front of the entrance and taunted the SWAT officers forming the perimeter. We held our breath knowing that the snipers lying up on the roof across from the market must be lining up the crosshairs on their rifles.

And then, after a few minutes of a poor Michael Jackson moon walk, he pointed the bottle at the nearest cop and took a long drag, casually turned his back on them all, and swaggered back into the store. Ken and I couldn't believe the balls of this guy.

We had brought a new microphone down to the scene, which the SWAT guys had inserted into an air duct on the roof. For the last hour we had been sitting in the command post entertained by their conversation. The two of them were arguing about how to get "outta this mutha-fucker and back to the hood." It was like listening to fourth graders making up rules for dodgeball. It would have been more humorous if they didn't have hostages. Listening to them now worried us that they might get stumped and do something foolish—like shoot up the place and kill the hostages.

The microphone had worked fine until one of the robbers turned on the overhead fan, which clipped off the wire. We could only guess their reaction as the mike dropped onto the floor in front of them. We were also concerned that, without a search warrant, the mike could be construed to be an illegal interception of communications—that in the twisted mind of some liberal-ass judge a hostage taker had some expectation of privacy. No one would indict us for that, right? Well, maybe. But as a law enforcement officer, you can get a real uncomfortable feeling thinking about becoming a defendant.

We had been using a small carryout chicken joint in the strip mall as a command post and the front entry was filled with cops milling around and bumping into each other. The negotiators had set up camp in the kitchen next to the deep fryer. It was total chaos and claustrophobia.

Periodically, a tall skinny black guy with long stringy Jheri curls would speculate on what the robbers were probably thinking and planning to do. Everyone would stop what they were doing to listen. The negotiator, an overstuffed senior member of the drug squad wearing a shoulder holster and a

"Wild Turkey" t-shirt, would put the crooks on hold and cover the mouthpiece. Even the SWAT team leader would walk over to listen.

After two or three times, I asked one of the officers who he was. He laughed, "He's the guy who owns this chicken joint."

Jesus, the world of law enforcement is stopping to listen to Chicken Man! And then it occurred to me that he probably knew a helluva lot more about what these guys were thinking than we did.

Suddenly, it finally happened. After twelve hours, as if they had just experienced an epiphany, the two guys agreed to surrender. They were finished. It was over. They were coming out—but only if "Wild Turkey" would meet them at the front door of the market. No SWAT guys. Without a hesitation, the negotiator agreed, slipped out of his holster and handed his weapon to another officer. He threw on a bulletproof vest and rushed out to the front door of the market.

And out they came, hands held high. An empty-handed Mr. Popov came first. They dropped to the pavement and proned out like dead tuna. It was finally over. There were handshakes and backslapping all around, and everyone lined up to congratulate the silver-tongued Wild Turkey for his success. Even Chicken Man chimed in with, "Yo, y'all done good, dude," as he shook Wild Turkey's hand.

The crowd held back at the street behind the police tape cheered the cops' success and the peaceful outcome.

I was hooked. I'd found my career as a hostage negotiator.

I'd later join the best the Bureau had; but it wasn't going to happen overnight.

CHAPTER 1

"JUST A GODDAMN YANKEE"

It was 1971, one of those miserable, humid, Mississippi days in August when the mosquitoes get up early and the sweat trickles down the middle of your back before you even pull out of the driveway in the morning. I was a rookie FBI agent assigned to the Resident Agency in Oxford, in the northwestern part of the state. A fellow agent, Ken Hughes, and I were sitting in the kitchen of the county sheriff's office discussing our plans for the day. In this county, you stopped by the sheriff's office to say hello and tell him what you were planning to do. That's the way it was in Mississippi back then even if you were the FBI. You didn't mess with the county sheriff.

The sheriff offered us breakfast, but I could never eat anything in a jail thinking about what the trustees in the kitchen could put in it. And the smell of burned bacon was starting to make me nauseous. Every sheriff's office in Mississippi always smelled like burned bacon.

As a huge black trustee with ripples in the back of his neck brought us a second cup of coffee, the sheriff turned to Ken. He was short and muscular, about as wide as he was tall, and when he shook your hand he stared you in the eye and squeezed it like he was trying to force blood out of your eyes. If you relaxed your grip he'd laugh and clamp on tighter.

"Ah, Ken, we got us a prisoner out back I'd like you to help us interview."

Ken eyed the sheriff cautiously, "Oh yeah?"

"Yeah, he says he's a traveling preacher man, but, ah, we don't think so 'cause he's got a shit load of them girlie books in the trunk of his car."

We all laughed.

"When did you pick him up?"

"'Bout a week ago," the sheriff said. "Passed out drunk in his car in the back parking lot of the Jitney Jungle." The Jitney Jungle was a local grocery chain primarily patronized by blacks. "Now what the hell would a cracker like him be doing over there?"

A week ago? He hadn't been interviewed or charged with a crime or even gone to court yet? My Mississippi education was beginning.

"What'd you arrest him for?"

The sheriff grinned and hesitated. Then after a few seconds, he snorted. "J.D.L.R."

Both he and Ken laughed. Ken looked at me, "Know what he means?"

I racked my brain trying to remember my legal training in the FBI Academy but was embarrassed to admit that I couldn't recall. I shook my head, trying not to feel stupid.

They both laughed again.

"Another goddamn Yankee, Ken," the sheriff said, looking at me and shaking his head. "At least he ain't a Jew boy from New York like the last one you brought around." He grinned at me, pleased with himself. Years of chewing Red Man had done its job and he needed some serious dental work. His breath could have started a fire.

"J.D.L.R.," he chuckled again. He looked from Ken to me with small blue pig eyes rimmed in red. I suspected he could be meaner than a snake.

"Okay, what's 'J.D.L.R.'?"

He hesitated, looked over at Ken and then back at me, and suddenly spit it out.

"Jes' Doan' Look Right."

We all laughed, although I couldn't believe his prisoner had been in the county jail for a week just because he didn't "look right." After Ken and I stopped laughing, we waited for a while for the sheriff to stop.

For several minutes, the sheriff tried to convince Ken that the prisoner had probably transported pornography interstate, which would be a federal crime and could justify the FBI getting involved. But Ken was wary of becoming involved in local jurisdiction cases, especially those with questionable arrests, interrogations, and searches. He politely but firmly refused to get involved and the sheriff finally relented.

"Okay, what the hell, then we'll just charge him with disorderly conduct or somethin'," he said. "Get the judge in here, Leonard," he called to the trustee. "We'll throw his perverted ass outta the county."

With that Leonard walked out to the front porch of the office and woke up a wizened old man in bib overalls sleeping in a rocker under a tired sign that read "Sheriff's Office." With caution and obvious respect, the huge black trustee awakened the Justice of the Peace gently and spoke a few words to him. The old man opened his eyes, focused his vision, straightened his hat, and began to slide out of the rocker. With great effort but refusing assistance from the trustee, he stood erect, gradually turned around, and shuffled into the office.

Leonard set up the courtroom. He spun a large desk around in the hallway, pushed an upright chair with a pillow on the seat behind the desk, placed a Mississippi flag on one side, and an American flag on the other. With a flair suggesting that he had done this before, he produced a gavel from inside the desk and wiped it off on his striped pants. At the conclusion of these preparations, he ushered the judge into his seat. Ken and I took our seats in the front row of the courtroom by turning our chairs around in the kitchen.

The sheriff then treated the judge to a detailed briefing of the prisoner, the crime, and the investigation, all of which lasted about a minute. The judge nodded, rubbed each eye methodically for several minutes, readjusted his glasses, and assumed a regal bearing.

"Bring me the prisoner."

A few minutes later, Leonard returned with a disheveled white guy about forty-five years old, alcoholic-skinny, wearing green Sears work pants, a dirty white t-shirt, five or six days of beard, and shoes with no laces. He was handcuffed with his hands in front and he shuffled in the shoes to keep them on. He was a classic Joe Shit the Ragman, the kind of drunk that opens the bar at eight in the morning, drinks draft beer and double shots of Wild Turkey, and sleeps in the back seat of his car three or four nights a week. Just this side of homeless. He looked like he'd had been arrested about twice a week since he was fifteen and as guilty as homemade sin. He oozed a life as wasted and used up as an old mattress lying alongside the freeway.

Leonard marched him up in front of the judge and stood behind him. The judge spoke.

"All right now, boy, I understand you been up to no good around here. The sheriff has advised me that you been peddling them girlie books and smut to the children of this here fine county, pervertin' their young minds. Your kind is what's wrong with America. Now we're also sick and tired of you stinkin' up our county jail."

The guy stood there, weaving back and forth.

"So we're going to offer you a deal, son. You can plead guilty to disorderly conduct right here and now, and your plea will be accepted by the court. Most likely you will be sentenced to five days in the county jail, which you done now, and so, of course, we'd be giving you credit for your time served. A stipulation of your plea will be that you will be required to leave the county. Forthwith!" The judge seemed to enjoy the sound and legality of "Forthwith."

"Now, of course, if you ain't interested in this here deal, which I personally consider to be very magnanimous on my part, you can plead not guilty, in which case you will be returned to your cell here to wait for the arrival of the circuit judge, who will conduct a trial. Now it's incumbent upon me to advise you that the circuit judge, ah, he comes by 'bout every month or two, and he come by just last week, so now it may be a while."

Joe Shit the Ragman tried to focus on the judge. The mental fog created in a Mississippi county jail was beginning to clear. I noticed that he had brought an aroma into the room that made my eyes burn and felt like something infectious that was going to stick to my clothes.

"What's it gonna be, boy?" The judge sounded aggravated having to wait for an answer.

At this point, the sheriff jumped in. "Judge, I do believe this dumb shit is too goddamn stupid to understand the gift you're offering to him. What's the matter with you, boy?" He moved towards him and I thought for sure he was going to slap him upside the head.

The prisoner finally spoke. "I'll take the deal."

"You guilty now, right, boy?" asked the sheriff, suddenly sounding like he needed to be convinced.

"Yeah, I guess so." he muttered. It was the shortest confession I was to hear in my entire career.

Bam! The judge slammed his gavel down on the desk.

"Guilty of disorderly conduct. The court accepts the defendant's plea. Five days custody, time served. And you are hereby ordered to depart the county. Forthwith!" The fourteen dollars in the prisoner's brown paper bag held by Leonard would be used to pay "court costs."

The sheriff smiled at Ken and me as if he had just solved the crime of the century.

Leonard escorted the prisoner down the hall and sent him out the door. My guess is he hustled out of the county without once looking over his shoulder or worrying about who now had possession of his "girlie books."

I couldn't believe what I had just seen. Mississippi justice. This was the Twilight Zone. It was 1971 and J. Edgar Hoover had sentenced me to a year in Mississippi. Having been born and raised in Michigan, I wasn't a Southerner. I was "nothin' but a goddamn Yankee."

"Y'all just don't understand. You're a goddamn Yankee, boy." I was to hear it a hundred times that year. Rarely used to embarrass, it was more often used to explain why I just didn't understand the Mississippi interpretation of racial issues. Race permeated everything in Mississippi from police brutality to discrimination in housing, from voter fraud to indentured servants, from segregated schools to white and black drinking fountains, and to Ku Klux Klansmen.

It was another year before I was able to escape to Los Angeles, but the Mississippi memories would be seared into my personal history forever.

CHAPTER 2

THE REPUBLIC OF NEW AFRIKA

The late 1960s and early 1970s, with the anti–Vietnam War rallies and a new black power movement led by the Black Panthers, the Nation of Islam, and the Black Guerilla Family, were a turbulent time for America. The State of Mississippi had its own black radicals, the Republic of New Afrika (RNA). Formed in Detroit in 1968 by former acquaintances of Malcolm X, this group called for the creation of an independent black nation consisting of the states of Georgia, Alabama, Mississippi, Arkansas, and Louisiana. The RNA advocated cooperative economics and community self-sufficiency, but its manifesto also demanded that the U.S. government cede the five states and pay four hundred billion in reparations to African Americans for the injustices of slavery and segregation.

Unfortunately for the RNA, most of the residents of those Southern states weren't very interested in the concept of giving up their states to radical African Americans. Led by President Imari Obadele, the RNA had moved into a house on Lewis Street in Jackson, Mississippi, and stationed a guard armed with a shotgun on its front porch twenty-four hours a day. This wasn't a violation of any law, but it certainly made the neighbors and police department nervous. Patrol units driving by the house reported that the guards came close to pointing the shotgun at them.

A few months after the RNA moved in, the FBI in Jackson received word that a fugitive wanted for murder in Detroit had moved into their house. The police had interviewed informants who had been inside the house and learned that the occupants had built bunkers and gun ports in its front and sides. Executing a search warrant for the murder suspect was going to be dangerous. Although SWAT teams were in the embryonic stage of development in law enforcement, neither the FBI nor the Jackson Police Department had an organized SWAT team at the time—or hostage negotiators. As a result, officers of the Jackson Police Department and FBI agents led by Special Agent in Charge Elmer Lindberg devised a simple arrest plan using an armored vehicle and a number of brave and courageous officers. They planned to drive up to the house and simply order the occupants out with a bullhorn.

It was summer 1971, before the crisis management failures of the Attica prison uprising in New York and the Palestinian terrorist attack on the Israeli athletes in Munich. The police response to both had been an embarrassment for those agencies involved and challenged law enforcement to search for new approaches. About the same time two New York City cops, Harvey Schlossberg and Frank Bolz, were searching for a new solution to hostage situations. The NYPD had also bungled a couple incidents of their own and they knew there had to a better solution than busting in the front door and shooting up the place. Within a couple years Schlossberg, who had a doctorate in psychology, and Bolz, who had an advanced degree in kick-ass policing, were teaching restraint and talking to New York cops about new techniques of negotiation. Recognizing a good thing, the FBI Academy joined in and the hostage negotiation model was born into law enforcement. In the wake of the race riots, violent anti-war demonstrations, assassinations of public figures, and the street violence of the 1960s, the American public was more than ready for a non-violent solution to police confrontations.

Unfortunately, the RNA situation occurred before the hostage negotiation paradigm arrived in Jackson, Mississippi. The police who arrived at the RNA house with a search warrant for the murder suspect were met with gunfire from several occupants inside the house firing out the portholes. Within a few minutes of the opening volley, Jackson Police Lt. Lou Skinner was killed, another officer was injured, and FBI agent Bill Stringer was shot in the upper leg. After several more minutes, the gunfire slowed and the occupants eventually surrendered without further injury.

However, as too often happens, the fugitive was not on the scene. He was later apprehended in Detroit. Agent Colby Mosier and I were returning to Jackson from an assignment in Natchez when we heard the raid going down on the radio. We put the red light on and screamed back to Jackson but didn't arrive until it was all over. Gun smoke still lingered in the air. It was a traumatic scene with the injured agent and officers, multiple suspects in custody, a huge crime scene, and numerous witnesses. What went wrong was the only thing we discussed for days, and it became apparent that law enforcement was going to have to reexamine its approach to highly dangerous hostage and barricade situations.

As a "First Office Agent" (FOA) in Jackson I was assigned to various training agents who shared their experience, taught me how to be successful, and showed me how to stay out of trouble. Ron "Mad Dog" Johnson, Hal Ratchford, Sam "The Attorney" Jennings, and Cecil Moses were great guys. Some of them had opened the Jackson office in 1964 when the three civil rights workers were killed in Neshoba County. It became the first civil rights investigation in the newly opened Jackson FBI office. Previously, the state of Mississippi had been covered by agents from the Memphis and New Orleans offices.

James Chaney, Andrew Goodman, and Michael Schwerner had come down south to the Philadelphia, Mississippi, area to participate in the voter registration drives. In the early 1960s, only 5 percent of voting-age blacks were registered to vote. For years they had been thwarted in their efforts to become registered voters by a loose-knit statewide conspiracy of white racists who insisted on conducting absurd literacy tests designed to fail blacks. In a collective effort to turn this around, the National

Association for the Advancement of Colored People (NAACP) and the Student Nonviolent Coordinating Committee (SNCC) organized busloads of northern college students to go down south to register black voters. It was the summer of 1964 and they called it Freedom Summer.

While there, Chaney, Goodman, and Schwerner were arrested on a bogus speeding violation. According to later trial testimony, Neshoba County Sheriff Lawrence Rainey notified several local Klansmen that he was planning to release the three after they'd been jailed for a few hours. Once the civil rights workers pulled out of the parking lot of the county jail that night, several Klansmen began to follow their station wagon and eventually forced them to stop. What happened next depends on which Klansman you decide to believe. Forty-four days later, their beaten and bullet-riddled bodies were found buried in a red dirt dam a few miles away.

After the killings, Hoover publicly declared war on the Klan. The agents worked twelve hours a day, six and a half days a week, taking time off only to attend church with their families on Sunday morning. The film *Mississippi Burning* accurately portrayed the violence going on in Mississippi at that time with the black church burnings and standoffs between the Klansmen and the FBI agents. The whispers around the Jackson office were that when the investigation into the disappearance of the three civil rights workers stalled, a group of agents kidnapped a Klan member, took him out to a swamp in the woods, and showed him a briefcase containing thirty thousand dollars. They also shoved a shotgun in his face and encouraged him to make a decision. In a remarkable display of intelligence for a Klansman, he chose the money, told them where to find the bodies, and the rest became blackened into Mississippi history. Roy K. Moore, the Special Agent in Charge, was publicly praised by Hoover for solving the case, but it was really the courageous street agents who went toe to toe with the Klansmen that began to take back the state from these brutal racists.

A long and intensive FBI investigation finally resulted in a 1967 federal grand jury indictment of eighteen Klansmen for violating the civil rights of Chaney, Goodman, and Schwerner, but only seven were convicted. Local authorities refused to charge any of the suspects for the murders. In June 2005, forty-one years after the killings, the local district attorney demonstrated how much Mississippi had grown up by finally charging Edgar Ray Killen with the murders. Killen, a local Klan member and Baptist preacher, was the mastermind who had arranged the ambush. After a condensed four-day trial in Philadelphia, Killen, now eighty years old and wheelchair bound, was convicted. He received a sixty-year sentence from a judge who, as a child, had attended church services at which Killen had preached.

The Ku Klux Klan never really went away though. After I transferred from Jackson to Oxford, I continually carried a dozen "Kluckers" in my caseload. This amounted to periodically checking their whereabouts and running down informant reports that the Klan leaders were going to kidnap and "hang a nigger" on Saturday night. I couldn't believe I was really hearing this stuff in 1971.

The Kluckers were often self-employed because they had difficulty getting along with others. Not everyone could tolerate their uneducated, racist, ignorant ranting and raving. They usually lived somewhere out in the woods where nobody would bother them, six and a half miles "beyond the holler" in the middle of nowhere. They all seemed to live at the end of a gravel road. It wasn't unusual to find the front yard decorated with a dead car, a broken washing machine, and a one-eyed dog that ran out to greet me by biting the tires of my Bureau car, a'67 Ford with a whip antenna—and no air conditioning. That old blue dog never seemed to cool off during my entire year in Oxford, but at 110 miles an hour on I-55 with all the windows down it would wail like a horny stallion as I waved to the oncoming Mississippi Highway Safety patrolmen. Speeding on the interstate like Richard Petty was a favorite game for Mississippi cops. I think it had something to do with the thrill of being offered more than one lane to use.

Interviewing a Klucker usually consisted of listening to

verbal insults of Mr. Hoover, the Supreme Court, civil rights, and blacks in general. It didn't accomplish much, but my visits did serve to remind them that the FBI was still around. The sad part of all the media coverage of the Klan in Mississippi was that it never presented the whole story. There were many proud Mississippians who constantly apologized to us for the behavior of those racists. Unfortunately, the good folks never made the news.

After several months in Jackson and a year in Oxford, I'd had enough of Third World Mississippi. I was transferred to the Los Angeles field office and Robbin and I celebrated our escape by selling our old VW bug and buying a new Ford Gran Torino (with air conditioning) to drive out to LA As we drove through the city square one last time, we pulled up behind a beat up pickup truck belching black smoke into the air. It had a shotgun hanging on a rack in the rear window, a black dog standing stiff legged in the bed, and a tattered bumper sticker on the tailgate which read, "The Bible says it, I believe it, and that's it." We looked at each other and laughed.

Life had to be better in Hollywood.

CHAPTER 3

WOUNDED KNEE REVISITED

It was an unusually rainy morning for Los Angeles in February 1973 and my fellow agents and I were hunkered down in the bullpen planning the day and trading insults when the call came in. A renegade group of two hundred Indians had taken over the village of Wounded Knee, South Dakota, within the Pine Ridge Indian Reservation, home of the Oglala Sioux. Led by radical members of the American Indian Movement (AIM), they had taken about a dozen people hostage.

FBI headquarters was asking for volunteers to back up the agents from Rapid City who had headed to the village, which consisted of a few houses and a general store run by a white family. After spending three years in the army, including a tour in Vietnam, I should have learned to resist volunteering for anything. But the thrill and excitement of the confrontation was overwhelming. Within an hour I was at home packing for one of my many journeys around the country to wherever trouble was brewing. These open-ended crises were called Bureau "Specials" and agents from all over the country would fly in to work the case. Over the years these "specials" became more and more costly due to the growing number of personnel deployed and would eventually require special funding from Congress as they occurred.

Apologizing to Robbin, who was seriously pregnant with our first child, and begging for forgiveness, I departed for the

13

siege at Wounded Knee. Only later would I realize what a historical confrontation this would be.

Wounded Knee was already a historical site because of the 1890 massacre of approximately three hundred Sioux by the U.S. Seventh Cavalry and as such held great significance for Native Americans. AIM, which was founded in 1968 by Russell Means and Dennis Banks, became a militant political and civil rights organization. In late 1969 AIM came to the attention of the public when they temporarily occupied Alcatraz Island off San Francisco, claiming legal rights to the land under an old treaty.

The 1973 occupation of Wounded Knee began as a protest against allegations of corrupt leadership by Oglala Sioux tribal chief Dick Wilson and his cronies. Their opponents claimed that federal funds from the Bureau of Indian Affairs (BIA) in Washington were being siphoned off by the tribal leaders and never seemed to get to where they were destined, or needed. By the time the siege was over, seventy-one days later, two people had been killed, twelve wounded, and over one thousand had been arrested. The 1973 Wounded Knee incident put AIM on the map and into the focus of the FBI as a truly dangerous domestic terrorist organization.

Even in the aftermath of the incident, Pine Ridge continued to be a potential powder keg of confrontations between AIM members and the FBI. During the summer of 1975 another gunfight occurred in which two FBI agents, Jack Coler and Ron Williams, who were looking for a murder suspect on the reservation, were ambushed and killed by several Indians. After being brought down, the agents were finished off at point blank range. Leonard Peltier was later convicted of the murders and sentenced to double life terms. Although he has become a cause célèbre of far left, anti-government sympathizers, his guilt or innocence remains a controversial issue for all those involved.

After arriving at the Rapid City airport, two local agents drove me and a couple other agents out to Hot Springs. I was amazed at all the federal agents and sheriff's deputies walking around with M-16 rifles and shotguns like the government had captured the town. All the firepower made Hot Springs look like downtown Saigon in 1968—and no one paid any notice. We had dinner and a couple beers with an agent named Mike from New York, who had been here from the first few days. Mike had been driving guys back and forth to the airport and had already shacked up with the hotel bartender—he seemed to have figured things out in a hurry. We hoped he could brief us on what was happening in the village, but instead he got drunk and bragged about beating the shit out of cabbies in New York. We figured he was just another typical New Yorker, but later found out it was true. He was a legend in the New York office as a psychotic street fighter. It wasn't until years later that the FBI began to conduct psychological examinations of applicants.

Early the next day we drove out to the village of Wounded Knee. Several roadblocks had been set up around the small village nestled in a large meadow. The FBI and federal marshals had established and were manning the roadblocks, numbered RB-1, RB-2, and so on, around the entire perimeter. The Indians and sympathizers in the village had built bunkers of their own around the edge of the village. We both looked at each other through the sights of our rifles and shotguns. Occasionally we fired. Most days we just had stare downs and shouted profanities. And tried to stay warm. The weather would change every five minutes, ranging from rain to snow to sunshine, all around 30 to 40 degrees.

Initially, we thought we had the Indians cut off from sympathizers and supplies, but almost every night our patrols ran into people bringing food and ammunition into the village. It was a risky assignment, as we never knew if the confrontations would result in a gunfight. Most nights we just turned them back, unless they were carrying guns or ammunition in which case they were arrested. These "rat patrols" operated independently with little supervision and were ignored for the most part by the FBI command structure, which was inexperienced and overwhelmed with the enormity of the crisis.

As the old Hoover gunslingers from the Dillinger days retired, the FBI's ability to respond to crises had deteriorated. The challenges had changed. The FBI headquarters staff had not kept up with training competent crisis managers to respond to the field and take over a critical situation or investigation. It wasn't until the early 1990s that they began to specifically train FBI command personnel in crisis management. Up until then the Special Agent in Charge (SAC) of the location in which the incident occurred was in charge, regardless of his or her experience or ability. Supervision of the agents' activities around Wounded Knee and at the roadblocks was minimal and there were no policies, procedures, or rules of engagement (ROE) in place specifically designed for the incident, something that later played a major role at Ruby Ridge, Idaho. We operated under our basic rules of engagement consistent with FBI guidelines for the use of deadly force, which required threat of death or grave bodily injury.

Government negotiators from the Department of Justice in Washington, D.C., carried on a daily dialogue with the Indians inside the village as well as with high profile sympathizers outside Wounded Knee who claimed to control the AIM people inside. Those of us on the perimeter weren't briefed on the negotiations, so we had no idea what was transpiring. We just showed up at our assigned roadblock each day. There was no real negotiation command post or trained FBI negotiators on site. This concept didn't evolve until years later. The command post in Rapid City primarily consisted of the SAC from the Minneapolis Division (which covered South Dakota), a couple FBI supervisors, and various FBI SWAT agents who had been flown into Rapid City and handed an M-16 rifle. Although I had lived with an M-16 for a year in Vietnam, many of the other FBI agents had never trained with one. Also, there were no organized FBI SWAT teams at Wounded Knee—just hard-charging agents who had volunteered to put down the second Sioux rebellion. It was classic cowboys and Indians.

As we drove into the Pine Ridge Reservation each day, I marveled at the depressing reservation towns: Oglala, Manderson, Pine Ridge, Porcupine. Juxtaposed against the natural beauty of the Black Hills, they were pathetic, dead-end, municipal road kills. The decrepit little houses with dead cars in the front yard were missing boards from the outside of the houses that had been used as firewood. The kids ran around outside in diapers in freezing temperatures. The Indians drove rickety ass pickup trucks and rusted out cars with fins. I had heard about alcoholism on our Indian reservations but I had never seen it firsthand. It didn't take long to realize that if all our Native Americans were like the Oglala Sioux, they sure as hell had good reason to drink. Educational opportunities were limited, and job skills were few. Employment was almost non-existent. A small moccasin factory seemed to be the only industry on the reservation. Escape from the reservation was difficult and a rarity. Even the young ones seemed helpless and hopeless. There were no successful role models, and none on the way. It was obvious that America was trying hard to forget about the plight of its American Indians by turning its face away from the reservations.

We passed a "Buffalo Crossing" sign on SR 87 each day and it gave us an opportunity to warm up on the way to work by cranking off a few rounds. By the time I left Wounded Knee the sign had been completely shot to shit by the agents driving up to the reservation and firing outside the car window as they passed. The whole place felt completely dead and lawless. Nothing seemed to matter. Every day was an endless creepy gray dawn where the damp cold crept inside your jacket and refused to leave.

One of those mornings, after I'd been at Wounded Knee for a little over two weeks, we arrived at RB-1 to learn from the night shift that there had been sporadic shooting all night. The Indians had become frustrated with the negotiations and had been sniping at RB-1 and the armored personnel carriers (APCs) parked there. The South Dakota National Guard had graciously offered them to us as protection, although I'm sure they'll never make that mistake again.

During the hours of boredom, we practiced driving the APCs by playing chicken on the open prairie populated by thousands of prairie dogs who would all sit up and stare at us, and then simultaneously disappear into their holes. It was a game for them and entertainment for us. Although we fired guns at everything else in South Dakota, we never bothered these funny little guys, or the buffalo. These magnificent, prehistoric-looking beasts grazed along the road like cattle and never ceased to fascinate us. They had a right to be angry because of the historical efforts to drive them into extinction, but instead they appeared mellow, unconcerned and uncomplaining about their tenuous place in our world. We weren't about to take the life of one of these survivors. We also figured it might be a hanging offense for a white man to shoot a buffalo in South Dakota.

It didn't take a degree, a license, or much training to drive the APCs, which had an accelerator and two arm handles that controlled the tracks. Turning consisted of pulling back on one of the handles to stop one of the tracks. Pulling back on both simultaneously provided the braking mechanism. Acceleration was just pedal to the metal. We'd drive straight at each other at about 35 mph and then swerve to one side or the other at the last second. They were impossible to roll so we became fearless fools. Riding inside as a passenger was another story though. It was all steel, cramped, claustrophobic and dangerous without a helmet. Of course, none of us had a helmet. To add to the danger, we occasionally buttoned the hatch down and drove with limited vision by looking out through a 3-inch thick glass plate with almost no peripheral vision. We never seemed to tire of this and the South Dakota National Guard never took them away from us. They should have. We were like kids abusing a little brother's new Christmas toy.

A couple hours into the shift, Jan Wilhelm, Chuck Kemp, and I decided to drive down closer to the village to conduct some reconnaissance on the shooters. We left the APC out of sight about fifty yards from the Indian bunker on the side of a ravine and crawled to where we could see the Indians inside their bunker. Smoke drifted slowly out of the bunker and we listened to them talking loudly. Sounded like an argument. Unfortunately, within minutes they saw us and opened up with several shoulder weapons. It started like most firefights—like microwave popcorn. A couple rounds, then beginning to increase, and then all hell broke loose.

The rounds first started snapping overhead and then zipped into the ground around us as they came closer. We hugged the bottom of the ravine and fired back. It was like Vietnam all over again. Then the other agents and marshals at the roadblock opened up. After a few minutes, we realized that we had left our radios in the APC and couldn't call for help. And each of us had only brought three or four extra magazines with us. It rapidly became obvious that it was going to be very difficult to get back to the APC without being hit.

We hunkered down and waited it out for half an hour. I decided to save my last magazine for my escape. When the shooting finally slowed a bit, and became intermittent, we nodded to each other, jumped up simultaneously and zigzagged like jackrabbits back up the hill to the APC. With rounds whistling overhead and slamming into the ground, the fear made me feel like I was running in waist deep water. Miraculously, none of us were hit. We collapsed against the side of the APC to catch our breath and grinned at each other. We didn't say anything but I know we all believed in God again.

A few minutes later we jumped into the APC and hustled back to the roadblock where we downplayed our incursion into Indian country. As survivors we were ecstatic, although somewhat embarrassed at our foolhardiness. Later we learned that an Indian named Buddy Lamont had been killed during the exchange of gunfire. A few hours later the Indians called Washington to arrange a truce to bring the body out. The three of us watched silently and said nothing as it was removed in the back of a pickup. It wasn't covered up and Lamont's head was swollen as large as a pumpkin. It was a sobering experience. It wasn't just harmless cowboys and Indians anymore.

Surprisingly, very little investigation of the shooting was ever conducted, probably because of the lack of organization and chain of command during the entire incident. In later years, an agent involved shooting (AIS) would result in an extensive administrative investigation by the FBI in which all the shooters would be intensively interviewed and each round fired by each shooter would be accounted for. The post incident reports of Ruby Ridge and Waco would later serve as excellent examples.

The occupation eventually ended in May when the government promised to investigate the AIM allegations of corruption in the Bureau of Indian Affairs and to hold hearings on broken Indian treaties. What the siege provided for the FBI was the justification for the development of the FBI's SWAT program, which was just getting off the ground at the FBI Academy in Quantico, Virginia, when Wounded Knee occurred.

When it was all over after seventy-one days, those of us who had participated agreed that the FBI needed a better way to respond to this kind of major occurrence. The lack of organization of not only the SWAT teams but also the lack of qualified command personnel was a serious problem that continually played out in major incidents around the country in the following years. In the aftermath of Wounded Knee in 1973, the FBI Academy staff developed a regional SWAT program, and eventually created the elite and highly trained Hostage Rescue Team (HRT) in 1982. It also created the international Crisis Incident Negotiation Team (CINT) of super negotiators in 1985, but it wasn't until the early 1990s that it began to focus on training command personnel for major incident crisis management. The FBI, like any large organization, changes direction very slowly.

A couple of years later, Chuck Kemp and I bumped into each other in the football team's weight room at the University of Nebraska in Lincoln, but I never saw Jan Wilhelm again. He left Woodward, Oklahoma, and transferred to Rockford, Illinois. Years later, I learned that he had been shot in the face by a bank robbery fugitive as he entered an apartment and almost died. He was gravely injured but recovered fully and eventually returned to duty.

The last time I saw Russell Means he had left South Dakota to play the part of an Indian in *The Last of the Mohicans* with Daniel Day-Lewis. He was one of the lucky ones. Hollywood saved him from a slow death on the reservation.

CHAPTER 4

PATTY HEARST AND THE SLA

It was a late spring morning in 1999 and I was sitting in my office at MGM Studios in Santa Monica. I'd retired from the FBI in 1995 and was working as the director of corporate security for the studio. As I paged through the *Hollywood Reporter* and sipped a coffee from Starbucks, I watched the gorgeous actresses walk past my window on their way to the casting office to audition for the next James Bond film. I was interrupted by a call from Steve Shaw, the VP of Human Resources.

"Jim, we think Emily Harris is working here at MGM."

"Emily Harris? You gotta be kidding."

I hadn't thought about Emily Harris in thirty years. Emily Harris was the Symbionese Liberation Army (SLA) fugitive who, along with her husband Bill and others, had kidnapped Patty Hearst in San Francisco in 1974. After an intensive investigation involving every office of the FBI, they were apprehended in San Francisco just miles from where Patty had been kidnapped. I had spent a year and a half looking for Emily and Bill in LA

I couldn't believe it. "Steve, what the hell are you talking about?" I remembered that the *Los Angeles Times* had recently published an article on the former members of the SLA, a "where are they now" piece. They had profiled most of the members, including Emily, and had described her as working in the LA area as a computer programmer. The article had included several pictures of the former SLA members, but none of Emily.

"She's been working here for two years as a contractor for IT," Steve said. "One of the IT guys made the connection based on a *Times* article. Supposed to be an excellent programmer. Good at tracking film rights. Well thought of. No problems."

Unbelievable. She was right under my nose. After twenty-eight years, and now when it no longer mattered, I found her on the second floor directly above me in the 2450 building at MGM. I would have loved to sit down with her and ask her a thousand unanswered questions from the investigation, but what Shaw didn't know was that Emily was the suspected shooter in an old 1975 bank robbery in Carmichael, California, a suburb of Sacramento. In the bank that day, a forty-two-year-old woman named Myrna Lee Opsahl had been killed with a shotgun while depositing receipts from her church. Emily had allegedly wielded the shotgun. Although Emily had done seven years in prison for the Hearst kidnapping, she had never been charged with the murder of Opsahl.

What made this particularly interesting in 1999 was that a few months earlier the FBI had arrested another former member of the SLA and longtime fugitive, Kathy Soliah, for attempting to bomb a couple of LAPD patrol vehicles. Soliah had married, raised a family, adopted the alias of Sara Jane Olson, and was living freely in Minnesota—a real soccer mom, married to a doctor, and acting in the local playhouse. I knew that things would be heating up for Emily after Soliah's arrest as Soliah would certainly be thinking about making a deal with the D.A.'s office. Emily had to be lying awake at night waiting for the FBI to knock on the door and hook her up for Opsahl's murder. And here she was, right here at MGM!

The Symbionese Liberation Army was born in Berkeley in 1973 when some radical anti-war white college kids got together in a bewildering association with Donald DeFreeze, an escaped African-American convict, and publicly stated they were going to conduct a "war against America," although no one really knew what that meant. DeFreeze assumed the name of Cinque, the leader of a famous slave rebellion. He also gave himself the rank of field marshal. The SLA's slogan, "Death to the Fascist Insect That Preys upon the Life of the People," never made sense to me. They used the term "symbionese" to suggest that all kinds of people can live together in harmony, which did make sense, but then they went out and killed people, which certainly didn't. Their symbol was a seven-headed cobra, representing the principles of unity, self-determination, collective work and responsibility, cooperative purpose, production, faith, and creativity. Obviously, they seemed to be spending more time on their new club than their college studies.

The SLA's first known act of violence and war against America was the murder of Marcus Foster, the Oakland superintendent of schools, in November 1973. Their second crime, for which they became infamous, was the armed kidnapping of media heiress Patty Hearst from her Berkeley home on February 4, 1974. They shot up the place, needlessly beat on her boyfriend, and after a few days made their ransom demand: $2 million worth of food distributed to the poor and needy in San Francisco by her parents, owners of the Hearst publishing network. Within days Hearst complied by setting up several food distribution points. It was one of smartest ransom demands I had ever seen. No one had to risk getting caught picking up the money. The kidnappers just walked down to the corner and watched the Hearst trucks dump off food to the homeless at several locations in San Francisco. Then the SLA disappeared. Went underground. With Patty.

That's when I got involved. I was working major fraud cases at the time Patty was kidnapped. Because the FBI office in LA began to get swamped with investigative leads, I was pulled over to the major case squad handling kidnapping investigations. I stayed there for ten of the most exciting years of my Bureau career.

Descriptions of the kidnappers were sketchy but included males and females who were armed to the teeth. Initially we were looking for Patty Hearst the kidnapping victim. Then two months later, the SLA robbed the Hibernia Bank in San Francisco—accompanied by Patty wearing a black beret, carrying a rifle, and now looking every bit the revolutionary. We began thinking that maybe the kidnapping was bogus, and just a means for her to join this group of domestic guerillas— something to make her little rich girl's life a little more exciting.

What we didn't know then was that Patty had been locked in a closet for weeks after her kidnapping, sexually assaulted several times by Cinque, subjected to constant threats by the other members, denied adequate food and water, and forced to join the group during the bank robbery. At her trial she claimed the gun she carried was unloaded. It has also been suggested that Patty's behavior was caused by Stockholm syndrome, by which hostages bond with their captors.

This concept developed out of a four-day hostage incident in Stockholm, Sweden, in 1973 in which several hostages were held in a bank vault with the bank robbers. One in particular, Kristin, protected the hostage takers, pointed out police snipers, and refused to cooperate with the police. She criticized the lack of response of the police and verbally assaulted the Swedish prime minister during a call with him. After it was all over she visited one of the robbers in jail and eventually married him. Nobody could understand it but the police shrinks loved this stuff.

During a hostage incident, the hostage is psychologically overwhelmed and shocked by the capture and forced confinement. Any movement or activity has to be requested of the hostage taker, and the hostage becomes childlike, with a complete loss of control due to the underlying threat of injury or death. As time goes on, any kindness by the hostage taker produces strong emotions of appreciation by the hostage. As these emotions increase, the hostage begins to identify with the hostage taker and develop affection. This attachment can also occur for the hostage taker, who can develop feelings of association with and protection of the hostage. Both begin to share a distrust of and hatred for the police—and of course, the negotiator. The Stockholm syndrome can begin to develop after as few as thirty minutes. Young women have the greatest potential to be affected, but children seem to be immune, probably because they already exist in a parent/child relationship and have not yet developed independence. Hostage negotiators have to be aware of this subservient relationship, of dominance and control, which is often present to varying degrees in hostage incidents.

In any case, things had become more serious. This was one heavily armed group of revolutionaries.

We were working twelve-hour shifts every day, pulling over and jacking up every black pimp with a white hooker in LA hoping to find Cinque with Patty. I was paired up with an old-time bank robbery agent named Parr, a stocky muscular guy who always wore a short-sleeve white shirt like Andy Sipowicz from *NYPD Blue*. He never wore his suit coat so his .357 revolver and handcuffs were easy for everyone to see, and he could not have cared less. Parr also had a large vertical vein in the center of his forehead that looked like a subcutaneous night crawler that grew when he was pissed. Which seemed to be most of the time. When he looked at you it was like being hit with a laser. The first time I met Parr was a few months before at a bank robbery in South Central. "Male usual," he grunted, as we pulled up to the bank, relating the description of the suspect, meaning "a black male." We cruised South Central LA together looking for likely suspects. Parr was fearless, stomping into pool halls and bars filled with hostile black males. He pissed all over them and no one ever came at us. "Fucking whip dicks," he called them. I couldn't believe it. By the end of the day my adrenalin was on empty. Parr just laughed at me. He later quit the FBI and his family and ran off with a female informant. Last I heard he was back east driving an eighteen-wheeler.

Besides the FBI full court press, the SLA also became the focus of intense media attention. Reporters kept asking the FBI why we hadn't found them. The pressure on us cranked up a notch after every front-page headline.

After the Hibernia bank job, we had identified the primary members of the SLA and knew who we were looking for. Cinque was the obvious leader and our main focus. We knew they had to have a support network, possibly some of the New Left people left over from the anti–Vietnam War groups. Maybe some old "SDS'ers" (Students for a Democratic Society). We also figured they would probably be staying together and we were surprised that no one had stumbled onto them, since it was an odd group, the hardcore black, Cinque, and several young white women.

Then Patty and the Harrises stopped off at Mel's Sporting Goods in south LA to pick up a few last minute things and everything changed.

Mel's was a typical sporting goods store on Crenshaw in the middle of Inglewood. We used to call it "IngleWatts" because it neighbored Watts and its residents were similar—black and Hispanic. It was a very tough town. You didn't mess around in Inglewood at night unless you wanted trouble. It was on page 51 of the Thomas Brothers LA street guide, and as fugitive hunters on the C-1 squad we used to laugh about how we seemed to spend most of our lives in Los Angeles on page 51.

On the afternoon of May 16, 1974, three months after Patty's kidnapping, Bill and Emily Harris, and Patty, stopped by Mel's so Bill could buy some clothes. Patty stayed in the VW van across the street. As they walked out, Bill shoplifted a pair of socks. An alert employee noticed and confronted Bill, and a struggle ensued. Then Emily jumped in and it turned into a third grade sandbox fight with everyone flailing about. Bill pulled a small revolver from his waistband but was actually disarmed by store employees, who were able to place a handcuff on one of his wrists. Patty, who had been daydreaming in the van in a parking lot across the street, finally looked up and noticed the fight. She immediately picked up a rifle and cranked off several rounds into the sign above the front door of the store.

When the employees ran back into the store to call the cops, Bill and Emily dashed across the street and jumped into the van with Patty. One of the male employees climbed into his car and followed the van as it made its escape from the area. He eventually observed the occupants abandon it and carjack another vehicle. As Bill jumped in the car he yelled at the frightened driver, "We're SLA, we need your car." Later interviewed by the cops, the carjacked victim and the employees from Mel's all stated that they were certain that the woman who fired the rifle was Patty Hearst. Other witnesses positively identified the other two as Bill and Emily Harris. The Inglewood police department immediately notified the FBI.

That night Patty, Bill, and Emily pulled into a drive-in movie where Emily sawed the handcuff off Bill with a hacksaw and they tried to figure out what to do next. Years later, Patty (not surprisingly) admitted to investigators that they hadn't watched much of the movie.

In the meantime, the FBI went ballistic. Within an hour every FBI agent and cop in LA got the word that the SLA had arrived in town. And there wasn't any more doubt about whose side Patty was on. Inglewood immediately became the safest town in America as hundreds of cops and agents poured in looking for the vehicle carjacked by Patty Hearst and the Harrises. Everyone hoped to be the one to find them.

Unknown to us, after the Hibernia bank robbery the group thought things were getting too hot in the San Francisco area, so they decided to drive down to LA. Cinque told them that he had a few friends in Southern California who could put them up for a while until things cooled down. They had traveled in two white vans. Separating in LA, they had agreed on a rendezvous point and time. While Cinque and the others searched for a safe house, Patty and the Harrises had gone shopping. After the shooting at Mel's, Patty and the Harrises were unable to connect with the others. Realizing the cops would be streaming into Inglewood, they drove further south and eventually ended up in a non-descript motel next to Disneyland in Anaheim where they quietly camped out of sight for a couple days.

Meanwhile, Cinque and the SLA members were also running out of luck. Unable to locate his contacts, they finally ended up at the South Central residence of Christine Johnson on 54th Street. But they had banged around the neighborhood enough to attract the attention of several of the neighbors. White college-aged girls stood out like neon lights at night in South Central LA. They spent the night at Johnson's, but time was running out. Police patrols and FBI agents were combing the area, and the search intensified throughout night. No one was more amped than I.

A search of the van abandoned by Patty and the Harrises had disclosed a parking ticket showing an address on 84th street. Within an hour a huge entourage of SWAT officers and agents converged on the house but discovered that it had been abandoned a few hours before. Hot food was left on the stove. Patrols kept swarming the area and FBI agents began interviewing the neighbors for additional information on the fugitives. We were hot on their trail like bloodhounds.

Then, in mid afternoon, the Newton Street Division of LAPD received a telephone call from Christine Johnson's mother. She wanted to report a bizarre situation. A black guy with several white girls carrying guns had moved into her daughter's house located at 1466 E. 54th Street. Yes, with guns, and no, these kids weren't from the neighborhood.

Minutes later, LAPD plainclothes officers probing the neighborhood found two suspicious vans in an alley a couple blocks north of 54th Street just west of Compton. They trumpeted their discovery and nearly every LAPD cop and FBI agent in LA responded. We staged at the local official police impound yard and watched the SWAT teams arrive. They arrived car after car, two in each, cocky, muscle bound weight lifters, bug-eyed with anticipation. While the FBI SWAT team consisted of only about eight members at the time, LAPD seemed to have a hundred. The excitement was electric. Everyone was convinced it was going to go down hard, although the surveillance units at the house had reported no activity since their arrival. They speculated that Cinque and the others might have already escaped or that they had the wrong house. We hung around watching the SWAT guys suit up and lock and load. The anticipation of the confrontation was immense. As the SWAT units pulled out of the yard to deploy, the rest of us followed them slowly, taking up secondary perimeter positions around the corner from the house.

Still wearing my standard issue FBI suit and tie, I got out of our unit and walked with my partner to the northeast corner of 54th and Compton. Although it was about 5:30 PM and we hadn't slept in thirty-six hours, we couldn't have been more awake. The house was a small bungalow on the south side of 54th, about the third one in from Compton. As the cops took up positions, the street emptied of people like an old cowboy movie before the showdown. After what seemed to be about an hour, one of the LAPD SWAT officers marched up the middle of the street like John Wayne, faced the house, and bullhorned a demand for surrender:

Occupants of 1466 East 54th Street!

This is the Los Angeles Police Department speaking.

Come out with your hands up!

Comply immediately and you will not be harmed.

A minute later the front door opened and a young black male walked slowly out of the house, hands raised, and into the arms of SWAT personnel. He was hustled off to a waiting paramedic van. After a second announcement, an older black male exited the house and was also taken into custody by SWAT guys. We had no idea who these two were, but neither appeared to be Cinque. It had to be the wrong place.

Finally, after several additional announcements, LAPD fired in two CS tear gas projectiles. We waited, wondering if it was still occupied at all.

Seconds later all hell broke loose. The occupants began pouring fire out of the house into those across the street and spraying the street. The SWAT guys opened up in response on all four sides of the house. The area turned into a war zone. I pulled out my Smith & Wesson Model 19 .357 magnum, something I had bought back in Mississippi as a new agent, and in an instinct of self-defense, pointed it in the direction of the house. I crouched behind a chain link fence (which offered absolutely no cover or concealment) at the corner and watched the shooting. Seconds later, I was lying on the ground with a news photographer crouched over my shoulder shooting video. I couldn't believe his courage or stupidity. Hundreds of rounds were impacting all around us. I flashed back to Vietnam again. Hunker down behind some protective cover, hold your weapon over your head and crank off a few rounds overhead at an unseen enemy. Periodically look up to make sure they weren't charging at you.

The shooting would periodically die down and then start up again. After about an hour several members of the FBI SWAT team arrived to back up LAPD. Minutes later when LAPD requested more gas, the FBI team jumped into the fray and fired a dozen 40mm tear gas grenades into the house and then backed off. LAPD resumed return fire into the house.

After approximately a half hour the shooting ceased, and everyone looked up expectantly. Suddenly, a young black woman, later identified as Christine Johnson, who had apparently been awakened by the gunfire, ran out the front door of the house. SWAT officers called her over to the side of the house and immediately took her into custody. Minutes later the war started up again. Strangely, we had just witnessed a non-negotiated truce between the two sides.

Smoke started pouring out of the rear of the house. Probably the tear gas grenades had started a fire. We assumed the gas would surely force them out of the house.

An hour into the firefight LAPD began to worry about having enough ammunition and the SWAT guys yelled for re-supply. Officers from the Southeast and 77th Street Division arrived with more. The firefight had continued with no apparent casualties on either side. (Actually at one point two SLA women had appeared at the rear door, fired at the officers, and were killed. This was unknown to us on the north side, however. We later learned that there were six members of the SLA in the house.) It suddenly dawned on me that I had been in the FBI three years and this was my third shooting incident. The RNA in Jackson, the AIM at Wounded Knee, and now the SLA. Was I becoming a shit magnet? I still had seventeen years to go to retirement!

Sporadic fire continued from the house. Some of it sounded like a heavy machine gun and when it opened up everybody hunkered down a little tighter. The houses in the immediate area were pockmarked with a lot of fire and the street began to look like downtown Beirut. The smell of gunpowder was everywhere. Gradually the firing from inside the house subsided as the structure began to burn. We all watched intently, expecting someone to coming running out.

Then, as the fire burned down, ammunition in the house began to cook off. We continued to wait for someone to burst out of the house.

No one did.

After waiting until it was apparent that no one could have survived, a pumper from the fire department moved up and began to soak the embers. One of the firemen stood up on the truck and directed the nozzle into the embers like a deer hunter posing with his foot on the head of his kill. He failed to hide a grin from the news photographers who had crowded into the area. It had been about an hour and a half of non-stop shooting. We stood in amazement. I had witnessed history from a front row seat. And I never fired a round. This was a SWAT operation. I had no part in it; I was just another observer.

Was Patty Hearst in those charred remnants of that house? It was three days before we had an answer based on the comparison of dental records. We finally determined that Angela Atwood, Donald DeFreeze, Camilla Hall, Nancy Ling Perry, Willie Wolfe, and Patricia Soltysik had perished inside. Where the hell was Patty? It was another eighteen months before that was answered.

I had been partnered up with Joe Alston, one of the most experienced and competent agents in the Bureau, who was assigned as the Los Angeles case agent. Joe was a world-class badminton champion who had his face on the front of *Sports Illustrated* in the '50s. His badminton was not the four beers backyard barbecue stuff, but the kind with vicious 200 mph smashes with an opponent ten feet away from you. Joe handled all the major kidnapping cases in the LA office and no one was better at coordinating a kidnapping investigation and a ransom payoff. His enthusiasm was contagious and he enjoyed the hell out of life. Nothing was ever a total waste; everything had some benefit. He was a joy to work with every day. He had a million dollar grin, an infectious passion for the job, and heel plates on his wingtips that always sounded like he was tap dancing. Armed with a huge backlog of investigative leads that seemed to multiply each day, Joe set the direction for the investigation of the Hearst kidnapping. Once the major players were identified and developed, he designed the FBI strategy that ultimately led to her arrest.

Patty ran from one end of the country to the other with the Harrises and SLA supporters for the next year and a half until September 18, 1975, when agents from the FBI's San Francisco office finally captured her with Wendy Yoshimura in a little row house on Morse Street in Daly City. Moments earlier they had arrested Bill and Emily jogging a few miles away. Even revolutionaries have to stay in shape.

The strange odyssey was over only nineteen miles from where it started eighteen months before. Before long, the remaining SLA members were prosecuted, convicted, and went to prison, including Patty, who got seven years in spite of being represented by renowned lawyer F. Lee Bailey. They all did their time, and they were released. But the 1975 Opsahl murder case stayed open.

With the arrest of Soliah back in Minnesota in June 1999, things started to happen. After the D.A.'s office in Sacramento had tried Soliah's brother, Steven, for the Opsahl murder and he won an acquittal, they were gun-shy about trying Emily. However, Opsahl's son, Jon, and two D.A. prosecutors from the Los Angeles county D.A.'s office were convinced it could be done. They began to put public pressure on their counterparts in Sacramento, and the LA Times ran a detailed story about the prosecutorial arguments between the two D.A. offices. After Soliah's arrest, the prosecutors began to locate and re-interview the original SLA members and set up a line for "let's make a deal." The rule is the first one in line usually gets the best deal.

Things started to happen. The former revolutionaries were now fifty-year-old family members who had no interest in spending the rest of their lives in jail for their misguided ideas of thirty years ago. Emily began to feel the heat and provided her roommate with plans to handle her affairs if she was jailed. And then the knock at the door finally happened. Emily was arrested and charged with the first-degree murder of Myrna Opsahl. She was jailed in LA County and then transferred to Sacramento.

My immediate thought at MGM was to safeguard her personal effects for the authorities. It would have been an embarrassment to find them auctioned off on eBay by an unscrupulous coworker. I was also concerned that her computer might hold the answer to the whereabouts of James Kilgore, the last remaining SLA fugitive. (He surrendered months later in South Africa.) The Sacramento county D.A.'s office called me the day after her arrest and advised that they would obtain a search warrant for her effects, but nothing happened and after a few months Emily became another distant memory.

On February 15, 2003, Emily Harris and several other former SLA members were led into court in Sacramento and pled guilty to second-degree murder. At her sentencing, the *Los Angeles Times* reported that Emily appeared remorseful, saying, "For the rest of my life, I will feel a deep sense of sadness." The judge then sentenced her to eight years in prison; the others received lesser sentences. After all, Emily was the one who had pulled the trigger of the shotgun that killed Myrna Opsahl, and she was the one quoted by the others as saying just after the shooting, "It really doesn't matter. She was a bourgeois pig anyway. Her husband is a doctor." After twenty-nine years, the SLA was finally dead.

Patty Hearst had her sentence for bank robbery commuted by President Jimmy Carter in January 1979, and she was pardoned by President Bill Clinton on his last day in office. She married her bodyguard, moved back East, wrote a book about the SLA, and became a stay-at-home mom and an occasional actress.

CHAPTER 5

WANNABE SKYJACKER

Continental Airlines Chief Stewardess Barbara Sorenson stood in the doorway checking the manifest and making the first-class passengers comfortable on Continental Flight 52 from Los Angeles to Phoenix on the morning of March 5, 1981. The Boeing 727 was sitting at the gate of the terminal as the passengers boarded with their carry-on luggage. The rear ramp was down to allow for the entry of maintenance personnel. When a tall man with a ski mask entered the airplane with a black gym bag in one hand and a gun in the other, Sorenson knew she was in trouble.

The masked man immediately announced, "I'm hijacking this airplane. I have a bomb in this bag. I want five million dollars. Shut the doors and get this plane away from the gate."

He pointed his semi-automatic at Sorenson and then backed against the bulkhead. Sorenson was momentarily stunned, wondering how he had walked into the airport wearing a mask and carrying a gun. But then her training kicked in and she moved into action. She stuck her head into the cockpit and notified the crew that a hijacker had just boarded the airplane with a gun and a bomb. Surprised, but not foolish, the pilots immediately slammed the door shut, climbed out of the cockpit window and slid down the emergency cable. Sorenson was left standing behind in disbelief.

Although it was standard procedure for cockpit crews to try to escape—a plane isn't going anywhere without a pilot—Sorenson was furious that they had abandoned her. The pilots' union and the flight attendants had been at odds during new contract negotiations and Sorenson later described the pilots' "run for your life, save yourself" reaction as typical. Now Sorenson was left without a crew to fly the airplane, and she knew the hijacker wouldn't be too thrilled about that. Without telling him that he had lost his crew, Sorenson walked to the back of first class, closed the curtain, and quietly notified a second flight attendant in the coach section of the hijacking. The second flight attendant walked to the rear of the plane and immediately called the Continental LAX gate from the phone in the plane.

"We have an armed hijacker on board Continental Flight 52 at the gate. This is not a test or a training exercise. Please make the appropriate notifications." She hung the phone back on the wall and turned to the passengers, totally unaware of how their lives would change in the next several hours.

It had started—an aircraft hijacking. The first call went to the FAA and the second to the FBI. The Secret Service, the State Department, and every airport in the U.S. were notified. An aircraft skyjacking rapidly becomes a major crisis.

Minutes later, a uniformed LAPD officer from the airport substation appeared at the rear of the 727. After taking a cautious look inside, he began to evacuate the passengers down the rear stairs and away from the plane. Because of an aircraft's design, visibility toward the rear is extremely limited from inside the plane. Assaults on a hijacked aircraft are planned directly from the rear because it is impossible to see approaching SWAT officers. And Sorenson had closed the curtains between first class and coach. As a result the hijacker did not see the escaping passengers. Within minutes, and unknown to the hijacker, the quick thinking efforts of Sorenson and the LAPD officer had resulted in emptying the plane of all but eight passengers in first class, the other flight attendant, and Sorenson.

Fifteen minutes after the hijacker walked into the airplane, we got the call at the FBI office in LA. The FBI has total authority and control over the response to any hijacked aircraft in the United States. Although the FAA assumes the primary decision making role while the aircraft is in the air, when it's on the ground control of the situation belongs to the FBI.

No other kind of hostage incident creates more suspense and generates a greater response than a skyjacking. The combination of the uncertainty of the outcome, the large number of hostages, the curiosity of the identities of the passengers on board (VIPs or celebrities), the unpredictability of a deranged gunman or the twisted motivation of a terrorist, wondering if it will crash in a ball of flame, and the threat to a common mode of travel, all combine to create an enormous crisis for numerous governmental agencies. It also creates unprecedented media interest. The FBI, FAA, the air carrier itself, the local air traffic controllers, other aircraft traffic in the air and on the ground, the local police and sheriff's departments, and the media respond in hordes. The Secret Service may wake up the president to notify him. An aircraft hijacking is a law enforcement emergency like no other.

When we all arrived, the plane remained at the gate with the rear-boarding ramp down. While most of the arriving agents evacuated the waiting passengers from the immediate gate area inside the terminal, as the first FBI hostage negotiator at the scene I ran down the steps and onto the tarmac. With me was Ed "Brylcreem Eddie" Best, the Special Agent in Charge (SAC) of the LA field office. Best was wearing a dark suit with a tie and a collar tiepin like it was 1940. He looked immaculate. I wondered if SACs all wore tie pins. Best and I walked up to the rear ramp and encountered the LAPD officer who had evacuated the passengers from coach.

Best identified himself to the officer, thanked him for his efforts, and then said, "The FBI will take it from here." This guy just saved a planeload of people and Best was playing the FBI superiority game. Confused, but accepting Best as the FBI authority, the officer walked away. I could only wonder what would happen to his career after he surrendered a hijacked airplane to the FBI.

As we walked up the rear stairs, Sorenson met us and provided our first status report on the hijacker. She was amazingly calm. "He has stayed in first class with eight passengers and another flight attendant. He definitely has a gun and said he has a bomb in a bag. He also has something that looks like a detonator. He wants five million dollars. He has insisted the plane leave the gate and has been threatening the passengers with the gun. He has a bit of an accent. He is dressed in black and wearing a mask." She took a deep breath.

Best backed down the steps and ordered nearby airport personnel to tow the plane to runway R-74, the designated hijack location isolated at the far west end of the airport. This required pulling up the rear stairs and buttoning up the plane so the tug could pull it away from the gate. I was strongly opposed to moving the aircraft. As a SWAT agent and negotiator, I understood the importance of keeping the rear entry ramp open. The primary challenge for any SWAT team is to determine an access point to enable them to make a rapid entry into a hostile location. In this case, the door was already open. The only thing it lacked was a neon "Enter" sign. It's extremely difficult to force an entry into an aircraft after it's buttoned up. I diplomatically said so to Best. Why not just evacuate those in the immediate vicinity of the gate to prevent injury if this guy actually had a bomb?

Best was insistent. "We're moving this aircraft." It seemed a simple ploy to gain control of the situation and to keep it away from LAPD.

A few minutes later the tug arrived. We walked down the stairs and watched as the door closed and the rear ramp was pulled up from inside. As she closed the door, Sorenson peered out the small window with the look of a kid being dropped off at an orphanage. The tug slowly backed the plane away from the gate. I didn't recognize the two guys on the tug, but my guess was that the passenger with the yellow overalls two sizes too small and wearing wingtip shoes was an agent trying to get a good look at the hijacker.

Best, Steve Ducker (the agent in charge of the FBI office at LAX), and I followed the plane in an airport security vehicle. Once it stopped at the west end of the airport near Pershing Drive, we looked at each other. What the hell do we do now? How do we talk to the hijacker? The crew had bailed out of the cockpit and the doors had been shut. Even if we had had an FAA radio there was no one in the cockpit to communicate with.

We got out of the car and looked at the aircraft. No one said anything for a while. I knew Ducker was pissed. He understood what we had given up as a result of Best's power play. Ducker was typical of a lot of agents: smart, perceptive, aggressive, someone who could have gone up the promotion ladder, but preferred to stay on the street where he could make a difference. He was short and wiry, salt and pepper brushy hair, and always seemed to know more than those around him. He wore a shoulder holster like a New York homicide detective giving a TV interview.

After a few minutes, I pulled out a notebook and wrote in large letters on a piece of 8 x 11 notebook paper: "OPEN REAR DOOR TO TALK."

I walked up to the side of the aircraft. I held it up to the passengers in first class who looked at me curiously and then nodded as if they understood. I walked to the rear of the airplane and waited a few minutes. All of a sudden the rear stairs dropped down and a flight attendant bounded down the steps.

"He's still in first class," she said breathlessly. "He's holding a gun in one hand, and some kind of bomb detonator in the other. He hasn't hurt anyone but he's scary. He has a mask on and he doesn't talk much."

She was shaking uncontrollably and the corners of her mouth twitched. She was a wreck and we couldn't risk her returning. Although she was worried about leaving Sorenson alone on the plane, she was also visibly relieved when we refused to allow her to return and rushed her away.

Best walked up the stairs. I watched him and doubted that he was wearing his gun. It would have ruined the lines of his suit. This guy probably didn't know where his gun was. Then it dawned on me—my own gun was still in my briefcase left on the seat of my car sitting in front of the Continental terminal with the blinkers on. I hoped I had remembered to lock the car. The SWAT team hadn't arrived yet to provide any firepower and I felt vulnerable and defenseless. I followed Best up the stairs and hoped he wouldn't notice. Two unarmed FBI agents just walked into an aircraft hijacked by a guy with a gun and a bomb.

Sorenson met us at the top of the stairs with a nervous smile. It was now just Sorenson, eight folks in first class who were probably wishing like hell they'd flown coach, and the hijacker. We started by telling Sorenson that she had to tell him the pilots had jumped ship. We couldn't fly the plane. The best we could hope for was that he'd abort his plan. Showing no fear, Sorenson walked forward to the front of the plane and talked to the hijacker for several minutes.

When she returned she said, "He wants the crew to come back. And he said to remind you of the hostages in first class. And he wants the $5 million."

Best, Ducker, and I remained in the rear of the plane. With Sorenson's help, over the hours we gradually reduced the number of hostages through a series of negotiation techniques. The first was to create an illness. We coached Sorenson how to do this by insisting that the weakest looking passenger be released. Chest pains were always a favorite. A sick hostage creates a control problem and an ethical dilemma for the hostage taker and also allows him to demonstrate his good faith by releasing the hostage. This worked well for the first of the hostages but it didn't take long for the others to catch on. Within minutes everyone on board had begun to experience heart palpitations—it was contagious. The strong desire to urinate also became a problem for everyone. For some unexplained reason, one of the hostages was allowed to come to the rear to use the restroom. We immediately captured her and sent her off the plane. Sorenson came back and registered a complaint for the hijacker.

"He's pissed. He said she promised to return."

"Tell him she refused to return. That it was her choice," I instructed. Sorensen duly returned to the hijacker.

Another hostage who came to the rear restroom insisted on returning, claiming that she too had promised the hijacker that she would return. She had been showing him how to make origami while they waited for a crew and five million dollars. We had to physically pull her down the stairs out of the aircraft because she was afraid the hijacker would injure the remaining hostages. A few hours later, he allowed a couple to leave together. We had pushed the control issue. A hostage taker only needs one hostage to keep us from going in after him. Any more than one creates control problems for the hostage taker. He's got enough to think about without worrying that one of several hostages may escape or attempt to overpower him. He bought this explanation also and a couple more came down the aisle. Things were going smoothly.

That was about the time Best brought Jerry Mortensen and Don Findley, two of our SWAT snipers, into the aircraft to discuss a sniper shot. Ducker couldn't believe what he heard. He had a look on his face like he'd just found the jalapeno in his fish taco. We both protested, pointing out to Best how successful the negotiations were going. Bringing SWAT guys closer in to muscle up to this guy could back him into a corner and negatively affect our negotiations.

"No," said Best. "He could come out shooting. We've got to get this option in place. We don't know what this guy is going to do." I kept thinking about the bomb the hijacker claimed to have, and the fact that we were standing in a plane that had just been fueled with thousands of gallons of jet fuel.

Through all this, Sorenson continued to surprise us with her strength and courage. Time and again she left the rear of the plane with us to return to the hijacker and attempt to convince him to surrender. She also kept encouraging him to release other hostages. Wearing the mask, holding the gun in one hand and what appeared to be a bomb detonator in the other, he remained sitting against the bulkhead in first class. After ten hours he had not moved, eaten, or drank anything. Never even used the restroom. He talked only a little, and then only to Sorenson.

Best was on and off the aircraft to check on the negotiations and the tactical setup. As the agent in charge of the incident, he really needed to be in the command post, but later he insisted he had to be "where the action was." The SWAT snipers had taken positions on either side of the aisle and would have a clear shot if the hijacker stood up or came out of first class. This gave Ducker and me some comfort and allowed us to move fairly freely about the rear of the plane. In late afternoon we watched in amazement at the caravan of media vans lined up on Pershing Drive getting ready for their "Live at Five" shot. We suddenly realized that this whole carnival was waiting for our performance. It was a heady moment.

Several hours into the incident we watched as a Brink's armored truck pulled onto a corner of the tarmac, apparently bringing the five million dollars. Did this idiot really think he was going to fly off with ten duffel bags of used 20s? We chuckled at the sight of Kevin Kelly, the agent in charge of the money, making a great show of pointing out directions and instructions for the Brink's guys. We certainly didn't think the payment was going to happen, but we did think that we might have to show the hijacker the truck or the money at some point. They couldn't have found a better guy to handle the money. Kelly's honesty and ethics would have made the local cardinal look like a sinner.

Early on, Sorenson had opened the curtains so we could see up to the galley and just barely observe the legs of the hijacker. The snipers could probably have forced a shot, but the threat of a bomb changed everything.

Sometime in mid afternoon Sorenson had carried a field phone up to the hijacker, but he refused to use it. We weren't surprised by this, as a hostage taker often fears he will be identified if he talks to the negotiator. And many times recorded negotiation tapes have been released to the media before the incident has been concluded, providing just that opportunity. This hijacker's accent could have been identified by those who knew him so he had good reason to refuse. Others feel inadequate and unable to negotiate for themselves. They often insist that a hostage talk for them. Only when confronted with their identity, which makes the masking of identity and their ultimate escape impossible, or when the frustration boils over, would they grab the phone from the hostage.

By about 9 PM we had negotiated the release or assisted in the escape of seven of the eight remaining passengers. Neither Ducker nor I had eaten anything all day. It hadn't even occurred to us. We had lived off the nutritional ice chips in the rear galley. Adrenaline puts hunger on hold.

When the last passenger remained, we discussed an escape plan with Sorenson. She agreed to position herself in front of the hijacker and divert his attention so that the hostage could make her escape. The problem was explaining this to the hostage in the presence of the skyjacker. By now we also assumed that the hostage had begun to identify with the hostage taker, the Stockholm syndrome referred to earlier in the Patty Hearst case.

Without hesitation, Sorenson agreed to set up the escape, ignoring the obvious fact that she would become the last remaining hostage.

"You do know what this means, right?" I asked.

She looked me in the eye, smiled nervously, and nodded. We spontaneously hugged briefly, and she walked back up the aisle. Then we waited. And waited. Finally she managed to quietly push the last passenger down the aisle to the back of the plane. It had taken ten hours. And now only one hostage was left.

We had encouraged Sorenson to develop a relationship with the hijacker as a method of self-protection. Tell him about yourself, your family, and ask him about his, we had suggested. Show him pictures of your kids. It's more difficult to deliberately hurt someone you know. Sorenson played him well. After an hour we thought she might even be coming on to him. She lounged in one of the leather seats in first class and seemed to have become comfortable. She even showed him a little leg. During this time Ducker and I took turns talking to her on the field phone while the other briefed the boss at the base of the rear stairs. It became apparent that she had lost her fear of this guy. We thought she was never going to come out. We needed to develop a separation plan.

So we started to build her frustration with the situation and the hijacker. Sorenson had been worried about her husband's reaction when he was informed of the hijacking. He had some health problems and she was concerned about his welfare. We pointed out to her that it was the hijacker in front of her who was causing her problems and that all this is his fault. She caught on immediately and began giving this guy the "coming home late Saturday night" diatribe. After half an hour she had worked herself up and had begun to scream at him.

Still using the field phone and watching her up the aisle in first class, I began talking to her about an escape right down the aisle when he put the gun down, which he had done periodically. She had been drinking a Pepsi and I suggested she offer him one—to his gun hand. He had kept the gun in one hand and the detonator in the other. When he put down the gun and took the drink, she was to run. The minutes seemed like hours while she built up her courage. I pushed her hard on the phone, but she couldn't make the break. She had become semi hysterical. And then when it happened I almost missed it.

We were at a critical point and anything could stop the momentum. I was trying to wave Best away from the steps. We were all on the edge. Any movement could fuck it up. The SWAT snipers were bug eyed in anticipation of sending him off to meet Jesus. And then she finally offered him the drink. He put the gun down on the floor and reached for the can.

Bam! She fled screaming back down the aisle towards us. Unfortunately she took only three steps before she tripped on the curtain and fell on her face on the floor. The SWAT snipers stood up and pointed their guns directly at the hijacker—as Sorenson hysterically low crawled to the back of the airplane. Ducker and I dragged her down the stairs with no apology. Eyeball to eyeball with the hijacker, the snipers gradually backed off the plane.

Outside the aircraft, the SWAT snipers took up defensive positions and Ducker and I jumped into one of the FBI cars positioned around the rear of the plane. Someone brought me the field phone and I rang into the hijacker. This time he had no choice but to use the phone. He immediately cursed at me for stealing his last hostage. All the trust he had with Sorenson had been betrayed. The goddamn FBI!

I just listened patiently. After a few minutes he calmed down and then went into a depressive suicidal monologue. I launched into suicide prevention, searching for the triggering event within the last forty-eight hours: Why are you doing this now? What have you lost that you feel you need to do this? There is always a loss of something—a wife, a family, health, a job, a reputation. There is always a catalyst for the act of suicide—an overwhelming hopelessness and helplessness. It won't get any better and there is nothing I can do about it. The negotiator has to find the hook. What is there to live for? A wife? Children? Children are a good reason to live. They need you. Who is going to take care of your dog? There is always something. It just may take a while to find it. And you have to hope the ambivalence about jumping off the bridge or pulling the trigger (and it wavers, 80/20, 90/10, etc.,) doesn't overwhelm him before you find the hook. So you ask him to put down the gun at least while you talk. He can always pick it up again. But just put it down for now. And keep talking. About anything.

This guy was concerned about his two children in Denver and he seemed to be more embarrassed for his failure than remorseful. After about an hour, he appeared resigned to failure and finally agreed to surrender. A few minutes after 11 PM, and fourteen hours after he had walked into the airplane, Victor John Malasauskas walked down the ramp, pulled off his mask, and spread-eagled on the tarmac. It was finally over.

Born in Lithuania, Malasauskas had worked for an aerospace firm in the South Bay area of Los Angeles and held a responsible position. He had lived the good life, played tennis in the marina, and partied with the ladies. Trouble was, he had falsified his resume. When his fraud was discovered and he ran out of a job, he needed money to keep up his lifestyle. On a skiing trip to Colorado a few months before the skyjacking, he was amazed that a large knife he had placed in his ski boots passed through the magnetometer at LAX. So when he decided to hijack the airplane he packed his 9 mm automatic in his ski boots and pushed them through the magnetometer. The operator (diverted by his conversation) missed it and he was immediately inside LAX with a loaded gun. He said later he laughed at how easy it was. His "detonator" was determined to be a television remote. Over the years, it seemed like every wacko who threatened to blow up a simulated bomb used a television remote. Once inside the terminal, he was so excited that he couldn't decide whether to walk around with his trophy for a while or to get on with the hijack. Overanxious, he made the mistake of getting it on.

After being charged with federal air piracy, Malasauskas drew a public defender that wanted some trial experience and refused to let him plead guilty. Instead of copping a plea, which would have probably given him ten to fifteen years, he went through a full-blown jury trial that boiled down to my testimony. It was a simple issue. His attorney asked how we knew Malasauskas was the hijacker. I testified that after all the passengers had exited the aircraft, I continued to negotiate with the hijacker. After Mr. Malasauskas exited the plane, my conversation with the hijacker concluded. A search of the plane then came up empty. Therefore the FBI concluded that Malasauskas was in effect—the hijacker. Even the jury figured this one out. Of course there was also the confession that he tearfully poured out to Wayne Cassetty and me back at the FBI office that night. He was convicted of air piracy and sentenced to life in the federal prison system. I thought I'd never see Victor John Malasauskas again.

Ten years later, he walked into the reception room of the FBI office in Los Angeles and asked to speak to me. I couldn't believe it when the receptionist called. I asked her to spell the name. At that time we didn't have a magnetometer in the lobby of the federal building, which could determine if he was armed, and I wondered if he had returned in retaliation. I grabbed my old partner Kevin Kelly, and the two of us cautiously walked into the reception room.

But Malasauskas greeted us like old friends. He said that he had to come back to thank us for not killing him on the airplane. He had reconnected with his children and he wanted to volunteer to go to Lithuania, his mother country, which was being threatened by the Soviet Union, and work for the FBI. After a few minutes and a couple prison stories (he said that as a skyjacker, he had been considered a big-time inmate), we promised to refer his services to the CIA. Victor John Malasauskas became history.

Continental, the FAA, and a citizen's group later awarded Barbara Sorenson citations for bravery. She deserved every bit of it. Her courage and nerve in the face of death was extraordinary and inspirational. Although there was talk about Sorenson and I taking a dog and pony show on the road for FAA, it never happened and I only saw her again at the trial. I often wonder if this courageous woman ever flew again. She didn't need to. She'd done it all.

CHAPTER 6

YEAR OF THE GUN

1984 was a bad year. It was the year I got scared. Everybody had a gun and I started to obsess over getting blown away by one of these maniacs.

Assigned to kidnapping, extortion, and fugitive investigations since 1977, I'd seen my share of bad guys. The FBI's fugitive program was designed solely to assist local police departments search for wanted persons who had fled their jurisdiction. Once the local felony warrant had been issued, and there was specific information that the subject had fled the state (the cops couldn't say he must be out of state simply because they couldn't find him), the FBI would step in and file its own federal warrant charging the suspect with unlawful flight to avoid prosecution or incarceration. When the suspect was located and arrested, the FBI would dismiss its federal warrant and return the fugitive to the local agency. The sole purpose was to aid the local cops. In the early 1980s, under Director William Webster, the FBI began to prioritize its investigations, including our fugitive program. The FBI stopped looking for car thieves, forgers, and burglars and began to focus on the violent criminals—murderers, rapists, and robbers. With them came the guns, and I started burning up my luck.

One of the first that year was a murder fugitive out of Seattle, a black dope dealer named Antwon who had killed his partner over a deal gone bad. Shot him with a cheap 9mm semi-automatic, rolled him up in a rug, dumped him on a deserted road, threw a can of gas on him, and then set fire to the whole thing. What an idiot. He might as well have called 911. Five minutes later, someone drove by on the interstate, saw the fire and called it in. Ten minutes later the cops unrolled the body from the rug. It took them only a couple days to figure out where the hit came from and when it became apparent that Antwon had fled the state, the cops asked the FBI to help locate him. A day later Antwon, a small-time dope dealer, had become an FBI federal fugitive described as "armed and dangerous." Investigative leads regarding every adult person that Antwon had been associated with, friends and relatives, every address he ever used when he was arrested or registered a car, and every employer (if he had any) he had worked for, were sent out to various FBI offices. All of a sudden there were a whole lot of people looking for Antwon.

A few months later, my partner Ralph DiFonzo and I drove down to South Central Los Angeles on a telephone lead for Antwon. The FBI in Seattle had subpoenaed the telephone records of Antwon's girlfriend and come up with an LA address. The number came back to a neat little bungalow in a quiet section of Watts, the scene of the horrendous race riots in 1968, something we never forgot when we skunked around in that area. There were still a lot of people down there who didn't appreciate the FBI poking around in their 'hood, and hundreds of armed gang bangers just looking for trouble. We were very cautious and never went into the projects without an army of cops and agents.

Ralph had sent a black informant, who worked an ice cream truck, down to the address a couple times to look around but he hadn't seen anything—no Antwon, no Washington licensed cars or any activity. Normally we'd show Antwon's mug shot to a couple neighbors first but Ralph figured it was a dry hole and he just wanted to get rid of the case. In hindsight, we should have shown the photo, even though neighbors aren't always helpful or honest. But once you've shown the photo you're committed to knock on the door. If you come back an hour or a day later, the neighbor has alerted the fugitive that the FBI came by looking for him and he's long gone. Instead we drove through the narrow alley behind the house but we didn't see anything interesting, just the usual trash, dead cars, and pit bulls favored by young black gangsters. We parked on the street a couple doors away and walked up to the front door.

After a couple knocks, a short black guy, about thirty, opened the door six inches. We tensed but he wasn't our guy, who was well over six feet. We edged into the house, talking fast while the little guy gradually backed up. He said his name was Jackie. Within a couple minutes he copped out to being the brother-in-law of Antwon. But no, he hadn't seen him in years. Didn't know he was wanted for anything, let alone murder. Jesus Christ, murder? We laughed at his phony concern. He was a little jumpy, but people usually are when they have a couple of FBI humps poking around in their house. Who knows how much dope or how many stolen TVs he had in the back room? After a couple minutes though, I asked Jackie if he was alone in the house. That's something I learned from an old timer a long time ago. Let him tell you he's alone, and when you hear the toilet flush or the TV shut off, you know he's a lying asshole. Jackie said he was. Alone, that is.

While Ralph started to put the screws to him, I wandered into the dining room, and then headed towards a back bedroom. If I had looked back I would have seen Jackie's eyes start to grow out of his head. But I didn't. As I moved further into the house, the hair on the back of my neck stood up and I pulled out my .357, Model 19, a revolver with a very large four-inch bull barrel. A real persuader. The bedroom looked like a goat had thrown up, or maybe burglarized by a band of gypsies. Shit was all over the place, clothes hanging out of the drawers. I stopped and listened—for anything. Sometimes you can feel these guys hiding right in front of you. Like behind the clothes in a closet. Holding their breath. I moved in quietly before I noticed the bathroom door partially open. Four, maybe five inches. I fought the urge to give a quick look under the bed but then the door slowly opened and two large brown eyes stared out at me. Holy shit!

"FBI!" I yelled in total fright, shoving the .357 out in front of me.

He swung the door open further and I started to squeeze the trigger. Then he slowly raised his hands and showed them to me. Huge white palms. White? He had a needle sticking out of his elbow. I couldn't believe the gun didn't fire. I wanted it to. The hammer must have frozen. I had every right to blow this guy away and everyone would have shaken my hand and told me I was a hero. Dumb bastard, making that furtive movement, he deserved to get blown away. My brain must have registered "no gun, no threat" and cancelled the nerve transmission to my finger on the trigger. But I'd thought he had a gun. And if he had, Antwon would have had me. Instead he was minding his own business shooting up heroin in the bathroom when Ralph and I walked in and ruined his day.

"Ralph, I got him!" I yelled. "C'mere." I leveled the gun and lined up the front sight right between those large brown eyes. He sat frozen on the toilet in front of me. Antwon! His large shiny head had sunk down like a pumpkin sitting on his knees. He held his arms up signaling a touchdown.

"Don't shoot me, man. I ain't got a piece," he begged.

Seconds later Ralph charged into the room, screamed with surprise and anger when he saw Antwon, and stuck his gun in his ear. "You motherfucker! You motherfucker!" he kept screaming as he dragged his ass out of the bathroom. He rolled him over on his stomach, kicked him in the kidneys a couple times South Philly style, and cuffed him up.

Suddenly Jackie also appeared and started yelling for us to stop kicking him. "Watch it, man, he's got shot in the shoulder!" he yelled.

Ralph turned around and charged at Jackie. "You're going too, you lying little shit!" he screamed, as he threw Jackie over the bed and hooked him up too. Antwon remained on the floor moaning. His arm was bleeding a little and foamy yellowish drool was coming out of the side of his mouth.

I stood back shaking a little and taking it all in. Antwon moaning, Jackie complaining, and Ralph screaming. I felt like I was watching a cheap movie from the front row.

A few minutes later we were en route to LAPD headquarters downtown with both Antwon and Jackie handcuffed and seat belted into the back seat. I drove and Ralph sat up front in the passenger seat, turned sideways, pointing his gun at both of them, threatening to blow them both away. They were definitely not enjoying the ride. Antwon had been shot a few days before while sticking up a mom-and-pop Korean grocery. Pop had cranked off a couple rounds with his own .22, nailing Antwon in the bicep as he busted out the door. To avoid getting arrested, he hadn't received any medical attention and he was really starting to hurt. Ralph kept jerking Antwon's wounded arm around to remind him what an asshole he was. He started to moan like he was having a seizure, eyes jerking. And then Antwon started in on Ralph about Jackie.

"C'mon, man, he ain't done nothing, man. Let 'im go. C'mon. Jackie ain't involved, man. He didn't do nuthin."

It got old. Antwon alternated between moaning and pleading for Jackie. Jackie kept begging to be released and Ralph kept trying to shout them both down.

Suddenly Ralph leaned into the back seat. "Okay, asshole. You want me to let Jackie go. Okay, man. Here we go."

He unbuckled Jackie's seat belt and pushed open the rear door, right next to him.

Jesus. I'm looking over my shoulder, driving 75 on the eastbound Santa Monica freeway with two brothers handcuffed in the back seat of my car, and one of them about to be pushed out onto the freeway by my partner.

"Ralph, shut the damn door!" I started yelling, hanging on to the wheel with one hand and trying to pull Ralph back from climbing into the back seat and pushing the door open further. "Ralph, pull it shut!"

I really thought he'd push Jackie out. Ralph was freaked. His eyes bulged like a bullfrog trying to shit a chicken bone. Jackie was struggling to stay inside the car by laying his head on Antwon's lap and bracing one foot against the doorframe. Both looked panic-stricken. He kept dodging Ralph, who was trying to push him out with one hand while holding a gun in the other. It was probably only a couple minutes but it seemed like forever. I thought about pulling over to the shoulder but I kept thinking he would stop. We passed the Vermont and La Brea exits before he finally pulled back. As I swept onto the Harbor north transition the wind caught the open door and it clicked partially shut. Both Jackie and Antwon kept moaning. Ralph twisted around into his seat, leaned back, and laughed insanely.

A few minutes later we pulled into the rear of Parker Center police headquarters, badged our way through the guard shack, and finally stopped with Jackie and Antwon gasping in the back of the car. By the time we got them up to the office of the fugitive investigators on the third floor, they had started to breath normally again. We booked a humbled Jackie for harboring a fugitive—he'd probably spend about thirty-six hours in jail before being kicked loose—and then spent an hour with Antwon, who wouldn't give us much of anything about killing his former partner. Although we had made a quick search back at Jackie's house, we never found the gun he had used in Seattle. He just kept rolling his eyes at Ralph and mumbling, "Sompin ain't right, man, sompin ain't right." He was still moaning when they took him down to the hospital ward for treatment of his arm.

Ralph always denied he really tried to shove Jackie out of the car that day, but he never convinced me. He was sure as shit certifiably insane that morning I damn near dropped the hammer on Antwon.

In May we went down to Corona del Mar on a dope raid. A Colombian dope cartel had been pumping cocaine into an insatiable Orange County market and drawn the attention of everybody—the cops, DEA, and the FBI. Several suspects and locations had been identified and a huge multi-agency task force was going to execute numerous search and arrest warrants. I was the leader of the SWAT team assigned to arrest one of the primary suspects, Ronald "Turbo" Ting. Ting was a white male, about twenty-five, described as a cokehead, paranoid, crazy, always armed, unpredictable and very dangerous. We listened intently during the briefing by Bucky Cox, the case agent, but it was a typical description of a dope dealer. As far as we were concerned, they were all armed and dangerous. We were fortunate to have a couple days to study the house from exterior and aerial photos taken by the Special Ops guys. We planned simultaneous entries with two teams, one at the double doors in front and the other at the slider in the rear bedroom, which is where we figured he'd be at 6 AM. Whoever got to him first would freeze him down for the others. We had decided we didn't need to use flash-bang grenades since we figured he'd be asleep. But of course it never goes the way it's supposed to.

We pulled out of the police department parking lot, separated into about a dozen vehicles. The case investigator led the way to identify the correct location, followed by a marked black and white police unit, my SWAT team leader's vehicle, two vans with SWAT guys and equipment, then other investigative FBI agents, police investigators, the crime scene van, and lastly the paramedics. We also used a black and white to trail and stop traffic into the street until the entry was over. That's a whole bunch of people for a forty-five second raid. But it was our typical caravan for high-risk raids and extensive planning for safety and success had gone into it.

We unloaded quietly a couple houses down from the location and hustled up to the residence, carrying various weapons and entry tools. After giving the backyard guys a thirty second head start, Wayne Cassetty kicked in the front door easily and we streamed in the front door while the rear entry team broke the glass of the sliding door with sledge hammers in the rear bedroom.

The formula for a successful SWAT dynamic entry is surprise, speed, and superiority of numbers—and if necessary—maximum force.

It would have been okay but for Ting's paranoia, which made him keep a gun stashed under his pillow. By the time the guys in the rear had punched the remaining glass out of the slider and pulled back the drapes, a naked Ting had jumped up and, kneeling on the bed, pointed a 9 mm semi-automatic at them, struggling to make it function. Cassetty and I had gone to our left on entry and were surprised by another suspect in the first bedroom. We had to wrestle with him for a minute before he was hooked up. I could hear SWAT agent Jim Burns, who had been the third man in the front, yelling for Ting to drop the gun.

Then I heard a shotgun blast and I knew someone was down. I rushed into the bedroom and found Ting lying on the floor, hit in the neck. After unsuccessfully trying to disarm him with one hand, Burns had been forced to shoot. After we cleared the rest of Ting's room and a bathroom, I rolled him over and put on a set of plastic flex cuffs. He looked dead. No breathing, no pulse, and rapidly turning gray. Certainly he'd be DOA. When the rest of the house had been secured, I radioed for the paramedics. Having accompanied us in the caravan they were only a minute away. They immediately entered, attempted to stabilize him and inserted an IV, but both looked up and shook their head as they loaded him on a gurney for transport to the hospital. His internal bleeding would likely be fatal.

The search recovered a modern version of a vicious looking medieval crossbow and several other handguns. Ting had a fascination with weapons. Burns and I walked into the backyard where I had gathered the other members of the SWAT team. We had a short tactical debrief before I sent Burns back to the FBI office in Santa Ana for the post shooting interviews.

I made a crude drawing of the house interior and then drove back to the FBI office with Bill "Skeeter" Ayers, dreading the intensive interviews. It was amazing how many confrontational and accusatory questions the attorneys could come up with. I called Robbin during the ride back to tell her I'd be home late. If you're involved in an shooting incident, you can figure on being held captive for at least twelve hours for the debriefing, interviews, and a walk-through at the scene. It's a very stressful experience.

"How's Burns doing?" she asked. The SWAT team was a

close fraternity. Of all the members on the SWAT team, Burns wasn't the most aggressive guy. He was an experienced bank robbery investigator, a solid, almost mellow guy. He never thought he needed a notch on his gun. He suffered considerably after this shooting as a result of the scrutiny and criticism that made him question his actions.

That night I drove home from Orange County in the number four lane at sixty-five mph like a senior citizen. By the time I hit the top of the Sepulveda Pass looking down into the lights of the San Fernando Valley I had begun to mellow out a bit, but the fear had started to creep into me.

I was convinced that Ting would die. A close up—almost contact—wound with a shotgun is a devastating injury. A double 00 buck round consists of nine to eleven .32 caliber pieces of lead. But an ER surgeon with experience in gunshot trauma from a tour in Vietnam zipped him open from shoulder to hip, sutured and cauterized everything that was bleeding. Several hours and sixty pints of blood later, Ting was stable. He did eventually recover, but as a paraplegic sentenced to a wheelchair for the rest of his life.

Ten years later, his excessive force lawsuit against the federal government and everyone in the vicinity of the shooting finally came to court in Los Angeles. Wheeled into court he was a pathetic figure, "Turbo Ting" no more. I felt especially sorry for his supportive parents who accompanied him to court everyday. A good kid from a good family gone bad over dope and greed.

After a month of painful testimony it was finally over. The jury was out for about an hour; just long enough to use the restroom, select a foreperson, and take a vote. Not guilty. Burns was finally vindicated. We had all suffered emotionally when first labeled defendants, but as the suit progressed over the years all of us except Burns had been dropped from it. Taking the brunt of the criticism from the family, the public, and the media had been difficult for him. Contrary to what the public may think, a shooting is a very traumatic experience for everyone involved, especially the primary shooter. They all scar you permanently. You remember the dates like your wedding anniversary.

1984 was an exciting year for another reason as we prepared for the Olympics that summer in Los Angeles. The FBI would be the primary investigative agency for any terrorist incident at any of the venues in Southern California. I was in charge of the hostage negotiation team if we were called in. We trained extensively, including a couple weeks with the Hostage Rescue Team (HRT) back at the FBI Academy in Quantico. It was a heady time.

In Los Angeles, the Olympics went off without any serious problems. The only incident was a fake bomb planted by a cop who wanted some recognition as a hero.

Right after the Olympics concluded there was also the embarrassing arrest of Richard W. Miller, a local FBI agent, for espionage. He was later convicted of passing some classified training materials to a female Russian émigré with a drinking problem, but I always thought he was just trying to get laid. He was a pathetic figure, an overweight dumbo in a grimy sweat suit who sold Amway products out of the trunk of his FBI car. He couldn't fit in anywhere and fucked up everything he did, so they shipped him down to the wire tapping room where he just waited for a phone to ring, clicked on a recorder, and waited for his Domino's pizza to arrive. We all laughed at the *LA Times* article that described him as having been assigned to a highly sensitive position wiretapping various espionage suspects. In reality, he had been banished to "the hole" where we sent all our failures.

A few weeks later, Rich Noyes and Jimmy Jones from the fugitive squad pulled a guy out of a sleeping bag on a swimming pool patio in West Hollywood. He was wanted for a dozen armed robberies in Kansas City. When they shook out the bag, a gun dropped out. The guy later admitted that he had the gun in his hand and would have fired at Jimmy from inside the bag if Noyes hadn't surprised him and gotten the drop on him from a ledge above the pool.

That's some scary shit and it didn't take me long to internalize that kind of threat. By this time I had started wearing a second gun strapped to my calf, a little five-shot, snub-nosed Smith & Wesson .38. I did this secretly, since a back-up weapon would have suggested to the other agents that I was paranoid or, worse, afraid. The fugitive squad was no place for someone without confidence. But I couldn't shake the feeling that it was going to happen again. Guns—it was all I could think about.

That's also when The Dream started. I had begun to have the same dream night after night. I was walking out of a drug store in San Francisco and then chasing a guy wearing a black jacket down an alley. When he turned around he pointed a gun at me, and I'd shoot at him. I would watch the bullets rip into his chest but he didn't go down. He just stood there impervious to the bullets. And then I'd wake up. It went on for years. I couldn't seem to shake it. I'd also started to self medicate my anxiety and sleeplessness by pounding down a six-pack of Coors at night. It was the only way I could sleep. The fear had been growing deep in my bones like a metastasizing cancer. Robbin watched my increasing anxiety and drinking with disapproval but trying to understand. I had finally told her about The Dream, but I didn't share it with anyone else. It would have been a sign of weakness—or that I was starting to lose it.

Sometime in the fall of 1984 our SWAT team had been called out to a bank robbery in Placentia, a neat little city deep into Orange County. The patrol cops had chased the robber into a duplex and were positive he was still inside. We rolled in, suited up in our SWAT gear—black jump suits, Kevlar ballistic vests, radio headsets—and armed ourselves with various assault weapons—H&K MP-5 submachine guns, .870 shotguns, 9 mm Sig Sauer handguns, and gas delivery weapons. For an hour we intently watched and waited for FBI negotiator Stan Fullerton as he fruitlessly bullhorned the guy from outside the house. After an hour we decided that if he was still in there, he obviously needed an incentive to come out, so we pumped in some gas and waited.

Many times in these situations the bad guy has already escaped before the arrival of the SWAT team. Sometimes he's found a place to hide from the gas. And sometimes he's too doped up or too crazy to be affected by it. You might find him sitting in the bathtub reading his Bible wondering what took you so long. Kicking a door can be like opening a Christmas present. Or defusing a bomb. You never know.

After waiting about an hour for the gas to work we masked up and slowly crawled into the first duplex. Crawling around inside some place you just gassed knowing there's some asshole with a gun in there waiting for you to play hide and seek will definitely get your blood pumping. Your heart rate on an EKG chart would be off the scale. The other problem with working in a contaminated environment is that communication is extremely limited. We were using the old military M-17 gas masks, which made us look like a herd of giant black preying mantis in slow motion. Verbal communication is difficult to understand. It sounds like you're Darth Vader talking through a sweat sock. You don't want to make any noise so hand signals work best. We slowly and methodically searched the first duplex with no results before moving on to the second. It's an extremely fatiguing process because you have to operate on the assumption that at each corner and behind every door you're going to find The Gun pointed at you. And all you can hope for is to beat him at quick draw. I couldn't help thinking about how Antwon could have beaten me that morning in the bathroom in that quiet little bungalow in South Central.

There appeared to be a crawl space between the attics, but after laboring from one duplex to the other, we still came up empty. We regrouped in the living room to start a second search. I had been leaning against a horizontal built-in wall unit in the hallway. About four feet long, it opened down—a place where you'd store books or linens. Suddenly, Doug "Big Mac" McClary put his hand on my shoulder and motioned me aside. Leveling the barrel of his MP-5 at the cabinet, he slowly pulled open the horizontal door. A pair of tennis shoes stuck out. Mac shoved me aside and pulled on the Nikes. A bank robber the size of a gremlin flopped out onto the floor and unrolled his arms and legs like a Transporter packaged by Fed-Ex. He quickly stuck his hands in the air and then his eyes snapped shut as the gas hit him. Mac hooked him up and I looked into the cabinet. There it was. The gun he had used in the robbery. He had just decided not to use it. We weren't good—we were just lucky.

I went outside with the others and pulled off my mask. Nobody said much of anything for a while. How in the hell had we missed that cabinet in the first search? We had walked all around this guy for over an hour and he had just decided not to take us on. His choice. It had been out of our control. We missed him. We fucked up. I walked over to my car, popped the trunk, and sat down on the back bumper. I started to pull off my equipment and then it hit me. I felt like every bit of luck Mr. Hoover had issued me was draining out of my ass.

A few nights later I sat down in my office at home and studied my disability and life insurance coverage. I decided to buy several thousand dollars of additional term life. Just in case. I felt like I had discovered pancreatic cancer in my guts before the doctor's diagnosis.

Roger Dale Stockham was a good helicopter pilot who came back from Vietnam with a chest full of medals and ribbons, and nightmares. He had struggled with normalcy, married, had a kid, and tried to work consistently. But it just didn't work. He had too many demons. So he took his psychiatrist hostage on the 12th floor of an office building in Century City with a confusing list of demands. It finally ended several hours later when LAPD's SWAT team detonated an explosive charge against the door and rushed in to capture him. It would have been over sooner, but their EOD guys had to carefully calculate the strength of the explosive, strong enough to force entry through the solid oak door, but not so powerful that it would blow Roger and the shrink right out of the windows onto Santa Monica Boulevard down below.

Several years later after being released, Roger kidnapped his eight-year-old son from his mother, stole a small plane from the airport in Santa Cruz, and transmitted a "hijacked" call sign to the LAX tower. He then nonchalantly landed the Cessna near the edge of a cliff in Rancho Palos Verdes. A few hours later, after investigation determined that the claim of the hijack was bogus, members of the LA Sheriff's Department SWAT team located Roger and his son on the cliff and drove him down to the county jail. The FBI had been called out when the LAX tower notified FAA that they had a skyjacked aircraft in the South Bay area. I stood on the side of a hill with a radio reporter from KFWB and watched the SWAT guys drag the burned out Vietnam vet and his son up the hill. One of the SWAT guys carried a small box filled with Roger's war souvenirs and mementoes that he had carefully packed with him on the plane. It was a sad scene. Roger needed therapy much more than the LA county jail.

We had forgotten about Roger until he suddenly surfaced again several years later when a small bomb was found in a trash barrel in Reno with a note from him claiming credit. It didn't take long for the FBI to get geared up to run him down again. We knew who we were dealing with this time.

Ralph DiFonzo and I, along with several agents from the Long Beach office, went down to the Long Beach, VA, hospital where we knew Roger had some old friends in the psych ward. We discovered that he recently had been in the area and had contacted a couple of them. We also received information from the local cops that someone had left several small incendiary devices around the grounds of Cal State University at Long Beach over the last twenty-four hours. It didn't take us long to make the connection and conclude that Roger had returned to Long Beach. We just didn't know what he was up to this time.

Unknown to us, however, was that he had called the NBC TV newsroom in Los Angeles to advise them that he was planning to hold a press conference in front of the Science Building at Cal State Long Beach that morning to explain his "Golden Triangle Theory of Southeast Asia." We later learned that this was his confusing conspiracy theory about American exploitation of Southeast Asia. NBC immediately dispatched a news crew to cover the conference, but it wasn't until they had almost reached the scene that they realized they had better notify the FBI. We received the information on the radio a few minutes later. While the other agents had headed off for breakfast and missed the first broadcast, Ralph and I had just picked up a cup of coffee and were still in the car. We immediately headed over to CSULB and were on the campus within minutes.

Two blocks from the Science Building we found him, walking down the street ahead of us. He was carrying a briefcase and walking like a man on a mission. He didn't hear us as we slid in behind him. We both jumped out of the car and jammed him easily. I took the briefcase out of his left hand and Ralph grabbed his right as we took him down.

Roger grinned at us but said nothing. It didn't sink in. He kept grinning stupidly at us, apparently uncomprehending. Ralph finally grabbed one ear and pulled out the earphones, listened to one, and then laughed. He held it up to me and I listened briefly—to the sounds of classical music. Roger, what an enigma!

I bent down and popped open the briefcase. What was I doing? The excitement of finally capturing Roger Dale Stockham had blotted out my memory of why were looking for him. He was a bomb maker!

I looked down at the inside of the case and observed something that looked like a blue ice container, two double DD batteries, and a series of wires. I froze. I looked up at Roger, who was still grinning like some kind of escaped maniac.

"It ain't real, man," he said. "I just needed something to get their attention. I figured once they showed up I'd threaten to set it off and they'd have to listen to me."

He knew he was crazy and he knew that the news guys would know it also. But they would have to cover a speech by some wacko if he had a bomb. That's the trouble with these guys. They may be crazy but they aren't stupid.

I looked down at the briefcase again and noticed that he had glued a small green tube of mercury on the top, which suggested that any movement would detonate the bomb. He also had a red push button crudely drilled under the handle, also to suggest that he had a second method of detonation. Primitive, but it sure as hell would have convinced anyone from a distance. Improvised explosive devices are the most dangerous since they follow no pattern. You never know if they used that green wire because they ran out of red.

I stood up and felt a tightness in my chest. I struggled to catch my breath. Holy shit. After all the real ones to get our attention, this was just a simulated incendiary device designed for a press conference. I walked over to the car and leaned against the door trying to stop the shaking in my knees. Roger stood just stood there grinning.

Minutes later the Long Beach PD bomb technicians arrived and suggested running a bomb dog by the briefcase even though some dumb shit FBI agent had already opened it. It was humiliating and humbling. And I deserved every bit of it. Once again, I had beaten the odds.

I can still see the face of Roger Dale Stockham today, with that lopsided lobotomized grin. "It ain't real, man."

Then the Colombians came to Rampart, a densely populated part of LA just southeast of Hollywood, an area primarily inhabited by Hispanics with a lot of Central Americans. One of the other guys on the kidnapping squad, Greg Pack, had been looking for a crew of Colombian kidnappers who had killed a guy in Florida. The cops there had screwed up the payoff so the frustrated kidnappers wrapped the victim's head in duct tape, suffocating him, and dumped him into a canal. They had also killed a guy in Houston by torturing him with a stun gun until he had a cardiac arrest and died. The three guys and a female were supposedly headed to LA to link up with a relative living in an apartment complex in Rampart. Pack had contacted the apartment manager who looked over the photos and promised she would call if they showed up. He had talked to her periodically but she said they hadn't been around.

Then one Saturday night, the manager called Pack around 11 PM. She admitted that the kidnappers had been living there for two months and that she had been messing around with the leader, a sadistic professional killer named Jesse. She finally called Pack after she found out that Jesse had also been banging a couple other women in the complex.

Pack called the rest of the members of the squad. A little after midnight, we met and briefed a couple blocks away in the rear of a Shell station on Melrose. We checked the radios, put on our ballistic vests, and locked and loaded before driving into the apartment complex. We gathered around the edge of the slimy pool—in twenty-five years I never saw anyone swim in an apartment swimming pool in LA—while Pack went in and talked to the apartment manager. He came out a few minutes later with a key to Jesse's apartment and a grin on his face.

"She's been fucking Jesse for two months," he laughed. "He was probably hiding in the back bedroom the last time I came by to talk to her." We all immediately agreed that we would never trust an apartment manager again. She told Pack this time that she'd only seen two guys and the girl. But she thought they were all in the apartment right now. She had seen Jesse with a gun, and yes, Jesse was a badass.

We crept up the stairs to the second level and found the apartment. Dim lights. Television on. Voices. Suddenly the lights went off. We held our breath. Had they heard us? No movement. We should have backed off and called them out. But we didn't. Pack slid the key into the lock and in we went. Five of us: Pack, me, Noyes, "Vinegar Joe" Varley, and Regis Boyle.

A guy we later learned was named Hector surprised us as he came out of a bedroom on our left. As Pack and I were wrestling with him I heard Noyes yell, "He's got a gun!"

I turned around to see Noyes struggling with Jesse in the middle of the living room. Both were standing, each holding onto the other's gun, which was pointed straight up at the ceiling. Then they went down, Noyes shouting again for help. I leveled my shotgun at the two but with only the low light of the TV and both wrestling around I didn't have a clear shot. Then Boyle came out of nowhere and jumped into the pile to help Noyes subdue him. After Jesse was handcuffed, Noyes stood up and held out a snub-nosed, chrome-plated .357 revolver—a 1980s Secret Service duty weapon. Where the hell did he get that?

Then it started to sink in, I never saw Jesse on my right when I'd entered the darkened living room. Went right by him looking to the left. Shit! He could have picked off every one of us as we streamed in.

After the others left with Jesse and Hector, Noyes and I remained inside the apartment and other agents stayed in the parking lot, waiting for the remaining two kidnappers to come back from a night of partying. We rotated sitting on a packing box, the only furniture in the place, standing up to stretch every half hour or so. Around 2 AM, we heard light footsteps and then a key in the door. In walked a small female. Before she could flip on the lights, Noyes clamped his hand around her throat and shoved her against the wall. Holding a cocktail glass in one hand and her keys in the other, she looked surprised but said nothing.

"What's your name?" Noyes snarled at her. She stared at him with fury and hate in her eyes. Then spit in his face.

Noyes picked her up by her throat, spun her around, and shoved her face into the wall while I cuffed her. I thought he was going to pluck her head off like a chicken. She gagged a little but never said a word. We hustled her into the back bedroom and stuffed her face into a blanket while we waited long enough for the fourth kidnapper to park the car and come up to the apartment. But when no one showed after a half hour we left the apartment and drove the female, later identified as Julietta, back to the FBI office. Other agents stayed with the manager for a while, but we called them back in when it became apparent that the fourth suspect was not coming back. We later learned that he hadn't accompanied the others to LA.

Julietta turned out one of the toughest dopers I'd ever met. A year before, she and her boyfriend had been kidnapped by some other Colombians over a deal gone bad and had been chained together under a house in North Hollywood for forty-three days waiting for a payoff. I imagine they got to know each other pretty well. Back at the FBI office we interrogated her for hours but she never gave us a damn thing and we shipped her back to Florida with Jesse and Hector a few days later.

I never testified in the homicide trial in Florida in which they were all convicted, but Noyes did. He still talks about taking that fucking gun away from Jesse. And why the hell he didn't pull the trigger on us we'll never know unless Jesse, who is now sitting on death row in Florida, decides to talk about it.

For the last several months I had begun frequenting a local indoor shooting range, sometimes with one of my daughters. It was a somewhat unusual father-daughter bonding activity, but we enjoyed it and especially our time together. The year's experiences had convinced me I would be tested again and I had become obsessed with improving my firearms proficiency. We fired the guns for hours. And I never missed my team's regularly scheduled firearms training either. I knew it was going to happen, and when it did, I was going to be ready.

But the Year of the Gun didn't end until December, when the Los Angeles SWAT team flew up to Washington State to arrest Robert Mathews and his wild group of neo-Nazi racists, survivalists, and white power advocates called The Order. By the time the smoke had settled, I was convinced that I'd never survive long enough to collect a pension. I'd been in the shit for too long.

CHAPTER 7

ROBERT MATHEWS AND THE ORDER

It was an ominous December 7 when the FBI's Hostage Rescue Team (HRT) had flown into exclusive Whidbey Island, Washington, and set up a perimeter at three locations where several members of The Order had holed up. They had federal arrest warrants for almost all the members of the group, which was a spin-off of the Aryan Nations. After the initial contact, the occupants at two of the locations had surrendered without a fight. But at the third, the HRT had found Robert Mathews, the hardcore leader of The Order. He wasn't going to give up easily. Or at all.

Based at Quantico, the HRT had been formed in 1983 to carry out the rescue of hostages in extremely dangerous hostage and barricade situations that exceeded the capabilities of the regional FBI SWAT teams. They were also trained to execute arrest warrants on suspects posing a high threat level. The Order certainly qualified for a response by the HRT. When they had been located on Whidbey Island, FBI headquarters immediately deployed the HRT to surround them and to make the arrests. But this was shaping up to be a long, dangerous siege, and the HRT was going to need some help.

The Los Angeles SWAT team got the call late in the morning but by 3 PM we had a U.S. Customs C-130 aircraft waiting for our team at LAX. We screamed down the 405 freeway to the airport, loaded our equipment, counted noses, and climbed aboard. Once inside we belted into the aluminum tubing and web seats. The aircraft crew chief stood in front of us, looked around, and shouted instructions over the noise of the auxiliary power units inside the cabin.

"Okay, I assume that all weapons are unloaded. Everybody belt up. Once we get airborne you can get up and move around, but I don't recommend it because there's no place to go. Don't worry about the web seats. The checkerboard creases in your ass won't be permanent. The head is up front, looks like a small sink, and is basically a urinal. If you need to take a crap, you can pull the plastic sheet around you. And if you do take a crap, you have to clean the bucket when we arrive at our destination. You can forget about complimentary beverages and peanuts. We're going to be airborne about for three and a half hours. I'll take your questions now, gentlemen."

We all laughed, but no one asked anything. We were soon lost in our own thoughts and prayers—and hoping our nervous stomachs could handle the three-hour flight. We were about to take on an anti-government, survivalist group of heavily armed and violent fanatics. Members of The Order had already shot it out with the FBI on two previous occasions. They were a crazy bunch of zealots and no one expected them to come out meekly with their hands up.

The FBI had spent a lot of time training regional SWAT teams to respond when their neighbors called for help. The field offices around the U.S. all have local SWAT teams, which can be blended into regional SWAT teams for major events. The LA team worked with San Diego and San Francisco most often, although we had been to Las Vegas on a biker raid a few months before. Portland and Seattle SWAT worked together and had already been deployed to Whidbey Island two days before with HRT in the planning stages of the confrontation. San Francisco had already left this morning as soon as HRT had called. Our assignment was to relieve the San Francisco SWAT team on the perimeter when we arrived. We touched down a few hours later at the Naval Air Base on Whidbey Island and were met by military buses and trucks that immediately took us and our equipment and us over to the bachelor officers' quarters. We checked in and then stowed our gear. The first meeting was held in the lobby. We were all hyped with nervous anticipation.

Myron Hitch, our SWAT team leader, stood in front of us. Hitch was a legend in his own time—everything a SWAT team leader ought to be. Stocky, muscular, neck veins like a drill instructor, predator eyes, could curse like a convict, and supremely confident. He was certainly one of the most intimidating agents that I ever met. He sought confrontation, enjoyed argument, and simply refused to lose. He always smelled like he had just run a marathon. Myron was convinced he could do anything. He made his own flash-bang stun grenades in his garage by drilling a hole for the fuse with a power drill without blowing up the neighborhood. His favorite movies were *Patton* and *The Great Santini*. He had half a black panther tattooed on his left bicep and none of us ever dared to ask about the other half. Myron had a Great Dane at home that peed whenever he looked at it. He intimidated the suits, the upper echelon bosses. He hated the FBI headquarters "slugs" that had never done anything on the street and he struggled when taking orders from them. A half eaten bagel had more common sense. The living room in his house was filled with boxes of extra SWAT gear. He lived and breathed SWAT. Every man has his pornography. For Hitch it was SWAT.

"Okay," Hitch started, "We've been negotiating with Mathews since about 10 AM this morning. He's refused to come out. Two others who were with him are out and they say he's got enough guns for a platoon and that he'll never surrender. San Francisco SWAT has the perimeter for now and we'll relieve them in the morning. 0700 hours. So relax, get some sleep, and we'll mount up here at zero six. It'll take about an hour to get out to the location. Any questions? Didn't think so. Okay, get going." Hitch stomped off to fuck with someone else.

We tried to get some sleep but most of us were too hyped. It was a long night wondering what was going to happen tomorrow. Most of us slept in our clothes, fearing we would miss the bus and incur the wrath of Hitch.

The parent group of our team's target, the Aryan Nations, was a neo-Nazi paramilitary offshoot of the Church of Jesus Christ Christian. Headquartered near Hayden Lake, Idaho, it was founded in the 1970s by Richard Butler, a disgruntled former California aerospace engineer. Butler's "Christian Identity" doctrine postulated that Anglo-Saxons, not the Jews, are the Biblical chosen people, and non-whites are "mud people" akin to animals. The Aryan Nations advocated anti-Semitism, preparation for a coming racial/religious apocalypse, and the establishment of a white racist state. Despite providing a training school for radical racists for years, Butler operated without interference by law enforcement authorities. In 1998, however, his luck started to run out when a couple of his armed guards fired on a car outside the group's compound and assaulted its occupants, a woman and her son. With the assistance of the Southern Poverty Law Center, they won a $6.3 million lawsuit verdict against Butler. In a bitter irony, he was forced to sell his 20-acre compound, complete with a gun tower and chapel, to a human rights group that demolished all the buildings and donated the property to a college. Butler died in late 2004, an unrepentant racist until the end.

Butler and his hate group had been responsible for graduating several militants and sending them out into the world to become involved in racially motivated shootings. One killed a state trooper in Missouri and another shot up a Jewish day care center in Los Angeles. Robert Mathews was a distinguished alumnus. After looking over Butler's operation, he decided it wasn't militant enough and in October 1983 he started The Order, also known as The Silent Brotherhood. Mathews began to recruit from a growing subculture of racists in the Northwest. He fomented a hatred of Jews and government officials and drew up a hit list that included Henry Kissinger and Norman Lear. Mathews was in a hurry to become a dangerous man.

The FBI was somewhat slow picking up on Mathews and his troops. Initially Mathews started in the counterfeit money business to fund the organization but decided it took too much work and time. Violence was easier—and more productive. Eventually totaling twenty-three at full strength, members of The Order held up a jewelry store in Denver, bombed a synagogue in Boise, robbed a bank in Seattle, hit a couple armored cars, killed an informant, and then gunned down a Jewish talk show host in Denver by the name of Alan Berg—all before the FBI realized they were dealing with an organized hate group. The Order's downfall was an armored car stickup in Ukiah, California, at which a shoulder weapon was left at the scene. After its owner was identified as Denver Parmenter, the FBI rapidly identified Parmenter's associates as other members of The Order. These included a new member named Tom Martinez, an incongruous selection because he was Hispanic, and a serious mistake by Mathews. Martinez eventually soured on the group's hatred and violence, and facing years in prison after being arrested for counterfeiting, became an FBI informant. It was Martinez who told the FBI that Mathews and the gang was holed up on Whidbey Island.

The FBI responded like it had found John Dillinger. By the time Mathews arrived at Whidbey Island, members of The Order had been involved in two shootings with FBI agents. When agents had tried to locate and interview one of his recruits, Gary Yarbrough, at his home in Idaho, Yarbrough came out shooting and then escaped, leaving his family behind. Yarbrough had been the security chief of the Aryan Nations at one time. The second shooting involved Mathews himself in Portland, Oregon. Martinez, who had been traveling with Mathews and several others, had been calling the FBI periodically to keep them advised of their location as they jumped from one hideout to another. Mathews was frustrated that he couldn't elude his pursuers, but never figured out who was tipping them off. Although they had planned to stay at the Holiday Inn—information Martinez had passed on to the FBI—Mathews changed his mind at the last minute, and they ended up at the Capri Motel. When the FBI finally found Mathews's car after searching all the motels in the area, the FBI agents from the

Portland office immediately converged on the scene, began evacuating the rooms surrounding that of Mathews, and putting an arrest plan together. Unfortunately they were too obvious and moved too slowly. Mathews happened to walk out of his room and spotted the agents in the manager's office. Grabbing a gun, he took off running down the balcony.

When the agents started firing, they missed Mathews and the first casualty was the coffee pot in the manager's office. Mathews jumped a fence and kept running without looking back. When he reached a nearby apartment complex, he took cover and fired at the agents chasing him. Art Hensel was the first agent around the corner into Mathews's line of fire and was hit in the foot, but SWAT agent Kenny Lovin managed to get off a couple shotgun blasts at Mathews, one of which clipped off part of his knuckle. In spite of an intensive search, Mathews escaped once again. Yarbrough, meanwhile, was arrested after jumping out of a window into the hands of a female FBI agent. For Martinez, who had partnered with the FBI, the long and dangerous ride with Mathews was over.

Kenny Lovin was one of our Bureau heroes. A blond, clean-cut, athletic, soft-spoken, good-looking guy, he had killed an airplane hijacker at JFK airport in the 1970s. Blew the guy away with a headshot while he walked across the tarmac with his arm wrapped around the neck of a flight attendant. The poor woman is probably still in therapy. Several years later he climbeda ladder into the cockpit of a hijacked airplane at the Portland airport, then rushed out of the cockpit and shot the hijacker in the chest with a single round. The passengers stood up and applauded. Lovin had the balls of a burglar and he was a national Bureau celebrity. In reality he was a very modest hero.

0600 hours. The roar of Hitch bellowing orders. We guessed he hadn't closed his eyes all night. Probably stayed up cleaning his weapons. Everyone was ready. We tried to shake off the jitters as we loaded into two buses in front of the Bachelor Officers Quarters (BOQ). The LA FBI SWAT team, coming to bail out the San Francisco boys. We laughed about HRT—Super SWAT—leaving the job for us regional SWAT guys.

The drive out to the cabin on Smuggler's Cove took about forty-five minutes. It was dark, rainy, and cold. Like most of the time in the minutes just before a SWAT raid, everyone was quiet, mentally rehearsing their responsibilities and pushing down the anxiety. We looked out the foggy windows at the rain. Nobody said much.

The buses stopped on a dirt road and we unloaded. The wet foliage was bright green like the Amazon rain forest. I had forgotten about the weather up in Seattle. If it isn't raining, it's getting ready to. I started shivering and didn't stop for the next twelve hours.

We loaded up our gear and marched in a column down a dirt trail for about a half-mile. Several FBI cars were parked at the end of the trail. Two negotiators were camped inside one of them seeking relief from the rain. The wire from the hostage phone ran a hundred yards further to the cabin, which rested on the edge of a bluff overlooking the ocean. It was an expensive, rustic, two-story building with large picture windows and a deck on the second floor looking out onto Puget Sound. Due to the confrontation with Mathews and a potential firefight, shipping traffic had been held back and the Sound was clear. We couldn't believe this maniac had stopped international shipping traffic. Two brand new oversize pickups were parked outside a shed on the south side of the cabin. We figured Mathews had probably bought them with bank robbery proceeds or their counterfeit bills. The San Francisco SWAT team was dug into foxholes around the cabin like the marines at Khe Sanh. They were hardly noticeable dressed in their camouflage and black fatigues.

While the rest of the team moved forward in small groups and began replacing the team on the perimeter, I stopped to say hello to the negotiators. They had been talking to Mathews since 10 AM on Friday. It was now 7:30 AM on Saturday. After allowing two others in the cabin to come out, Mathews had vehemently refused to even discuss surrendering. He was pissed that the FBI had found him, and the pain of his injured hand (the knuckle Lovin had hit) added to his aggravation. The negotiators were pessimistic about a surrender. Mathews seemed determined to shoot it out and to take as many agents with him as possible. He had constantly told them so. He seemed determined to become a martyr for The Order and white racism.

The LA team settled in and tightened the perimeter, moving the foxholes closer to the cabin. John Uda, "Skeeter" Ayers, Jim Burns, Hitch, and I crawled up to a shed on the south side. By 11 AM we had concluded the negotiations were going nowhere and the two SACs on the scene (from Portland and Seattle) agreed that we had waited long enough. After twenty-four hours of negotiation, we were ready to suggest another reason for Mathews to surrender—gas.

At Hitch's radioed command, all hell broke loose. Half a dozen agents around the perimeter fired tear gas simultaneously into various rooms of the cabin. I aimed my first round at the chandelier in the kitchen. We waited, naively thinking this would affect Mathews. After approximately a half hour, Hitch ordered another volley. Again we perforated the cabin windows. I kept loading up the kitchen by picking off pieces of the chandelier, which swung in the wind like a target in a carnival shooting gallery.

Eventually, we went to our 40mm M-79 grenade launchers to deliver the gas. Unfortunately, the larger projectiles only succeeded in ventilating the whole cabin for a strong wind now blowing in off the Sound. And it got colder—about 40 degrees—and of course it was still raining. Damn, it got cold. And wet. I continued to shiver. We pumped gas into the cabin for several hours with no response from Mathews. The bastard never even coughed. He laughed at the negotiators and said the gas hadn't affected him at all. We figured with all his military equipment and firearms, he probably had a gas mask.

We marveled at his stamina. He had been up for at least thirty-six hours talking to the negotiators, threatened with an assault at any time and attacked by the gas. And yet he had the balls to still threaten us. The man's dedication, devotion, and motivation were amazing. But he was wrong. And he was a killer.

Around 4 PM the sheriff's department decided to send in a dog. This seemed foolish to me as I figured Mathews, supposedly armed to the teeth, would simply shoot the dog. The handler crept forward while we continued to pound the cabin with more gas intended to keep Mathews's head down. He pushed the dog into a window on the first floor, only to have the dog jump back out a few seconds later. He repeated this a couple more times and finally gave up. That German Shepherd had no interest in meeting Bob Mathews.

An hour later, an entry team from the Butte, Montana, FBI office kicked its way through a door on the south side of the cabin. Masked up and led by Gary Lincoln, their SWAT team leader, they crawled into the first floor of the cabin.

Minutes after Lincoln's team entered the cabin Mathews opened up on it from the second floor, firing what sounded like an M-60 machine gun right through the floor. Lincoln and his bug-eyed teammates backed out, dodging and darting back to the safety of the perimeter. Lincoln pulled his mask off. "Motherfucker!" he growled. "We damn near died in there."

Gary Lincoln was not one to back away from a fight. Before going to Butte, he had been assigned to bank robbery investigations in the LA field office and was a member of our SWAT team. We knew him to be one of the more fearsome agents. The Bureau had recruited him from a Washington State logging camp, adding to his Paul Bunyan mystique. There wasn't much Lincoln was afraid of. Several years before we had cornered a bank robber in the attic of a bank in Downey. After hours of attempting to convince him to surrender, we flooded the attic with tear gas, but he refused to come down. Eventually someone had to climb up the ladder and poke his head into the attic. Lincoln didn't hesitate. Five minutes later he was dragging down a shirtless, hairy retard from the crawl space.

That was the last entry team we sent in. We huddled again with the agents in charge and decided we had to wait this one out. More gas. More waiting.

At about 6 PM, we brought in an FBI helicopter flown up from San Francisco to look the place over. It was beginning to get dark, which meant we faced the possibility of Mathews attempting to escape by shooting his way through the perimeter.

Everyone became more intense. As soon as the helicopter came in from the ocean side and made a close pass, Mathews opened up on it. The bastard had been outside lying on top of the deck to avoid the gas, completely unseen by any of us.

The helicopter pilot immediately pulled up and to the right to avoid the rounds. In spite of the surprise burst by Mathews, it was not hit. But he had given away his location. We immediately repositioned our snipers, but by the time they were set up he had disappeared again. We pumped more gas into the cabin and I watched the chandelier in the kitchen lose another piece. By now the wind was really blowing and we were reduced to Kentucky windage for shotgun-delivered rounds. Accuracy with the gas rounds had become difficult and we had saturated the place, but the wind was working against us by blowing the gas outside the cabin.

A few minutes later Mathews surprised us again by opening up on my team's side of the perimeter. Several rounds slapped into the shed we had been leaning against. John Uda and I stumbled over each other diving behind the shed. Where the hell was he?

More rounds came in and we were pinned down for several minutes. All we could do was just sit tight and hope the he didn't demolish the shed. A few minutes later he opened up on the other side of the perimeter and we got a chance to locate his firing position. Ayers began to methodically pump 7.62mm penetration rounds from his M-14 rifle into the upper bathroom window. A good ol' boy from Arkansas and a Vietnam veteran, Ayers knew what he was doing with a rifle.

But Ayers moved too slowly for Hitch. Frustrated with his measured methodical firing, Hitch pushed Ayers out of the way and jumped into the open, a 9mm semi-automatic in one hand and a .357 revolver in the other. Reminiscent of gunslingers in the old West, Hitch fired both guns alternately until they were both empty, screaming "Take that, cocksucker!"

Then he fell back behind the shed, popped the magazine out of the 9mm, and slapped another one in. His blue eyes bulged with excitement. He flashed a toothy grin at me and laughed,

"Ain't this shit great?" The man was mad.

Mathews continued to fire at the agents on the perimeter, one side after another, trying to prevent another assault. At times it seemed as if all sides of the perimeter were firing back at him as he moved from one window to another. I had given up on the gas and gone to rifled slugs for penetration. We began to wonder if we'd have enough ammunition. We constantly worried that Mathews would make a break for it and try to shoot his way out through the perimeter. As darkness began to surround us, several M-79 illumination rounds were fired into the cabin to light it up and hopefully locate Mathews. However, a small fire started on the ground floor and several minutes later the cabin was burning. The negotiators urgently increased their pleas to Mathews for his surrender, promising that he would be unhurt. But he only continued to scream profanities at them over the hostage phone and then continue to fire, moving from one position to another in the cabin. We were amazed at how long he held out. In fifteen minutes the fire was raging and the cabin was fully engulfed.

Eventually Mathews stopped shooting. We waited anxiously, totally convinced that he would come out, guns blazing. Even when the second story collapsed onto the ground floor, we were still on edge. This was a man motivated by hate. We watched silently, waiting. Then the cabin became an inferno. Rounds in the cabin began cooking off and forced us down into our holes and behind the trees.

Later, as it began to die down, we edged forward, wondering if he was going to rise from the ashes like in some horror movie. But it was over. Robert Mathews was no more. He had his chance and he had made his choice. He had tried to kill us and he had failed. We stood silently and watched the last flames consume the hatred and evil of the man. To hell with him.

Gathered around the smoldering embers like a warrior tribe at a campfire after a successful hunt, we suddenly realized how long it had been since we had eaten. We dug into the box lunches the navy had prepared for us. As we finished the chicken we threw the bones into the fire, laughing at how the FBI crime scene technicians would wonder what the hell Robert Mathews was doing with the fifteen chickens they found in the embers of his cabin on Whidbey Island.

The autopsy subsequently determined that Mathews's cause of death was several gunshot wounds although the body was also severely burned. Several other members of The Order remained fugitives, but within a year the FBI had apprehended every one of them at various locations around the country. The U.S. Attorney's office in Seattle eventually charged them with a multitude of crimes under the federal Racketeer Influenced and Corrupt Organizations (RICO) statute. All were convicted, sentenced and incarcerated for long prison terms. The Order, Robert Mathews's brainchild of hate, death, and destruction was no more.

CHAPTER 8

BIRTH OF THE CRISIS
INCIDENT NEGOTIATION TEAM

It was June 1985 at the FBI Academy on the Marine Corps base in Quantico, Virginia. With twenty-four other experienced FBI negotiators from around the country, I had been sitting in the academy's state-of-the-art classrooms for a week listening to guest speakers. We had been selected as the first members of the FBI's international Crisis Incident Negotiation Team (CINT). This team was designed to become the nucleus of the FBI's organized response to complex and potentially lengthy hostage and barricade incidents around the world.

The late 1970s and the early 1980s had witnessed an alarming rise in the number of long-term hostage and barricade incidents. The Hanafi Muslim sect had paralyzed Washington, D.C., for several days with its simultaneous takeover of three locations in 1977; Americans were taken hostage in Tehran in 1979 for 444 days; and a small, right wing survivalist group known as The Covenant, The Sword, and The Arm of the Lord (CSA) was involved in an incident in Arkansas in 1985. Perceptive members of the Crisis Management Unit (CMU) at the FBI Academy realized that the Bureau needed a small, mobile, and highly trained group of expert hostage negotiators to respond to these incidents.

The original CINT team members had been selected from a pool of more than 350 FBI negotiators based on resume reviews, personal interviews, psychological testing, foreign language fluency, and negotiation experience. Most were experienced agents who had been hostage negotiators for ten to fifteen years and had extensive operational, investigative, and training experience. We enjoyed the fact that the group was multi-racial and multilingual, with several members fluent in four to five languages. Our diverse investigative experience included foreign counterintelligence, counterterrorism, organized crime, drugs, basic criminal investigation, and informant development. Because most of us had been police instructors in the field, and we all possessed an excellent working knowledge of negotiation strategies, hostage and barricade techniques, and crisis management principles in addition to actual negotiation experience. Several of us had negotiated high profile aircraft skyjackings. All were experienced street agents. We were excited about the program's potential and proud to be considered the best the Bureau had.

The CMU arranged and coordinated semi-annual training seminars at the academy or other venues that could accommodate the team's special instructional needs. We conducted joint training with the CIA, the Department of Energy's Nuclear Emergency Search Team (NEST) and participated in numerous long-term training exercises in Albuquerque, New Mexico; Camp Pendleton, California; Indianapolis, Indiana; and at the Lawrence Livermore Labs near Oakland, California. Criminal profilers, specialists in various cultures, and mental health professionals from other federal government agencies experienced in personality profiling also provided instruction for the team.

The International Hostage Taking Act of 1984 had tasked the FBI with deploying agents overseas to conduct skyjacking and kidnapping investigations. This responsibility required CINT team members to interact with Department of State personnel and receive overseas operations training. It also required the members to learn how to work with foreign law enforcement and intelligence agencies. This training focused on developing critical threat assessments, devising strategies for responding to kidnapping ransom demands, coordinating the efforts of the U.S. embassy staff, as well as maintaining contact with the employers and families of the victims. Working overseas to effect hostage rescues created completely new and demanding challenges for the team. A primary issue to cope with was that law enforcement in the rest of the world doesn't always function as efficiently or as effectively as that in the United States.

Team members received updated passports, instruction in diplomatic procedures, cultural norms and sensitivity training, as well as numerous inoculations. All the negotiators attended the outstanding negotiator's course provided by the Metropolitan Police Department at New Scotland Yard in London. The Brits are the best at organization and planning for crises. Their experience with the IRA in Northern Ireland gave them an understanding of terrorism that made them natural trainers. I had attended the course in 1984 because of my negotiation team supervisory responsibilities during the Olympics that summer in Los Angeles.

Immediately prior to the Gulf War in 1991, the CMU scheduled a special training session for the CINT members at the FBI Academy that focused on the threats posed by Middle Eastern terrorists. We reviewed prior terrorist incidents in addition to the culture, history, politics, and religion of the area, and prepared for the potential of a hostage incident involving Americans anywhere in the world. The CIA provided a grim assessment of just how difficult negotiations with these guys would be. They were extremely motivated by their mix of religion and politics, something Americans struggle to understand since we cherish the separation of church and state.

In the first ten years after the inception of CINT, team members were deployed overseas on more than twenty incidents in efforts to arrange the release of Americans held hostage by terrorists and criminal gangs. We had thought our passports would take us to Rome, Barcelona, and Hong Kong. Instead they sent us to Zaire, the Philippines, India, Panama, Costa Rica, Guatemala, Bolivia, Mexico, Colombia, Honduras, Cambodia, Chile, El Salvador, and Ecuador. Some of the assignments were extremely dangerous, taking the negotiators to war torn areas. Fortunately, none of the CINT members have been killed, wounded, kidnapped, or contracted a life threatening illness. Most though, posted overseas, have suffered Montezuma's revenge more often than a sailor.

CINT members have also responded to numerous domestic sieges around the country. They were deployed to the Cuban prison riots at Oakdale, Louisiana, Atlanta, Georgia, and Talladega, Alabama; a standoff by religious zealots in Marion, Utah; a prison hostage incident in Lucasville, Ohio; the Randy Weaver barricade at Ruby Ridge; the Branch Davidian standoff at Waco; and barricade incidents with the New Republic of Texas and the Montana Freemen.

We trained together, we partied together, we were deployed together, and we became a family. The friendships of the original CINT members will last a lifetime. We'll never forget the creative insanity of John Denton, the combativeness of Margo Bennett, and the secret handshake of "Chicago Bob" Scigalski, which was so hysterical at the FBI Academy and so obscene in the Chicago airport. Our CINT experiences have given us great war stories and I will be forever grateful for the opportunity to belong to this talented and dedicated group of people. Although new troops have replaced most of the original CINT members, it is impossible to discuss the CINT without mentioning Fred Lanceley and Gary Noesner from the Academy CMU, who were so instrumental in convincing headquarters that CINT was essential to the FBI crisis management response. Lanceley, nicknamed "Abu CINT" ("The Father of CINT"), and Noesner, along with Dr. Dwayne Fuselier and Clint Van Zandt, kept CINT evolving into an incredibly successful concept. Without their vision, persistence, and leadership, CINT would never have been created or survived. Each of them has led the troops to various overseas deployments and set the standard for performance and success. Over the years the members of the CINT have saved hundreds of lives.

On the last Friday morning of that memorable June in 1985, with all of us anxious to return home, the classroom phone rang with a call from FBI headquarters. TWA 847, a Boeing 727 flying from Athens to Rome with 152 passengers and the crew aboard, had just been hijacked over Greece by two Lebanese terrorists. The FAA had requested the assistance of FBI hostage negotiators. It could not have been more dramatic or timely. CINT members Gary Noesner, and "Viktor" (a pseudonym, as this agent continues to be used for undercover work for the CIA) from the Washington, D.C., field office, left immediately for FAA headquarters in Washington to provide consultation and expertise.

Meanwhile, the hijacked plane, under the command of Captain John Testrake, flew from Beirut to Algiers and then back to Beirut as the hijackers demanded the release of hundreds of prisoners held by the Israelis. To prove their constant threats were serious, the fanatics beat U.S. Navy diver Robert Stethem to death and threw his body out of the aircraft in Beirut. Hoping to prevent more violence, Uli Derickson, the heroic lead flight attendant, purchased fuel for the aircraft with her personal Shell credit card during a stop in Algiers. Some of the passengers were released at various stops, but thirty-nine remaining hostages were held another seventeen days and openly paraded in front of the media in a lawless Beirut. The hijackers later handed them off to yet another terrorist group before exchanging them for some of the prisoners.

Back in Washington, Noesner and Viktor had remained in the FAA command post for the entire time while TWA 847 circled the Middle East threatening death and destruction, while the world watched the events evolve daily on TV. Although both hijackers were eventually identified, to date only one of them has been apprehended; he was later convicted and imprisoned in Germany. The skyjacking of TWA 847 was truly one of the most bizarre aircraft hijackings that ever occurred. When it finally ended, CINT had been officially born.

Several years later, Gary Noesner, my wife Robbin and I had dinner in West LA with Kurt Carlson, one of the hostages from TWA 847, and his wife Cheri. During the evening he recounted the details and some of the horrors of his experience. Listening to the rich and emotional personal recollections of such survivors was fascinating. It always refueled my commitment to and passion for the hostage negotiation program.

CHAPTER 9

KIDNAPPING IN PALOS VERDES

No one noticed Farooch (a pseudonym) as he drove his piece-of-shit pickup with its camper shell slowly down Palos Verdes Drive. They should have though, since it was so out of place. Palos Verdes was home to the Mercedeses, BMWs, and Jaguars of affluent Southern Californians. But later we couldn't find anyone who had seen a thing out of the ordinary. The fifty-one-year-old babysitter and the one-year-old baby boy were gone—vanished off the face of the Earth without a trace.

When the baby's parents, Lisa and Tony (also pseudonyms), had arrived home that evening to find the house empty, they had immediately called the Palos Verdes Police Department to report the babysitter and their son missing. It was too unusual not to find them at home at that time. Palos Verdes was a small town with a responsive police department, the kind of place where they still did security checks on your house while you were on vacation. They wasted no time dispatching an officer, who arrived just after the kidnapper called.

It took a few minutes for Tony to calm Lisa down before they could explain to the officer what had happened. The caller had said that he had the baby and the sitter, and that they were okay. But he wanted fifty thousand dollars to guarantee their safety and release. He said he'd call back in a few days with instructions on where to take the money. Then he hung up and Lisa started screaming.

All she could tell him about the call was that the kidnapper had some kind of an accent. After listening to the frantic couple, the officer immediately called his watch commander who, realizing that the small police department had neither the resources nor the experience to handle a full-blown ransom kidnapping, called the FBI.

An hour later, Rich Noyes and I, assigned to the C-1 kidnapping squad, were southbound on the 405 from the federal building in Westwood headed down to the Palos Verdes peninsula.

Farooch's call had not only confirmed the kidnapping but suggested his motivation. That's an important issue for the investigator, as the motivation for a kidnapping provides several clues. A ransom demand explains the reason for the abduction and suggests recovery of the victim may be possible. The lack of a demand is ominous. It suggests that the victim may have been taken for some other reason—to regain control and possession of an estranged spouse or girlfriend, to barter a child against the other parent, to kill the captive for vengeance, or to use the person for sexual purposes. Sometimes the victim is inadvertently killed during the abduction or accidentally overdosed by the kidnapper using drugs to sedate the victim. Young girls, and more recently also young boys, taken for sexual purposes, are rarely released unharmed. Infants, who can't identify the kidnapper, are sometimes abandoned in a location provided to the parents or in a place where they will be readily discovered.

Rich and I were relieved when Farooch stressed the money. Unfortunately, a ransom demand means something different to the family. A ransom demand cancels their initial hope that the victim will walk in the front door unharmed and with some explanation for being late. It also confirms that the family member is definitely in danger.

To violate federal law, a kidnapping normally has to have an interstate nexus, but the FBI may otherwise get involved in any kidnapping case if it is first reported to them or if a local police agency requests FBI assistance. If the victim is a young child, the FBI will jump right in without hesitation. For the most part, local police agencies appreciate the personnel and resources the FBI can offer, as long as they receive their own share of recognition and appreciation once a case is concluded. Unfortunately, the FBI hasn't always been good about this.

A kidnapping investigation evolves as the events unfold. The first step is confirmation that the victim is actually missing or has been abducted. (75 percent of missing adolescents return on their own within seventy-two hours, usually after having had a dispute with a parent.) The age and sex of the victim, the circumstances of the kidnapping, prior incidents, the stability, financial, and social status of the family—are all clues to the legitimacy of the kidnapping claim. Once a genuine kidnapping has been confirmed, the FBI goes into high gear, unleashing its resources and personnel.

An investigation grows like the branches on a tree. Phase one: agents move into the home with the family. Phase two: establish and restrict control of electronic communications to the family. Phase three: conduct a behind-the-scenes investigation of the family's employment, finances, criminal history—anything that might provide the reason for the kidnapping. Phase four: with surveillance teams and arrest teams, prepare for the payoff. Phase five: identify and investigate potential suspects, paying close attention to the family's employees and associates. Phase six: coordinate the crime scene investigation at the point of abduction (if known), and prepare to process the eventual recovery scene for potential evidence. Phase seven: pull all the investigative pieces together for the prosecution of the suspects.

Each phase has a team leader. The case coordinator conducts daily briefings each morning and evening as the information pours in and the investigation develops. FBI headquarters is advised daily of the investigation's progress. Local police agencies are kept in the loop. The criminal profilers at the FBI Academy in Quantico, Virginia, are provided the facts of the case and tasked with a criminal profile of a suspect. The secrecy of the investigation is guarded carefully and media interest controlled if at all possible. Most members of the media will cooperate when the life of the victim is pending. However, once a competitor releases confidential information, they will all run with the story despite the awareness that overt media coverage of a kidnapping investigation can threaten the victim's safety.

Being assigned to move in with the family is probably the most critical of all the phases. All the seeds of the investigation come from the family. I had been involved in several of these over the years and knew it to be an incredible roller coaster of emotions as each member of the family gradually begins to release their secrets. It's very rocky emotional terrain. In one case the younger sister of a kidnap victim withdrew from the family and refused to talk to any of the investigators. Gradually, with patience and gentle coaxing, it became apparent that she was disappointed and hurt by the fact that her sister had been kidnapped instead of herself. To her it meant that her sister was considered more valuable, even to an unknown kidnapper. Family dynamics can be very complex for the investigator in the house to sort out. Old wounds can be reopened and new revelations can create additional family conflict at a time when they all really need to pull together.

By moving agents into the family residence, the traffic in and out of the house is limited (most kidnappers caution the family not to call the police, or FBI, and it has to be assumed that they may be watching the house); the agents get to know the family members and conduct ongoing interviews which produce actionable intelligence (which may identify the suspect); strategy for the telephone conversations with the kidnapper can be planned, role-played, and repeated; and the emotional swings of frustration, anger, and fear of the family members can be managed. My experience as a hostage negotiator had prepared me for dealing with demanding and threatening suspects, so it was a natural decision for me to be assigned to the family residence. With the endorsement of the FBI Academy Crisis Management Unit, the FBI has since increased its use of trained negotiators during kidnapping investigations with great success.

When we got into the area we rolled slowly by the house, then parked a block away and walked back. It was a nice neighborhood with large landscaped lawns and long driveways. These were Neiman-Marcus people. We also realized that we had to keep the black-and-white police patrol units from driving by the house. Its takes some diplomacy to deal with the local cops, who always have a natural territorial stubbornness and want to hang around the scene.

Jon Uda, an agent assigned to the Redondo Beach office, had already arrived. Jon and the responding police officer had calmed Lisa down enough to talk to us, although we knew that her shock and hysteria had to lie just beneath the surface. A white female, who they had employed for over a year and appeared to be reliable, cared for their son. Both Lisa and Tony were adamant that they had no reason to suspect she was involved, although parents never imagine a trusted family employee could be. The babysitter usually took him for walks in the stroller in the afternoon, but they didn't know where other than down Palos Verdes Drive. Lisa was a stay-at-home mom, but did charity work during the day. Tony was a consultant and traveled frequently. Despite being only in their early thirties, Tony said they were very comfortable financially, with a net worth just this side of seven figures. Both said their son was the most precious part of their lives. Tony was short and stocky, with a wrestler's build and a boyish look. Lisa had that skinny rich look. While Jon and I listened to them ramble, Rich began to set up an office for us in a back bedroom, someplace to locate the radios, a cold phone, and a place to have private discussions.

As we developed more information, we began to phone investigative leads out to the FBI office. Fully identify the babysitter. Contact her husband, and stay with him. Don't minimize the fact that his wife is also a kidnapping victim. Begin a background investigation of them. Determine who else was aware of the kidnapping. If only the grandparents, contact them and ensure their confidentiality and cooperation. Conduct police checks and gather financial and background data on both the parents. Look for extra-marital affairs, debts, questionable associates, lawsuits—any derogatory information—but no overt interviews that could give away the fact that the FBI is involved. Identify the registered sex offenders in the area.

We also began to prepare for the next call from the kidnapper. Because the family members are often too emotional, we try to insert an agent to "represent" the family to the kidnapper. Although sometimes kidnappers will insist on talking only to family members, this ploy often works. They may also insist that a family member deliver the money, but when someone else delivers it instead, they rarely walk away from their big payday. Kidnappers usually assume family members have called the cops, but they are too invested and too close to success to walk away. Seeing the package (the money) distorts their judgment.

Regardless, we encourage the family to stay away from this, as they are not trained to make the ransom drop. This is where a negotiator can function so well in a kidnapping, to assume this role of dealing with the caller and making the drop.

The first location given is rarely used for the drop. Usually the kidnapper will send the money man from one location to another with a series of phone calls to ensure there is no police surveillance. It also gives the surveillance team the opportunity to pick up on a suspect at each drop. If the same vehicle shows up in the vicinity of two or more sites, you've got a pretty good suspect. But this drill requires constant contact with the suspect and has a tendency to wear out a family member who is running on emotion and adrenaline at this point. Trained negotiators are a better choice to manage what can become a Rubik's Cube of decision-making. An awful lot of things can happen—and most of them bad. There are certain rules for dropping off the ransom that can't be deviated from. Like dropping the money before the surveillance team gets set up. That's a good way to lose the money right from the beginning. Another technique of trained negotiators is to slow down the progression of events, which is really gradually taking control away from the kidnapper. That's a good thing. Slow it down. Make sure the package is covered.

Walk away if it doesn't feel right. Go back to the last point of contact. He may be frustrated, but he'll call because he wants the money. Be patient, and be ready for anything. Expect to be surprised.

Tony listened to our explanation and nodded in acknowledgement, but he insisted on speaking to the kidnapper and making the drop himself. Lisa just curled up on the sofa, expressionless. Unblinking. Still. Like a digital freeze-frame. I wondered if she had popped a couple Valiums.

We rushed to set up our telephone recording equipment and also confirmed that the tech agents were prepared to trace the call when received. Then we sat down to wait. And talk. Gently, after several minutes, I asked for pictures of the baby. And possibly foot prints if they had them. Lisa stared at me thinking about what that meant. Finally she got up, went into the bedroom and retrieved a picture. Taken when he was about nine or ten months old, it showed the baby wearing a Dodgers t-shirt and sitting on her lap. She couldn't find the footprints taken at the hospital when he was born. They had no pictures of the babysitter but the agents interviewing her husband would get that. When she brought the photo in, she sat down and stared at it for several minutes. No tears. Unusual. Then she handed it to me. I went into our makeshift office and called the command post to send someone over to pick it up. They would copy the photo in the lab and distribute an enlarged photo to every agent working the case. It could also be given to the media if we needed to go public later. When we received the footprints, they could be used to positively identify a body. Today we use DNA.

We began the short course for Tony and Lisa, explaining that we had to insist on some proof of life from the kidnapper, some confirmation that the caller really was the actual kidnapper—something from the babysitter maybe, or listening to the kid giggle, cry, or make a sound that a mother could recognize to confirm that they really had them and that they were alive. They would also have to insist that they needed time to gather the ransom money. The more calls made, the greater the chance of tracing one. They also needed to know that the caller might threaten them to force meeting his demands. They should try to disregard that. It may be as stressful for the kidnapper to make the phone calls as it is for the parent to receive them. Kidnappers often talk longer with each call, appearing to loosen up.

Arguing to reduce the ransom amount can work against you, since it could prolong the negotiations, or encourage a frustrated kidnapper to kill the victim. But to immediately agree to any sum would also be suspicious. So it takes a little negotiation. The decision to actually pay a ransom, and the decision to let the kidnapper walk away with it without being arrested, are huge decisions for the family. Nevertheless, they are decisions for the family, not for the FBI. All we can do is give them our best advice. Although we considered the amount demanded, fifty thousand, relatively small (two hundred fifty thousand would have been more respectable), we couldn't underestimate the seriousness of any kidnapper. Two years before we had become involved in a kidnapping case on the east side of Los Angeles in which the father had received a two thousand dollar ransom demand for his fourteen-year-old son. It was difficult for the local police department to take seriously as they suspected it was just an angry kid playing games with his father. Two days later, the boy's body was found in a neighbor's garage after the cops screwed up a payoff attempt. We knew that we couldn't dismiss any claim based on the amount of the ransom.

Tony and Lisa were good listeners and quick learners. Unfortunately, two days went by without a contact from the kidnapper and everyone's stress level began to increase even further. We also began to develop a routine. Everyone ate dry toast in the morning. We snacked on cheese and grapes in the refrigerator. I can't recall seeing Lisa eat anything for three days. Rich and Jon and I slept on the floor like family dogs, waiting for a call and talking to the FBI office in LA. Tony seemed to find sleeping an escape for him and I had to remind myself that everyone copes differently. Lisa would disappear for an hour or two periodically, and then return to talk. And talk. About everything. About anything—about her son, her hopes and dreams for him, what they would do when he returned. One chapter of conversation after another, linked together randomly. We heard much more than she ever needed to share with us. When it was all over, she said that she had spent those disappearing hours in the shower, crying uncontrollably, washing her tears away. Her emotional release. She compartmentalized and scheduled her grieving while waiting for her son to return. The human reaction to trauma and grief is remarkably individual and unique. Tears, laughter, anger, denial, guilt, withdrawal, and threats. It's completely personalized for each victim. The agents involved weren't immune to this either. Dealing with the emotional highs and lows of the family also played out on those of us in the house. But the only firewall of emotional protection would be ceasing to care and we could never do that.

Although the investigation was picking up steam behind the scenes, we still hadn't developed a good suspect. But on day three, a little after 9 PM, the phone rang. We all bounced up and shook off our growing lethargy. Tony beat me to the phone.

"Do you have the money?" the accented voice asked. I listened with the earpiece. The caller sounded Middle Eastern, like Lisa had described in the first call. Same guy.

"Yes, we have it ready," Tony said. I watched the tape whirl slowly in the recorder and the needle wave back and forth as he spoke. I wished he had let it ring a few times to allow the tech guys more time to get a trace.

"All right then. Good. Tomorrow night, at eight o'clock, take it in a black suitcase to the dumpster behind the Carl's Jr. on Century Boulevard by the airport. By the nude girls."

Then he hung up. No time for Tony to ask for anything. No time to insist on clarification, to drag it out. Or confirm the proof of life.

"Wait a minute. Stand by. He may call right back again, to avoid a trace, to finish his message," Noyes cautioned Tony.

We waited for several minutes, all of us staring at the phone, telepathically trying to make it ring again. In the home with the family of a kidnapped member, waiting for the call from a kidnapper, the telephone becomes the focal point for everyone and takes on incredible importance. When hope is dying, a ringing phone can bring the family back to life. It becomes a life preserver thrown to someone drowning. When it doesn't ring, the phone becomes a love/hate object. It's failing to do its job. But everyone stays within arm's reach. Everyone stares at the phone like a junkie focusing on his next fix. It can stop the hurt. It can be salvation.

Rich looked at me and shook his head.

"Could it be that simple? Giving us the location twenty-four hours in advance. Twenty-four hours to prepare a surveillance for the drop location. What's up with this guy?"

Did we get a trace? Minutes later the tech guys called on the cold phone. No trace. Of course not. Dammit. At least we got a recording. Some evidence. A fairly identifiable voice: Middle Eastern, male, thirties.

"Same guy as the first call," Lisa said after listening to the recording.

We all knew the location. You couldn't drive down Century Boulevard into LAX without noticing the "Nudes, Nudes, Nudes" billboard just west of the Carl's Jr. fast-food restaurant. The strip club was a popular hang out for the horny traveler with a couple hours to kill before flying back home to the missus. The kidnapper might have even made the call from there although we couldn't hear any background noise.

Rich immediately called headquarters to advise them of the call and to pass on the drop location. To be given the location with this much time to set up surveillance was an absolute gift. It reminded me of the time several years ago when a guy threatened to kidnap Walter Matthau's son, Charlie. He mailed Walter a letter telling him to be at the public telephone on Pacific Coast Highway at Cross Creek in Malibu on Friday night at six. Said he'd tell him then where to take the two hundred fifty thousand. We were able to look the place over for four days and design the surveillance.

Apparently the suspect didn't notice that the street population of Malibu had increased by fifty that night as hordes of LAPD cops and FBI agents set up on the phone booth. The phone rang promptly at six and was answered by one of the undercover officers. "Take the money to the top of the hill of John Tyler Drive at Pepperdine University. Leave it near the large tree," the young male caller instructed.

With a caravan of officers and agents in tow, the undercover officer drove up PCH, turned left onto John Tyler Drive, and stopped at the top of the hill, which was a new construction site. The rest of us parked on PCH. Walking slowly to ensure that he was seen, he walked over to the tree and dropped off the suitcase. As he walked away he transmitted on his wire that he had seen a guy hiding nearby in the underbrush. A few minutes later we all heard a muffled explosion up on the hill and saw a small black mushroom cloud. Everyone jumped out of their cars and ran up the hill to see the suspect running east into the university grounds. Fortunately, he couldn't outrun the police helicopter that landed just behind him and deposited two officers, who ran him down like a couple of linebackers. He had left the suitcase with the money behind when a small explosive charge rigged inside exploded when he opened it. In a typical demonstration of police humor, the officers had also included a note inside the suitcase for the suspect that read, "Gotcha."

After his arrest, the suspect, with black soot coating his face and hair blown up like Don King, the boxing promoter, readily admitted his involvement in the extortion. He related that he had seen Matthau on TV talking about losing a million dollars on horse races, and figured that if Matthau could afford to drop that kind of money on the horses, he could afford the quarter million the suspect needed to set up a business. The young entrepreneur had found Matthau's address by taking a "Homes of the Stars" bus tour and had selected the PCH location because it was close to Matthau's residence. He had tried to make it easy for Walter. And he had typed the letter in the public library to avoid any link to him. He just hadn't really thought much about his escape plan. Like most of them—he never figured he'd get caught.

Walter turned out to be a great guy and very appreciative of our efforts. A couple weeks after it was over he invited all of us to a swanky restaurant in Beverly Hills for dinner. He told stories and jokes and signed autographs for hours. Not all the Hollywood people are like that.

Having a jump on the drop location can give the surveillance team the time and the opportunity to design an observation and arrest plan. There was one considerable downside in this case, however. The location at Carl's Jr. was in the direct landing path of incoming aircraft to LAX. This meant the FBI surveillance aircraft would have difficulty loitering over the location.

That had happened to us before, during an aircraft extortion payoff at LAX. An extortionist claimed he had rigged a bomb in an aircraft to explode if it descended below 2,500 feet. If he was paid the money (it was a relatively small amount—something like $50,000), he would tell us how to disarm the bomb. We dropped the simulation payoff package at a specified location in the terminal and waited. After several hours and just before we shut the operation down, the suspect suddenly popped up. He grabbed the package, ran into the crowded street, jumped into a cab, and took off south of LAX on Sepulveda Boulevard. We were worried about our vehicle units being able to get through the traffic in the streets outside the terminal, but with aerial coverage standing by we thought we had it covered. However, just as the suspect took off, the FBI helicopter had to wait to cross the LAX flight-landing pattern and we lost him on the ground. After an hour we gave up.

A couple hours later, after he had opened the package and found three books of the Los Angeles Yellow Pages, the guy called us, really pissed off. We apologized for letting him escape. He told us to fuck off and slammed the phone down. Just to be safe we put the aircraft down at the airport in Denver, which is above 2,500 feet, but found no bomb. Fortunately, we never heard from the extortionist again. It was the only ransom package I ever lost.

We immediately sat down to discuss the pay-off procedure with Tony and Lisa. The caller had not specified a vehicle or a driver. This was a good thing. It allowed us to select both. It also suggested that maybe he didn't know what vehicles the family had. Or care. He was apparently focused on only three things— the time, the location, and the money. Which meant that we could expect him to be hanging around the dumpster at 8 PM. He would either try to be invisible or to look like he belonged there. He could have told us to find a note with more instructions at the dumpster. But no, he said to leave the money there. So apparently that was to be the final drop. He'd have to be there or have some mope there for him. In any case, he had to prevent someone else from discovering the package. So we knew he'd be in the immediate vicinity when the drop was made. Watching. The surveillance team was responsible for setting up the arrest. We had to plan the trip down to Carl's and hold the family together.

Another concern was that once we claimed to have the money, we had to be concerned about a rip-off, which is being robbed of the money on the way to the drop location. Tony insisted on driving the vehicle in spite of our protests. He couldn't be dissuaded. I think he secretly hoped to make an actual exchange of the money for his son. Hand to hand, man to man. He didn't want to just drop the money and leave. He was insistent. We finally agreed to it, but only with Jon Uda, a small wiry SWAT guy, hidden in the trunk armed with an MP-5. The car would be wired so Jon and Tony could talk to each other, as well as keep Jon in radio contact with the surveillance team riding alongside them.

Excited about this coming to an end, we all talked long into the night. We were too tired to sleep. Lisa finally gave in first around 3 AM, and eventually the rest of us crashed in various places we had found comfortable around the house. Rich had agreed to take the late watch until morning.

We woke up to the familiar smell of toast. In short order we were all up and met in the kitchen to discuss the preparation of the money. Lisa made scrambled eggs for all of us. It was the first time we ate a meal together. It was symbolic and we all silently felt it. We felt good about today.

The FBI has a long-standing agreement with Bank of America to maintain several million dollars of pre-recorded one hundred dollar bills for situations like this. Once notified, with an authorized wire transfer, the bank can put the package together in a couple hours. Later that morning, Tony and Jon drove to downtown LA to pick up the money, and then to the FBI garage to have Tony's BMW wired. Tony had decided to use real currency, figuring that in case the suspect escaped but had the money, he might let the baby go. But he also agreed to an arrest at the drop if the FBI guys at the scene thought it appropriate. That was a major decision. Lisa had disappeared again while Rich and I kicked around the plan in the living room. It all seemed too easy—giving us the drop location a day ahead. It had to be more complicated. Could this guy really be this stupid?

It took most of the day for Tony and Jon to pick up the money and the FBI tech guys to wire the car. They finally returned to the house about 4 PM. By then they had worked out procedures and codes for the drop. We checked and rechecked the vehicle in the garage and the money package, which also contained a transmitter that would be monitored by the surveillance team. We packed and repacked Jon into the trunk, trying to find the best position to allow him to jump out if he had to rescue Tony from a rip-off. We tested and retested the intercom until they were comfortable. By seven, Tony was ready to go and Lisa couldn't sit still. Tony's parents had come over in the afternoon to hold Lisa's hand. Although it crowded the house and added an extra dimension to the situation, we couldn't protest. Lisa was unraveling.

The surveillance team leader called and advised they were ready. The drive was about forty-five minutes to the airport. Rich and I went into the garage with Tony and Jon, checked the money, tested the transmitter, and looked over the car one more time. We looked each other in the eye and shook hands all around. We all knew anything could happen. Then we packed Jon in the trunk and slammed it shut. The garage door opened and Tony backed out. He gave us a thumbs-up and a nervous grin as he pulled away.

Once out of the garage, we monitored their progress by listening to the surveillance units calling out their location.

The trip to Carl's was uneventful. We expected Tony to call

out a dozen suspicious vehicles on the way but he controlled his anxiety and remained focused. Once on site, Tony made the drop just as planned while Jon remained in the trunk. Fortunately the surveillance team was in place and he didn't have to delay the drop while they made adjustments. When he got back in the car he complained to Jon about the number of people hanging around the dumpster. They appeared to be Carl's Jr. employees taking a smoke break, three or four of them. He had tried to be unobtrusive and hesitated a bit since he was afraid they might pick up the package out of curiosity. He finally dropped it when they wandered back to the restaurant.

As Tony and Jon headed back to the 405 south and Palos Verdes, Jon lay in the trunk quietly, listening to the surveillance team chatter. Rich and I listened in our office back at the residence. We didn't want the family to hear this radio traffic. Things can turn to shit real fast in these situations—a vehicle pursuit and collision, a foot chase, a shooting. These are very volatile moments—nothing you want to share with the family.

Minutes later, a surveillance unit in a hotel room overlooking the parking lot called out a suspicious individual walking from the restaurant towards the dumpster. He looked like a Carl's Jr. employee wearing a baseball hat, dark clothing and an apron. Thirty seconds later he came out of the dumpster with the suitcase and walked towards the alley. Another minute and he was in the custody of the FBI. Although he had not been identified, a few minutes later one of the agents on the scene described the suspect as appearing to be "Latino or Middle Eastern." Rich and I looked at each other. Could it really be this easy?

Within minutes the suspect was hustled into a large FBI camper that had been hidden in a nearby parking lot where the best interrogators in the LA FBI office had been waiting for him. A criminal investigation can take you in a lot of directions, but the real test for an investigator is the one-on-one interrogation. It's a game of psychological chess, a search for the door leading to that cathartic confession.

Rich and I were ecstatic. We walked into the living room

and reported to the family that some guy had picked up the package and that although we didn't have the baby and babysitter yet, we did have a suspect in custody. Everyone collapsed with relief.

Minutes passed. I went into our office and called the command post on the cold phone for an update. The suspect's name was Farooch, but he hadn't given them anything else. He denied everything. He was wearing a Carl's Jr. uniform, but the Carl's Jr. manager told the agents that he had no idea who this guy was. This had to be our guy.

Tony and Jon returned to the house and offered a play-by-play description of the drop. We were all excited that we had a suspect in custody. Relief poured out of all of us while we waited for the results of the interview. Sometimes confessions take a while, we cautioned them.

Time dragged. An hour later I called again. No change. He's still not talking. I started to get uneasy.

Another hour. The cold phone rang. It was Rich Bretzing, the agent in charge of the LA FBI field division.

"Jim, I think you need to prepare the family for the possibility that he has killed them. He has refused to cooperate and we're starting to think he doesn't have them to give up. We've offered a couple deals and he hasn't wavered. He hasn't admitted a thing. He may have killed them right at the start. I'll call you if anything changes."

I hung up the phone and sat there for a few minutes trying to think of what to tell Tony and Lisa. Did I really need to tell them anything? Was there any point to causing the parents to worry more than they already were? I mulled it over for a few minutes. Sometimes it's good to break it to parents gently and gradually that things may not turn out right. I called Tony into our converted office.

"Tony, I'm going to give it to you straight. Sometimes these guys find it difficult to control their victims and sometimes they never planned to release them in the first place. Sometimes the victims don't make it. It takes away their bargaining power, but you never know who you are really dealing with. I think we have to consider this as a possibility. This guy just isn't coming around, and we don't know why. Other than maybe he doesn't have them to give up. He's passed on what we offered to him. At least for right now."

Tony looked at me, and then dropped his head into his hands. "Do we have to tell Lisa?"

"Of course not. We can give it more time, and we can wait until something is confirmed. At this point, we're just speculating because he's been so uncooperative. Sometimes these things take several hours. At least he hasn't lawyered up."

"Okay," he responded, getting up and walking out into the living room to join the others. I wondered if he would be able to mask his feelings in front of the others. It would take a better man than I. I hung back for a while trying to understand the mind of the kidnapper.

Rich and I went back to listening to the radio in our office. Hours passed. Suddenly Rich said he thought he heard something about the surveillance guys now in Inglewood. Why Inglewood? We had dropped the ransom package just west of Inglewood. We focused intently on the radio. I called the command post.

"What are the SOG guys doing in Inglewood?" I asked.

"Stand by, Jim."

Suddenly Rich jumped up.

"Hamer says they found them. They're in a camper in Inglewood." Bob Hamer was one of the SOG surveillance agents on the street.

Several very long minutes later, the command post confirmed it. Both the baby and the babysitter had been located in a camper in Inglewood. They were in good condition and now in the care and custody of the FBI. We looked at each other and grinned. Rich and I trooped into the living room and announced the news to the family. We all stood for a group hug and to share a few tears. It was almost over. Now we just needed the baby home. Lisa and Tony disappeared for a private moment.

I called the command post and asked if the victims could be returned to the family prior to being taken to the hospital for examination. I was advised that they were on the way.

Farooch was also traveling, to the FBI office. He was accompanied by an Iranian restaurant owner from Palos Verdes. When it became apparent that the FBI was unable to convince Farooch to admit his involvement, a Palos Verdes police officer suggested that a friend of his, a local Iranian restaurateur, be brought in to talk to Farooch. With nothing to lose, we seized on it. With the assistance of the local cops, he was located and driven down to the camper. An hour later, after a hug and a kiss, and some small talk about his mother and their homeland, Farooch began pouring out his whole sad story and his financial failures. He gradually got to the part about the location of the victims in Inglewood, where they were tied up and held in his old pickup with the camper shell in a deserted parking lot.

It was hours after midnight when the agents finally arrived with the baby, along with the agent in charge, a couple of his assistants, and the Iranian restaurateur. The Iranian was reserved but smiled a lot and shook hands with everyone. Being there to witness Tony and Lisa reunited with their son was a moment I will never forget. The return of a kidnapped child to its parents is euphoric for any investigator. We all just stood around soaking up the emotions of the family, feeling intrusive and embarrassed, but too addicted to leave. We listened to the details of the investigation, the surveillance at Carl's and the arrest of Farooch. In an unusual twist, Farooch apparently didn't know who he had kidnapped. He had just grabbed a woman with a kid in a stroller from an upscale neighborhood and threatened her with a knife. Once he drove off with them, he asked the babysitter for the mother's phone number. He had no idea whether the family had the ability to pay a ransom, but figured they'd be able to get at least $50,000. All too often we give these guys too much credit.

The baby quickly lost interest in the conversation and fell asleep in Lisa's lap. She smiled and then announced that he was going to spend the rest of his life in her arms. The brass left, and Rich and I began packing up the equipment. We returned to the living room where the family had gathered, shook hands, hugged everyone a last time, and walked out into the chilly ocean air of Palos Verdes. We drove slowly back to the office, saying little but savoring the moment. It had been a long five days.

Months later Farooch pled guilty in the Superior Court of Los Angeles County and received a ten-year sentence.

Each year I receive a Christmas card from Tony and Lisa. And each year they write the same thing: "Thank you for bringing our little boy back to us." It has been an annual reminder that I had the best job in the world.

CHAPTER 10

THE CUBAN PRISON RIOTS

Small fires were burning inside the federal immigration detention center, creating a threatening red glow like an approaching wildfire.

Sonny Benavidez and I stood outside the double chain link steel fence topped with concertina razor wire, imagining the surreal scene that had occurred just minutes before our arrival. Rioting Cuban inmates had built an altar in front of the main gate, tied a hostage to a chair on top of the creation, and threatened to set him on fire.

Armed with machetes and knives, the inmates had screamed at the hundreds of worried FBI agents, Federal Bureau of Prisons (BOP) officers, U.S. marshals, and state and local police officers watching from outside the wire. The hostage, a Hispanic officer about forty years old, was at the point of breaking. Everyone watching was convinced they were about to witness a human sacrifice. Only an immediate decision to bring the armored vehicles up to the wire and prepare for a massive forced entry into the center had stopped the Cubans. After several minutes of posturing and threatening the hostage with machetes, they had untied him and retreated back inside the building.

Listening to the story related by the agents on the perimeter and seeing the scene set the stage for us. Everyone expected the frustrated Cubans to go ballistic again at any minute and start attacking their hostages. This was going to be an incredible experience.

It was November 1987. The federal detention center in Oakdale, Louisiana, had been built to house several hundred Cubans who had arrived during the 1980 Mariel Boatlift. An economic downturn had led to a mass exodus from the island. The problem was that of the approximately 125,000 Cubans who fled, most were violent criminals and mental patients that Fidel Castro had released. Those that the Immigration and Naturalization Service (INS) was able to identify were incarcerated in the federal penitentiary in Atlanta or here in Oakdale to await deportation. Some had already committed violent crimes in the U.S. Many had remained in jail indefinitely for years, waiting for an immigration hearing. Cuba refused to repatriate them and the U.S. refused to accept them as legitimate aliens because of their criminal records. So they were just warehoused without hope. In effect this really did make them political prisoners—"non-removables" some called them. Nobody wanted them.

Then in late 1987, as a result of State Department negotiations, which were kept under the public radar screen because of their explosive nature, Cuba suddenly reversed its position and agreed to repatriate them. Convinced that they would be killed or receive a life sentence if returned to Castro's Cuba, several hundred "Marielitos" took twenty-eight correctional officers hostage at the Oakdale detention center. Three days later, twelve hundred Cubans in the federal prison in Atlanta started a second riot and took 124 correctional officers and employees hostage. Their basic demand was that they did not want to be returned to Cuba by the American government. They also demanded individual release hearings.

The BOP requested additional tactical troops and the FBI as well as the U.S. Marshals responded. Our Los Angeles SWAT team flew into Oakdale accompanied by several negotiators. At the time I was acting as one of four LA SWAT team leaders under the command of the SWAT coordinator Myron Hitch. Agent Sonny Benavidez, an experienced negotiator, fluent Spanish speaker, and a CINT member had come along with us. Over the years Sonny had been deployed on a number of occasions to kidnappings and hostage incidents in Mexico and other parts of Latin America.

Sonny also had the emotional scars of failure that haunt every experienced negotiator. A few years ago he had flown down to La Paz, Bolivia, to assist in the recovery of an American held by terrorists. Shortly after his arrival, the cops captured the girlfriend of one of the terrorists. After a torturous interrogation in the police station that night, she finally provided the location of the terrorists and the hostage. Sonny and a couple of Bolivian cops jumped into a taxi—there weren't enough police cars—and mad dogged it out to the scene just in time to see the Bolivian army shelling the building with artillery. Naturally they killed the terrorists—as well as the hostage. They also threw one of the terrorists off the roof of the building, and he lay in the front yard of the hideout with a horrendous compound fracture of his femur. You don't forget scenes like that.

Sonny had also spent several weeks with a hard-working and loving family in Tijuana whose twenty-year-old son had been kidnapped by criminals demanding an outrageous ransom. Because they couldn't afford to pay the ransom, time ran out and the kidnappers lost patience. They killed the son and dumped him in a field outside the city. The autopsy disclosed gunshot wounds in the arms and legs indicating that the young boy had been sadistically tortured before the lethal shot. Sonny came back from that one with a deep sadness and a new appreciation for life. His empathy was genuine and his compassion sincere. A passionate and effective negotiator, Sonny Benavidez was the best the FBI had to offer.

We set up camp in a National Guard armory that should have been condemned. The place smelled like an old abandoned high school football locker room and the floor was dirtier than a recycling center. There were four showerheads in the shower room and three flush toilets to accommodate thirty agents. It didn't take long before we began to bitch about everything. One of the most aggravating was one of the SWAT guys with a prostate problem who would get up at 2 AM every night and flip-flop across the entire gym floor in his shower sandals to the toilet, waking everyone up. Finally someone got pissed off enough and cut the heels off his sandals. This not only stopped his noisy shuffle every night, but also made him walk on his toes like a girlie boy, much to our amusement. He threatened a vicious payback to the culprit, but he never identified the suspect since we all confessed to it.

We stayed there a week practicing entries while the negotiators worked with the Cubans.

Myron Hitch, the SWAT team commander and a training maniac, refused to be deterred by the daily rain, and we spent hours tramping around in ten inches of water behind the armory planning our assault into the prison if the Cubans harmed the hostages or negotiations broke down. After taking a good look at the place, which was designed to keep people in and to keep people out, we put our support behind the negotiators. None of us wanted to charge into that prison. Someone was definitely going to get hurt. This didn't deter Hitch though, he laughed and said obviously the Cubans never heard the expression "Never take a knife to a gunfight." He kept saying, "This is the dream I've been waiting for all my life."

Our entry point was to be through a vehicle entrance at the rear of the prison using a bulldozer to breach the double chain link fence and barbed wire. Once through the wire by using a two and a half ton military troop transport, we would then haul ass in an armored vehicle across the center of the compound to the maximum-security unit where we thought they were keeping the hostages. Inside the unit we would use various explosives and cutting tools to break into the cells, if necessary, to rescue the hostages. All of this was to be accomplished before the Cubans began killing the hostages with their homemade knives and machetes when they realized the assault had started. You can now understand why we hoped the negotiators would be successful.

On Saturday night several of us attended a Mass at the local Catholic Church and listened to an emotional prayer and plea for the safe release of the hostages. Many of the parishioners stopped us afterwards, tearfully thanking us and wishing us Godspeed. Everyone seemed to have a relative being held hostage inside the detention center. It was a considerable contrast to the welcome we usually received when we operated in South Central Los Angeles, where the residents would point at us derisively and chant, "SWAT, SWAT, SWAT." They loved us here. And no one asked about Mr. Hoover's cocktail dresses or his boyfriend Clyde Tolson. This was grassroots America—and the FBI was king.

We spent Thanksgiving standing outside the wire, watching the inmates standing around watching us. We ate turkey and bologna sandwiches off paper plates and traded war stories with the cops from the local parish. We were surprised that some of the sheriff's deputies had just driven up to the detention center on their own time. They borrowed a company car, put on their uniform, and joined the perimeter. After a few days, they would cycle on back home. Law enforcement in Louisiana was a little different than in LA.

The BOP guys really appreciated us showing up. Their brothers were the ones being held inside and everyone wanted to buy us dinner or a beer. Most had suggestions on how to resolve the standoff, none of which involved negotiation. Some of the BOP officers wanted to punish the inmates who took the hostages. A huge issue in the field of negotiations in a prison situation is that correctional officers often have a difficult time giving the inmate the respect and equal ground necessary for negotiations. Some can't suspend the belief that inmates are inmates and therefore deserve no respect. To change that attitude, and negotiate as equals, is often very difficult for correctional officers

One of the problems with the Cubans was their fiery and threatening nature. Initially this frustrated the government negotiators who kept trying to find the magic word for them to surrender. I grew up in Michigan with a number of Bautista Cubans who had fled Castro and I knew how emotional they could be. It was not a bad thing, just an ethnic characteristic.

What we eventually realized, however, was that we had to let them vent their threats for several days before any productive negotiations could occur. Once they got past that, things got easier. But the first few days pumped up the adrenaline of everyone, and that can be a dangerous thing whether you're holding a shiv or a loaded gun.

Every night back at the armory, I'd complain about the rain and Sonny would discuss the progress of the negotiations. Naturally the Cubans had lost complete faith in the federal government and any negotiator it fronted. They would come to the wire and yell at the negotiators. It was just insults and threats. There were no real negotiations. After a few days, three of the leaders had consented to a sit down in neutral territory in the reception room of the main prison, but they had made demands that the FBI and BOP negotiators couldn't satisfy: individual hearings for each inmate and immunity for the hostage taking. They always ask for immunity before surrendering in a prison incident and it's something a negotiator can never promise. This was going to take a decision by the Department of Justice and possibly the Department of State. There was even some talk that it may require an act of Congress.

They trusted no one. As far as they were concerned the American government had done nothing except throw them in prison and toss away the keys. Clearly, the government had to find a third party negotiator, a neutral party trusted by the Cubans. Eventually they found one in a Catholic bishop from Miami named Agustin Roman who had a long history with the Cuban population there. Bishop Roman had been monitoring the standoff and was well aware of the issues. When the FBI approached him to assist, he readily consented and flew up to Oakdale.

When he arrived, he came in like the Grand Marshal of the Rose Bowl parade with his entourage trailing behind. Sitting in an open military vehicle, wearing his religious garments, he was driven around the perimeter for all the Cubans inside to see. He waved at them like the Pope. Periodically the vehicle would stop and he would ask them to put down their weapons. As promised by the negotiators, he told them the government had planned to provide them individual hearings and said that they may possibly be released but not returned to Cuba.

An inner-city priest once told me that Hispanics may not attend Mass every Sunday, but they never leave the church. The Marielitos were no exception. They respected the bishop and one by one they began to pile their weapons near the front of the detention center. We were astounded at how many they had, but it didn't surprise the BOP officers. They knew that any one of these guys could make a shiv out of a dried roast beef sandwich and then hide it where the sun don't shine. Eventually the hostages were released, one at a time. They came out of the front of the prison to be tearfully reunited with their families. It was an emotional scene for everyone.

The Cubans then allowed the BOP officers to take them into custody. One by one they also began to file out the front gate, and finally, on a Sunday night, after nine days, it was over. At Oakdale.

Four hours later we had packed our gear and were flying to Atlanta for round two.

The hostage situation at the Atlanta prison was a whole different ballgame. An enormous federal penitentiary, it had a long list of distinguished alumni, including Al Capone. It was one of the most secure gated communities the federal correctional system reserved for hardcore inmates. It had a cold, dark look with huge thick impenetrable walls that looked to be twenty feet thick. Huge spotlights lit up the exterior perimeter. Several huge power lines snaked up the front steps into the main entrance making it look like a monolithic monster being refueled. We stood in awe of the twenty-two buildings, twenty-eight acres of maximum lockdown, and 1,400 screaming Cuban inmates roaming freely all over the prison. How the hell were we ever going to assault this bastard?

After a briefing in the command post, the U.S. Marshals' Special Operations Group (SOG) supervisor led our team leaders into the prison. Much of it was trashed, with several inches of water over the floor after the inmates destroyed their plumbing.

It's an irrational, self-destructive concept I've never understood, similar to the residents of South Central Los Angeles burning down their neighborhoods to protest against the police department. As we crept deeper into the prison we came to a checkpoint manned by two SOG marshals armed with M16s.

"All you guys gotta sign our 'reception book' before you go forward." one demanded.

"What's this for?" I asked.

"So in case you don't come back, we know who they got," he answered bluntly.

Okay, now we're getting serious.

We clicked the safeties off our MP-5's and entered the prison. I felt like we had crossed the border into a hostile country. We continued down the labyrinth of hallways, hoping our guide would remember the way back. Along the way, he informed us that their recon teams had occasionally run into groups of inmates trying to sneak out of the prison through the warren of tunnels under the prison. So far, they had chased them back and no one had been injured. But realize that we may run into somebody, he cautioned. These underground teams were labeled the Tactical Underground Reconnaissance Detail, which within a day was shortened to the "TURDS." Their mission was to locate and apprehend any suspects hiding in the tunnels—that is, to apprehend the "SHITS." It was dirty and scary work but the agents assigned to the TURDS prided themselves on their assignment as if they were the Navy SEALs of the FBI.

Eventually we climbed a series of stairs and there it was. The Yard. Groups of inmates huddled around hundreds of small fires. Every one of them seemed to be carrying a machete or some kind of weapon. Unbelievably, the prison had operated a broom factory where the inmates actually used machetes. Our guide pointed out various groups and leaders and explained how the gangs had maintained their identities and territories even during the riot. They all carried machetes and shivs for individual protection.

The scene was surreal and hard to believe. We could smell the fires burning in the crisp air and all the inmates looked threatening as they moved freely around in the shadows. Approximately 1,400 inmates involved in the uprising and the 120 or so hostages were being held at various locations. We watched the wandering inmates who periodically stopped and stared up at the guard towers. We could only imagine how the correctional officers in those towers felt, knowing their brothers were being held hostage down there somewhere in the bowels of this beast. A helicopter circled over the prison yard like a lightning bug searching for a place to land. We crawled back out and went down to the BOP command post where the LA SWAT team drew its assignment—rescuing the hostages held in the prison chapel. We were excited about drawing one of the most dangerous assignments. We were to be the point of the spear. Obviously somebody thought the LA SWAT team had its shit together.

The next day turned bad again though, when we spent some time with the Hostage Rescue Team (HRT) planning our assault into the prison. Led at this time by Danny Coulson, their Napoleonic leader, they were the best. The selection process convinced most applicants it wasn't worth it. They trained with Navy SEAL Team 6 and the Army's Delta Force, the Israelis, the German GS-G9, and the British SAS commandos. They were designed to respond to those incidents of potential violence that exceeded the capability of the local or regional FBI SWAT teams. Their training and equipment was incredible. When Danny was promoted to FBIHQ after the first few years, Woody Johnson took over the team. Although Woody was well qualified (and easier to deal with than Coulson), when the Cuban riots broke out FBI headquarters sent Coulson down to Atlanta to assist Woody on the tactical solution because of his previous experience.

As at Oakdale, the plan included a bulldozer assault on the vehicle gate. Following closely in an armored vehicle, our team was to rush through it, first to the library and then on to confront the convicts holding the hostages in the chapel. As the inmates had been observed welding some chapel doors shut and had also filled door locks with dental plaster to block keys, Explosive

Ordnance Detail (EOD) guys from the military were assigned to us to handle breaching explosives. The assault seemed impossible to carry out without the inmates having the time to kill the hostages. Once again, we hoped like hell the negotiators could pull this one off.

The Cuban inmates in Atlanta had begun to communicate with their brothers in Oakdale through CNN TV coverage. There was no direct contact, but three days after Oakdale started, the hostage situation blew up in Atlanta. From then on they watched each other closely through the television coverage. It became an incredibly effective method of communication for the inmates separated by hundreds of miles. Each day they could flip on the TV and see what the others were doing. And we had no control over it.

Eventually the scenario at Atlanta began to parallel the events, which had occurred at Oakdale. A significant difference though, was that the inmates in Atlanta were really hardcore. A Cuban named Meza had been known to periodically stab himself in the stomach with a shiv just to get to spend a few days in the prison hospital. He considered it a break from time in his cell— kind of like a vacation where he got to meet new people. He also often threatened to cut off one of his balls and throw it at the passing guards. And there was no doubt in their mind that it was going to happen some day. This guy was way beyond just loco.

There was another badass, a white guy named Silverstein. He was a buffed up psychopath who had killed inside prison and threatened everyone. The Cubans, who were scared to death of this guy, were concerned that his insanity would interfere with their negotiations. So one night they drugged him up, dragged him to the DMZ (a neutral area where the negotiations took place each day) and dumped him off. After the Cubans pulled back, the BOP officers grabbed him and immediately shipped him to another maximum-security federal prison in Marion, Illinois. In Marion some of these guys are allowed out of their cells for only an hour every week to take a shower. They just shove their meals under the cell door. It may be a little impersonal, but it's a whole lot safer for the officers.

There was only one death at Atlanta, and we didn't fully understand what had happened until after it was over. One of the hostages named Luis came back to Quantico several months later and made a presentation to the CINT members. Luis had been working as a civilian supervisor in the broom factory when the inmates overpowered him. Initially he thought it was a joke because he worked with all these guys every day and knew them. But when they turned him over to the riot leaders, his friendships disappeared and he thought he would be killed. He was kept in the chapel with about thirty-five others in terrible conditions. The toilets overflowed almost immediately so they just used buckets in the shower room on the second floor of the building.

A couple days into the riot, Luis was handed an envelope addressed to him. He said it was presented to him like he had won the Reader's Digest Sweepstakes. He opened it up to read that the Cubans had selected him to be sacrificed—he was to be executed—to emphasize their demands. He thought his heart was going to explode out of his chest. He couldn't breathe. The other hostages around him started to rotate and go out of focus. He told us without embarrassment that after a few minutes, he regained his composure enough to cry like a baby. The inmates told him to write a goodbye letter to his family. So he did. He wrote a painful letter to his wife, saying that he regretted that they had not started a family but that he had loved her with all his heart. He gave her financial instructions. He thanked her for loving him although he said he didn't deserve her love. He said he hoped that he had remembered to kiss her every day before he went to work. Then he presented the note to another hostage and begged that it not be lost. He said good-bye. They hugged and cried together.

An hour later, the Cubans came for him.

They took him out into the yard, hands tied in back, surrounded by hundreds of angry, shouting inmates. Luis was well aware of the prison policy that instructed the correctional officers in the towers to use deadly force if a prison officer or employee was being threatened with death or bodily harm. As they took him up to the base of the tower he looked up at the guard, knowing what would happen—and what could happen to him as a result. The inmates began to beat Luis, screaming their intention to kill him. They shook their machetes in the air at the officer above.

An instant later, the guard fired.

Luis said he didn't know whether he heard the gunshot or the impact, but he vividly recalled that the bullet exploded in the head of a Cuban standing right next to him. Brains and blood splashed over Luis. The inmates screamed in protest and Luis bent forward thinking that his throat would be slashed. But he was suddenly pushed to the ground and then dragged by the screaming Cubans back into the chapel. He couldn't believe his good fortune. He rejoined the others and said a prayer. A born-again Christian. But his relief was short-lived.

The next day they again dragged Luis out into the yard. "Why me?" Luis asked. He was only a civilian broom factory supervisor. He never learned why. Out in the yard, they repeated their threats to kill him in front of the guard tower. But this time nothing happened and after several minutes they again dragged him back into the chapel.

They were constantly threatened and Luis watched other hostages taunted and threatened with sodomy with various weapons including the machetes. Their living conditions became worse, and the shower room used as a toilet was almost intolerable. One of the hostages refused to talk or eat and began to slowly chew the flesh off his fingers. Late one night, Luis crawled over to this guy, cradled his head in his arms, and tried to feed him some canned tuna, but he refused to eat. He continued to deteriorate over the days and slipped into a catatonic state. When they were finally released the psychologists diagnosed this officer as having suffered the most severe emotional trauma of any of the hostages. Luis said he was still going through a long, sad recovery.

Luis's emotional description of the hostages' experience was incredibly moving for all the CINT negotiators, especially for those of us who had been there. At the conclusion of his presentation, during which he praised the FBI and thanked all of us personally, we gave him a tearful and standing ovation. Luis was one impressive guy. He later received several commendations for his bravery and his support of his fellow hostages. I've met a lot of heroes in this business, and Luis is definitely at the top of the list.

In the first few days of the Atlanta takeover, approximately twenty-six prison medical employees had locked themselves in the prison hospital. Once the inmates discovered their location, they attempted to break into the hospital's cafeteria. The employees tearfully begged the warden, Joe Petrovsky, to send a SWAT team to rescue them before the inmates got to them. In one of the most agonizing decisions made during the entire incident, Petrovsky and Weldon Kennedy, the FBI agent in charge, refused to do so, convinced that armed intervention would only encourage the inmates to injure or kill the other hostages. They believed that negotiations would be successful and that the employees would survive, even if they were taken hostage. They held off the SWAT team and the inmates eventually broke into the hospital and added those employees to the others held in other parts of the prison. Petrovsky and Kennedy's decision turned out to be correct. However, it was a terribly difficult decision and a heavy burden for them until all the hostages were safely released.

It took some time for the inmates to sort out their leaders. In the first few days, at least four separate alpha males (accompanied by their own cheering sections) broke loose from the pack and declared themselves as the leader of the insurrection. Twenty-four hours later they would disappear. Then the next day another one would appear and claim the same. This went on for days while the inmates argued and fought inside the prison. Unfortunately, the government negotiators were forced to play the game with these guys until they burned out.

Eventually, four inmate leaders with some credibility surfaced and insisted that they had the ability to control the rioters. The government negotiators reviewed their personnel files, built personality profiles, and eventually selected one named Charlie to be their primary contact. Through a slow process of building his value in the eyes of the other inmates (giving him privileges and the most important—respect), they subliminally controlled the rioters' selection and support of Charlie. As the inmates saw his stature grow in the eyes of the FBI negotiators, they decided Charlie would be their best representative in the negotiations. Of course, the FBI negotiators had selected Charlie because he seemed to be the one over whom they could exert the most control. These psychological games are a constant in the process of hostage negotiations.

The first few meets occurred through the bars of a sally port in the main prison with the inmates carrying weapons. Gradually the building of trust began and they agreed to a sit down meet with the BOP/FBI negotiators. The site chosen was again in a makeshift DMZ with bars on either side. It was a risk for both sides to go in. The inmate negotiators carried knives and machetes, and the government negotiators refused to go inside the DMZ until they disarmed. Eventually the inmates agreed to leave their weapons inside the prison. Each side entered the negotiation cage like tigers in the circus—wary, suspicious, and posturing.

Our primary FBI negotiators at Atlanta were Di Rosario and Pedro Toledo, both native Spanish speakers and experienced negotiators from Miami. After the surrender at Oakdale, they were joined by Fred Rivero who had been the primary negotiator there. Gradually, the serious talks began.

One of the most critical frustrations was the federal government chain of communication. At the conclusion of the daily negotiations, the FBI negotiators would return to their commanders on the scene and brief them on the progress of the negotiations. The BOP negotiators would return to their leaders and do the same. Each commander would then brief their headquarters personnel in Washington on the status of the negotiations. After the FBI Director received his briefing, he would contact the Director of the BOP, and they would discuss what each had heard from their men on the scene. (Naturally there were always inconsistencies that had to be clarified with the Atlanta teams.) They then went to Attorney General Ed Meese together, made recommendations and received instructions. The results of this meeting were then returned down the chain of command in the same manner and eventually found their way to the on-scene negotiators of each agency. Factor in the daily schedules of the Director of the FBI, the Director of the BOP, and the Attorney General, and you begin to understand why it took so long to resolve this incident. The practicality of the matter was that once the negotiators took a break to get an answer at Atlanta, they could take almost twenty-four hours off before they were ready to go back to work with the instructions from Washington. It was an incredible communication bottleneck. It really made the case for putting the decision makers right at the scene of the incident.

Meanwhile, the Atlanta inmates liked what they saw on CNN about how events had unfolded at Oakdale so much so that they also asked for the Miami bishop. But the government negotiators refused until they released some of the hostages. The inmates balked, but they kept talking and began to build a relationship of trust with the government negotiators.

As time wore on, various groups of inmates began to surrender to the BOP officers. They sensed the end coming and realized what was going to happen to them if this whole thing collapsed. Deals were going to be made, and they wanted to be first in line. This required them to escape from the inmate hostage takers who had threatened to kill anyone refusing participation and support. They would usually appear at night at one of the guard posts, eager to surrender. They also provided considerable intelligence about what was happening inside, where the hostages were located, who was guarding them, and what kind of weapons they had. Our intelligence grew significantly with each surrendering inmate.

Another force at both Oakdale and Atlanta was a cadre of immigration attorneys who were attempting to lobby on behalf of the rioting Cubans. In Atlanta in particular, there were a couple attorneys who were well known to the Cuban inmates from prior contacts, cases and court appearances. Although we were naturally skeptical of their motivation and of their professional egos, they became genuinely helpful and assisted the negotiators who were still attempting to obtain the trust of the inmates. Through their persistence and pressure, the Department of Justice finally agreed to give the inmates hearings regarding their immigration status and consider parole. We hoped this was all they needed to hear.

But unfortunately we still had to convince the Cuban hostage takers that the offer was legitimate. This took another two days and help from their immigration lawyers. And eventually we did bring in Bishop Roman, whose speech to the Cubans was broadcast throughout the prison. Right after he finished, the Cuban negotiators agreed to surrender. After eleven days, we had an agreement. We had refused a plan initially offered by the BOP, which insisted that the inmates all kneel in the yard. Those who refused would be shot. This had all the potential to turn into a massacre, but the FBI agent in charge, Weldon Kennedy, quashed that suggestion before it left the room. We all understood that the BOP wanted to exact their revenge but an orderly assumption of control was the key to a safe and successful resolution. We were there to prevent violence not to create it. Eventually the surrender was choreographed to everyone's satisfaction.

Fifteen minutes after the agreement, the first of the hostages came out. Some were laughing, some crying, some stoically stone faced. Some seemed stunned and confused. Many couldn't believe it was really over. Luis had told us that he had joined arms with several others and they marched out tearfully recalling Martin Luther King's famous words, "Free at last. Free at last! Thank God Almighty, we are free at last!"

The BOP immediately bused them to a reception center, gave them a brief time with their family, and then rushed them into a medical exam. The shrinks also jumped into the debriefing. Many of the hostages later complained that the psychological debriefing was unnecessary, and that they just wanted to go home to their families. But the American government had learned much from the Vietnam POWs and the Beirut hostages and realized the importance of a psychological debriefing. Initial exhilaration can give way to depression, emotional confusion, indecisiveness, resentment, marital problems, alcohol and drug abuse, and suicide. As a group, these hostages would later prove to be no different.

Once the hostages were out, the BOP took over. Bus after bus pulled up and squad after squad of BOP correctional officers dressed in jump suits and armed to the teeth jumped out. Jesus, they looked bad. They all carried chains of handcuffs and leg irons. We just stood back and watched them. Eventually the inmates came out, one at a time. Slowly and methodically they were stopped, searched by four officers and then led into a mobile booking van. When they emerged they were silent and humble, and suited up in new orange uniforms. All looked apprehensive. The whole process took over a day to complete, but methodical processing ensured safety for the officers and would serve the criminal prosecution of the ringleaders later. The BOP distributed the inmates around the country to various federal prisons while the Atlanta prison was repaired. Once identified as a hostage taker, and especially a riot participant, these guys were given special reception and treatment when they arrived at their new homes. We didn't ask the BOP guys for the details. The look on the faces of the inmates told the story. They knew what was coming.

Once the surrendering inmates were gone, the prison was ours to search for any remaining inmates who had hoped to escape. We also considered the very real possibility that inmates could have been killed inside the prison. Each FBI SWAT team was assigned several cellblocks. We locked and loaded and walked into the prison, psyched. This is what we had come for. Only trouble was the bad guys were gone, although we could still run into a lone holdout deep in this dungeon.

My first impression was one of utter devastation—a totally trashed prison. The suspicious muck on the floor was like wading through six inches of rancid thick black bean chili. With the plumbing destroyed, shit was everywhere. We also started remembering that half the Cubans were HIV positive. Suddenly this had really turned into one very dangerous job. Hitch decreed that all the boots were to be burned afterwards.

One by one, we scoured the devastated cellblocks and found complete devastation. One of the agents briefly picked up a rosary hanging on one of the bunks and examined it. But reminded of the curse that the Santería believers among the Cubans might put on him, he quickly dropped it as if it burned his fingers. Many of the Cubans were Santería worshippers. That's the voodoo religion with chicken feet, blood, dried black bananas, candles, and chanting. Many of the cells had pictures of fat naked women taped to the walls. These Marielitos were strange men. We spent half the day wading through the prison looking for inmate holdouts that we never found. It was empty. It was over. By noon we had pulled out and returned to the hotel, cleaned up, packed our gear, and headed to the airport. Oakdale and Atlanta were history.

Although the Department of Justice had resolved the immediate problem, their promise of individual hearings was an empty one. Few hearings actually took place after Oakdale and Atlanta and in 1991 the Cubans struck again. Inmates took twenty-six hostages at a prison in Talladega, Alabama, for nine days, an uprising that was finally ended by forceful intervention by the FBI's HRT. In 1996 Congress passed a law requiring the INS to incarcerate criminal aliens until they could be deported. In 1998, Cubans rioted at a detention center in El Centro, California, and took hostages again at a center in Jackson County, Florida; and in 1999 they took the warden and several correctional officers hostage for six days in St. Martinville, Louisiana. The Cubans detained in these immigration warehouses remain ticking bombs. The best they can hope for is a new and more receptive Cuba in the post-Castro era. For all those who are affected by this human rights quandary, it can't come too soon.

CHAPTER 11

HARVEY LEE GREEN
AND THE TRI-LATERAL COMMISSION

Harvey Lee Green was one of those guys who had trouble pushing a broom in a work release center. A Vietnam vet with an alcohol problem, a drug habit, and a dishonorable discharge from the Marine Corps, Green had come back from the war with extra baggage. Trouble was, life had no distance for Harvey. It was all about just getting across the street safely. He was kind of an African-American Forrest Gump. Unfortunately for us in the LA FBI office, Harvey Lee Green was living in Hollywood.

One ugly gray morning in the spring of 1988, while the pigeons were still picking at the night's leftovers under the bus benches, Harvey was sauntering down Hollywood Boulevard trying to find his way to work. He carried a bag of laundry over his shoulder. As he passed by a branch of the Bank of America, he was suddenly overcome by inspiration. He turned into the bank, waited patiently in line, and then when it was his turn announced to the teller that he was robbing the bank. He smiled and then made a point of telling her that he was carrying a bomb in the bag over his shoulder.

Some tellers freeze, some cry, some pee in their pants, and others just hand over the money. This one calmly pulled the robbery alarm triggering the police and FBI into action. And then she told Harvey it'd be a minute or two while she rifled through her cash drawer making sure that she gave him all the bait money. Because his pickled brain functioned in slow motion while the neurons searched for a connection, Harvey smiled at her and waited patiently instead of becoming agitated.

Harvey had also never heard of the Two Minute Rule. Every experienced bank robber knows that staying in a bank longer than two minutes exponentially increases your chances of getting caught. Get in and get out in two minutes, and you may be able to beat the black-and-whites responding to the robbery alarm that some teller down the line has pulled while you were looking the other way or cramming the money into that Carl's Jr. lunch bag, unless you have an off-duty cop standing in line behind you. Then it can really get interesting.

Los Angeles is known as the bank robbery capital of the United States, so cops all know what to do. So do the FBI agents. Friday is bank robbery day, and the record still stands at twenty-eight. Fourteen on Saturdays after the S&L's decided to remain open. In 1992 the Los Angeles area experienced 2,641 bank robberies. So everyone in Los Angeles with a police radio hears "2-11" (robbery) alarms all day long. In most cities, a 2-11 alarm will pump up the adrenaline of all the cops on the street. In Los Angeles, it just becomes an annoyance. You also have to understand that while driving around in the sprawling city of LA, you may still be ninety minutes driving time from a bank that just got robbed. So unless you're right on top of it, FBI agents would leave it to the local police patrol units to be the first to respond.

Nine times out of ten it's a simple "note job" where the robber shows the teller a note and simulates a gun or verbally claims to have one. The teller gives him about $2,000 in a bag containing a dye pack, triggers the silent alarm and he walks out of the bank, thinking that it was so easy he ought to do it again sometime. With any luck, within a couple minutes the bag of money explodes, spewing bills into the air and coating the robber with red dye. This produces a running red man for the cops to look for as they approach the bank. It's even more dramatic when the bag explodes inside a confined area, like a getaway car. This has a tendency to interfere with his driving, and also draws the attention of the people in the cars next to him, especially on a freeway. Today, everyone in LA has a cell phone, so the 911 operator gets thirty-seven calls in the first minute. The cops home in on him and Fox TV has another pursuit to spike up their ratings. Some Los Angelenos actually have a message service to notify them of televised police chases. LA loves its police pursuits.

If the robber's getaway is successful, typically within an hour he's bought the dope he needed the money for. When the patrol cops arrive at the bank they broadcast a description of the robber, fill out a one-page report, and leave. The FBI shows up an hour or two later, interviews the victim teller and any other witnesses, and pulls the film from the surveillance cameras. Hopefully they'll get some decent pictures and someone will be able to identify him. The FBI sends out about four hundred pictures of its serial bank robbers to every police department, probation and parole office, and correctional institution, as well as the local TV and print media if the guy gets pretty good at it.

Bank robbers generally rob until they get caught or killed. When they get caught, they are typically convicted of four to five robberies. Most do about four to eight years in a federal prison, considered a Courtyard by Marriott compared to the overcrowded and violent state prisons in California. They all want to do federal time. When they get out though, they rob again. It's in their DNA. Bank robbery is just too easy. And it's a rush, watching some poor, underpaid teller go catatonic with a gun in her face. Bill Rehder, the former bank robbery coordinator in the FBI office in Los Angeles, has put some of the same bank robbers away four times over his thirty-year career.

The real dangerous robberies are the "takeovers" when the robbers come in screaming, shoot a few rounds into the ceiling, and put everyone down on the floor. These thugs are often cranked up on cocaine and extremely dangerous. Any hesitation may result in people getting hurt. Los Angeles went through a period in the mid 1990s when several South Central black gangs were robbing banks to finance their drug operations. A number of these involved shootings. The major players would pick up a couple of mopes standing on the corner, load them up with crack cocaine and drop them off around the corner from the bank. Most of these guys were in their teens or early twenties and became known as the "Baby Bandits" to the FBI robbery investigators. But they were crazy and shooters and extremely dangerous inside a bank. They'd come in screaming and shooting and scare the piss out of everybody. After pulling the robbery, they'd run around the corner to get picked up by a getaway driver. They'd dump the hot getaway car in a nearby shopping center, jump into a switch car, head for the freeway, and get the hell back to the ghetto. The big dogs would give them a couple hundred from the robbery and take the rest. It was a dream job for these crack heads. Limited hours, great flexibility, quick bucks, and a little excitement. When a combined task force of cops and FBI agents finally identified the gang leaders behind the robberies and picked them up, the number of takeover robberies dropped dramatically.

Back in the Bank of America, Harvey was walking around in circles and talking in tongues. Hearing his announcement of the robbery, several people had immediately dashed out of the bank and called the police. Within minutes, LAPD black-and-white units from the Hollywood station had surrounded the bank.

Green paced back and forth enjoying his new supervisory position. He then made a generous announcement. "Okay, anyone with a family can leave." Needless to say, almost everyone immediately developed family ties and most of the customers stampeded out of the bank like a prison break.

I was a short distance away when I heard the FBI dispatcher transmit the "2-11" alarm and arrived within a few minutes. I immediately ran into Lt. Mike Hillmann, LAPD's famous SWAT team leader and negotiator. Hillmann was an LAPD superstar right out of Hollywood and long overdue to be awarded his own action figure. His Kirk Douglas jaw, heroic exploits, and supreme confidence inspired others. He looked terrific in uniform. He wore medals. He oozed sincerity. He was loved by the troops and the TV reporters. The female TV reporters swooned over him, and he loved the camera. What a competitor!

One of our FBI negotiators, Jack Trimarco, had stepped into a Fotomat kiosk across the street from the bank and established telephone contact with Green. This presented a problem. Hillmann and I shared a natural rivalry of agencies that had almost boiled into a fistfight at other hostage scenes. Both our agencies, and both of us, wanted to control the incident. At this one LAPD had the perimeter, but the FBI negotiator had the suspect on the line. There was no way this was going to work.

In a previous hostage incident at the Spanish Consulate in LA, the FBI had beat LAPD to the scene and I had assigned Rudy Valadez, a Spanish speaker, as the primary negotiator to initiate negotiations with the suspect inside. When the LAPD arrived, their commander requested a briefing from Valadez, who had connected with the hostage taker inside the consulate. Reluctantly, but in the spirit of cooperation, I pulled Valadez off the line. After a twenty minute briefing, we returned to find that an LAPD negotiator had taken over negotiations with the suspect and refused to relinquish control. We spent the next several hours engaged in an argument with our leaders about who was in charge. Only the surrender of the suspect settled the matter. Needless to say, we took a blood oath that day to never get fucked by LAPD again.

In the meantime, back at the Bank of America, LAPD's SWAT team had suited up and taken over the perimeter before the FBI SWAT team arrived. It was always a goddamn horse race with them. Now we had our own standoff. For several minutes Hillmann and I argued, ignoring Harvey Lee Green inside the bank.

While Trimarco continued to talk to Harvey, Hillmann instructed his negotiators to set up their own hostage phone. We continued to argue about who had jurisdiction. For the LAPD, a bank robbery was a violation of Section 211 of the California Penal Code. That made it theirs. If the bank was federally insured, it was a violation of Title 18, Section 2113 of the United States Code and the FBI had jurisdiction. The Bank of America was federally insured. So, we both had jurisdiction.

I had the negotiator and Hillmann had the SWAT team. Fortunately, we finally agreed to make an assessment of what was going on inside before taking any further action. The next thing that happened was truly remarkable.

Hillmann and I walked up to a partially open door at the rear of the bank and immediately observed Harvey with his back to us. He was standing in front of about a dozen remaining hostages who were sitting on the floor like third graders. He was expounding in dramatic fashion about President Reagan and the Tri-Lateral Commission, which he described as a secret organization making all the decisions for the government of the United States. He was holding a bag at his side in his left hand and was apparently oblivious to the fact that the rear door of the bank was open. And our presence.

Hillmann and I stood approximately thirty feet from Green, each of us with a clear headshot, yet neither one of us moved. We were both still smoking over who was going to take charge of this thing, and I don't think we could really believe we were that close. After several minutes, we backed out of the bank. The LAPD SWAT officer who replaced us also just stared at the scene inside the bank. Harvey had absolutely no idea how vulnerable he was. Outside, I couldn't believe we hadn't shot Harvey. Although each of us was truly committed to the negotiation process, given a chance to kill a hostage taker threatening to kill others, most officers would have taken that option. And LAPD wasn't known for having a lot of patience. The truth was, Harvey hadn't threatened to kill anyone yet. He had only asked that the President of the United States fly to Los Angeles, take a limo to the Bank of America, and hold a press conference to present him with an honorable discharge from the Marine Corps. I couldn't help but think—Harvey, whatever happened to a simple demand—like a million dollars cash and a fast getaway car?

After a couple of hours Trimarco had been able to convince Harvey to allow additional hostages to leave by promising him a press conference. At one point he cautiously informed Harvey that the hostages weren't his, they "belonged to the bank because they were customers of the bank." After being advised of this, Harvey had an epiphany and said, "You're right, Jack. They can all go." He then told the hostages they could walk out the front door. They belched out of the front door like they had been trapped in an elevator for twelve hours.

At this point, the SWAT guys normally start to hyperventilate, anticipating getting their hands on the suspect. However, Harvey still had that damn laundry bag. No one really thought that this dope could have made an explosive device, but all the statistics go out the window when it comes to making that decision. 98% of the time it's a fake. So why do we think this isn't the other 2%? We much preferred to let the bomb team make that decision after scoping it out, taking an X-ray, running a dog by it, and awaiting the arrival of the bomb robot and the water cannon. It's a lot safer.

The challenge was to separate Harvey from the bag. This would give the SWAT team an opportunity to overpower him. Trimarco kept him talking. Jack had a convincing sincerity that we all knew was bullshit, but Harvey liked him. Taking advantage of the fact that Harvey appeared to be chemically retarded, Jack gradually coaxed him over to the window to wave at Jack across the street, to "make a connection, you know, kind of like shaking hands." Harvey put down the bag when he went over to the window and seemed to forget about it. This gave LAPD's SWAT guys the opportunity they needed. Within seconds they entered the bank, introduced themselves to Harvey Lee Green, and the taxpayers starting paying for his room and board.

After picking him up, straightening his clothes, putting his hat back on (and probably stopping the bleeding), the SWAT guys escorted Harvey out onto Hollywood Boulevard for his "news conference." They all bunched around him while he explained that he was disappointed the hostages didn't understand the Tri-Lateral Commission but that "Jack was a stand-up guy." It lasted about fifteen seconds. Jack had promised Harvey he could do this, and he was good to his word. As soon as the news media turned their cameras off, LAPD walked him around the corner and gave Harvey back to the FBI to file federal charges. For some reason, it was always like that. After the LAPD news conference, we were left to pick up the pieces. We were also thrilled to inventory and book Harvey's "bomb bag" of dirty laundry.

The day after the Harvey Lee Green incident, I got up in the morning to see Mike Hillmann on TV, explaining how he had managed to convince Green to surrender and how LAPD's finest had once again saved the good citizens of the City of Angels from another violent bank robber. He never mentioned the FBI. Over the years, Hillmann and I became close friends but combative rivals, like a couple of welterweights who slugged each other for ten rounds to a draw and then shook hands, hugged, and walked away. Recognizing a superstar, Bill Bratton, shortly after becoming LAPD's new chief, promoted Mike to Deputy. Chief Jack Trimarco has since retired and been successful as an independent polygraph operator and a Fox TV news consultant. The whereabouts of Harvey Lee Green, whose life was spared during a turf battle that day in Hollywood, are unknown.

CHAPTER 12

RODNEY KING AND THE LA RIOTS

"Rodney King," the Brazilian police official said in broken English and rolling the "R." "What was so bad about that?" He shrugged his shoulders in nonchalance. "In Rio, here, ah, this, ah, is not so unusual." He smiled at me and then at the audience.

It was November 1993 and I was standing on a stage in front of two hundred police executives in Rio de Janeiro. Fred Lanceley, from the Crisis Incident Response Group (CIRG) at the FBI Academy, and I had just finished a presentation on the investigative procedures of kidnapping for ransom cases and had opened the floor for questions. Rio had experienced over 120 kidnappings in the previous year and was averaging three hundred murders a month. The drug traffickers who lived in shantytowns known as *favelas* up in the hills surrounding Rio would come down into the city and kidnap family members of wealthy business people. The victims were often killed after several months if the ransom was not paid. On some occasions the cops killed the victims as well as the suspects while trying to apprehend the kidnappers. In some cases, the cops were working with the kidnappers.

Police brutality in Rio had become outrageously commonplace. Orphaned street urchins, many under the age of ten and referred to as "runts," sniffed glue and robbed businesses and people on the street in the middle of the day. In July, cops had cornered eight runts in a storm drain and killed them. Several businessmen who had been victimized by runts had paid the cops to do so. A month later a frustrated death squad of police officers shot twenty-one people to death in one of the slums. Needless to say, tourism in Rio had been taking a big hit.

Fred and I had been driven around Rio by a Caucasian Mike Tyson who drove with one hand while holding a huge .45 semi-automatic on his lap with the other. A Neanderthal bodyguard in the front passenger seat cradled an Uzi submachine gun. Our cute little female translator from the embassy sat crushed between us in the rear and rambled on nonstop about how beautiful Rio was and how the violence in Brazil was overemphasized. Fred and I weren't buying it and instead wished we hadn't declined the offer of the Regional Security Officer (RSO) at the embassy to issue us handguns while we were in country. It was common for the embassy RSOs to unofficially offer a handgun to visiting FBI agents since we couldn't travel or enter the country with a weapon.

I had been introduced at the Rio law enforcement conference as being assigned to the LA office of the FBI. The first police officer up to the microphone, a dark-skinned Brazilian resembling an African American, smiled, asked me again to confirm that I was from Los Angeles, and then asked the Rodney King question. He found it amazing that cops beating a suspect at the termination of a pursuit would create such criticism and controversy. Cops shooting bad guys in Rio was an everyday occurrence. And there wasn't much of an investigation afterwards either. Rio had become a pretty lawless place. The cops didn't even police the *favelas*. Recovering drugs or hooking up a wanted fugitive wasn't worth a shootout. They were left to police themselves. And police themselves they did. The *favelas* experienced nightly shootouts, and the unlucky losers were carelessly dumped into the drainage ditches.

Even in Rio, the cops knew about Rodney King. He had become as famous in Copland as Danny Miranda, the guy who gave us the "You have the right to remain silent" fifth amendment advice of rights warning.

On March 3, 1991 LAPD and CHP officers arrested Rodney King and a couple of his homeboys after a vehicle pursuit in the north San Fernando Valley. When he finally stopped, Rodney's buddies got out of the car and followed the instructions of the officers. Unfortunately for Rodney (and for a whole lot of people later), Rodney didn't. So they took him on. When Sgt. Stacey Koon unsuccessfully tried to taser him, three other LAPD officers jumped in and administered fifty-six blows with their nightsticks. On the video of the incident, Koon seems to be studying his taser as if he were making an entry into his BlackBerry. He seemed to miss half the action while his cops beat the dickens out of King rolling around on the ground. The CHP officers, a husband and wife team, in a commendable display of good judgment, merely stood back and counted the blows.

When they were finished, Rodney went to the jail hospital with eleven head fractures and LAPD's community policing program was set back twenty years. Unfortunately for the officers, amateur videographer George Holliday taped the last eighty-one seconds of the beating from a balcony across the street. When he tried to give the tape to LAPD the next day, the desk officer at the Foothill Division was too busy to show any interest, so he walked out and sold it to a local TV station for $500. Media experts estimated that by the end of 1991, four out of five Americans had seen the tape.

The beating of Rodney King reverberated around the country in every police department. Every cop paid the price. The public trust had been lost in a very big way. And the criminal case, in which the officers were charged with excessive force, divided cops everywhere, including the LAPD, which provided expert witnesses to both the prosecution and the defense. When they finished the jury went out, watched the video fifty more times, and then came back with not guilty verdicts for all the officers. That's when South Central LA went ballistic—and then nuclear.

Shortly after the verdict was read, a riot started at Florence and Normandie in the heart of South Central, with blacks beating whites driving by. While the media reported the growing riot and TV helicopters captured it live from above, more violence exploded in the other parts of the city. Downtown. LAPD headquarters. Koreatown. Hollywood. Even down to Long Beach. But South Central really took the brunt of it. Infested with gangs and violence, it had been a volatile area for years. It seems as if each intersection is littered with a fast food joint and a liquor store. On the corner lot you can buy a framed velvet picture of Martin Luther King and behind the gas station you can buy a couch that fell off the delivery truck. Motel rooms rent by the hour. Many residents suffer from a lack of education, jobs, role models, and hope. That's why the gangs there have been so difficult to fight. The California Department of Justice has identified 463 gangs in Los Angeles with membership in excess of thirty-nine thousand members. 10,300 belong to the Crips and 4,200 to the Bloods, both African-American gangs located in South Central, which have a much stronger identity than the all too common fractured African-American family with an absentee father. Every weekend these surrogate families get together to go gang banging. Killing each other. And innocent others. It's not unusual for ten to twelve South Central residents to be killed on a weekend as a result of gang violence. And half of those killed are non-gang innocents who just happened to get in the way.

So when the city exploded that night it was no surprise to law enforcement that it started in the midsection of South Central at Florence and Normandie. Who can forget the images of Reginald Denny, the truck driver pulled from his cab in surprise and confusion, pulverized with a rock and a fire extinguisher by the frenzied mob? And the Asian gas station attendant, locked inside the bulletproof cashier's booth on Normandie, who survived a gun fired pointblank at him by rioters without effect. Six times! This is one guy who needed to buy a lottery ticket.

Both the LAPD and the Long Beach police department appealed to the FBI for help. The FBI responded by flying in the Hostage Rescue Team (HRT) from its home base at the FBI Academy in Quantico and by deploying its local SWAT team. The LA FBI SWAT team was sent down to Long Beach to provide security for the fire department on its arson runs. They had been fired upon several times the night before. I was still a team leader on the SWAT team and it was to be one of the most exciting assignments of my career.

It was mid afternoon of day two, and although things had calmed down a bit, parts of Los Angeles and Long Beach were still burning. We stood in a small group suiting up at the National Guard armory just off the 710 freeway in Long Beach. We knew how dangerous this was going to be. Riding shotgun for the fire department with unseen snipers shooting at the trucks—and us!

The Long Beach police commander stood in front of our SWAT team like General Schwarzkopf during a Gulf War press conference, rocking on his heels and relishing the moment. A real red meat eater.

"Gentlemen, what Long Beach experienced last night was a disaster. We almost got overrun last night. We almost lost the war. That is not going to happen tonight. And you're going to help us. These animals are not going to burn this place down. We are going to take back this city." The commander's anger and frustration boiled over from the embarrassment of having to run for cover the night before.

"Now last night, the rioting and looting was so bad we couldn't arrest everyone. So we've resorted to what we called our 'Beat and Release' policy [a play on the catch and release program of the Fish and Game Department]. Just chase 'em off and try to get in a lick if you can, because you're just not going to have time to hook 'em and book 'em."

We were stoked. The adrenaline was starting to push. It reminded me of getting psyched before a night patrol in Vietnam. It was also addictive. And it's what drove guys into the SWAT program. Routine policing just wasn't stimulating enough. SWAT offered pure adrenaline. Like loading up a house with tear gas, knowing some asshole with a gun was hiding inside waiting for you, and then going in to find him. That'll get your heart rate revving. When your entire body is nothing but nerve ends. When everything is vibrating. Those highs and lows made you feel alive. Really alive. And they kept you there.

After the briefing we quickly returned to check our weapons and gear. It was put-on-the-war-paint time.

We spent the next two days in the middle of total anarchy. Jim Burns and I were assigned to a firehouse as the fire trucks had received sporadic sniper shooting during the riots. A firefighter in LA had suffered a serious neck wound while responding to a call. We followed the trucks out on every call but we often pealed off during fire calls to respond to "officer needs assistance," "arson in progress," "looters at the Big 5 store," "shots fired," "vehicle pursuit," "armed suspects at the corner of," and a hundred other hot calls. While the city burned, we had a free pass to drive like Richard Petty from one crisis to another. Burns, who had grown up in Long Beach, knew his way around the city and we got to the scenes in a hurry.

Back at the fire station we traded war stories with the fire fighters. All of us were adept liars and we all knew it, but we still enjoyed sharing our adventures. And the ice cream. We never saw any four-alarm firehouse chili. It was always ice cream. When they returned from a fire, they rewarded themselves and us, of course, with a bowl of ice cream. Cops drink alcohol after a fight or a shooting; fire fighters eat ice cream after a fire. It's their celebration of survival.

Ice cream may make them sound like wimps, but they were some of the bravest men we saw. Regardless of the danger they continued to roll out to every fire reported without hesitation. And they turned out to be the most unselfish, hospitable hosts we had ever worked with. We really bonded with them. After all, everyone loves a fireman.

Eventually the National Guard set up barricades in the intersections and helped us enforce a curfew and secure the city. When the smoke cleared four days later, fifty-one people had been killed and over two-thousand had been injured. Property damage was estimated in the billions. The charred buildings in South Central represented the failure of cultures to coexist. The riot demonstrated just how fragile the relationship was that existed among the African-American community and the LAPD.

And it permanently scarred the LAPD.

The riots also seriously affected me. For years I had prided myself on working in the mean streets of the big city and surviving. Pulling a murder suspect out of South Central's Nickerson Gardens or Willow Brook was a challenge, a thrill and an accomplishment. But driving through burned-out South Central after the riots depressed me. I just wanted to leave. I didn't want to be around these people so eager to destroy the property, hopes, and dreams of others. For all the criticism of South Central, there are thousands of quiet residents who strive to survive, raise their kids, and send them to school, steering them away from drugs and gangs and unwed pregnancies. They go to work every day and to church on Sunday. They pay their bills on time and respect authority. They are the salt of the earth and they had to live among these psychopaths. I began to seriously consider leaving LA. By now I had the seniority to transfer almost anywhere. Robbin and I started talking about taking a look at Seattle or Portland. Maybe Honolulu.

And Rodney King? After settling with LAPD and the City of Angels for $3.8 million (most of which has reportedly gone to his lawyers), he has continued to bump into the cops periodically with several minor arrests for drugs, alcohol, and domestic squabbles. Eventually he landed in a small city east of LA where he lives a simple life apparently doing nothing.

CHAPTER 13

RUBY RIDGE

It was a cool August morning in 1992. Supervisory Special Agent Fred Lanceley, from the Crisis Incident Response Group at the FBI Academy, and I were crouched on the edge of a ravine at six thousand feet in the remote mountains of northern Idaho. Forty miles south of the Canadian border. Wedged between us was Marnis Joy, the sister of Randy Weaver. We had flown her from Missouri to Idaho the night before on a borrowed Lear jet in a desperate effort to talk her brother into surrendering to the FBI. Weaver was suspected of killing a federal marshal.

We knew it was going to be difficult, though. Weaver and his family had hunkered down in his homemade cabin stocked with weapons and he hadn't talked to anyone for the last five days. And we knew he didn't think much of the federal government.

It had all started the Friday morning before when Weaver and his twenty-four-year-old protégé Kevin Harris had become involved in a deadly shootout with a special operations group (SOG) of U.S. Marshals trying to arrest Weaver. The federal government's arrest warrant was based on his failure to appear for a court date on a weapons charge. The whole case was built on Weaver having sold two sawed-off shotguns (prohibited by federal regulations) for $450 to an informant for the federal Bureau of Alcohol, Tobacco, and Firearms (ATF) in 1989. By the time it was all over, Randy Weaver's refusal to turn himself in resulted in the death of a federal marshal, Weaver's wife, his son, and his dog, and the serious wounding of his friend Kevin Harris as well as Weaver himself. It also dramatically changed the lives of several FBI agents.

In the world of federal law enforcement, Weaver's weapons charge was known as a cheap case. There are typically thousands of outstanding arrest warrants for relatively minor crimes for lawbreakers on the run. A warrant is entered into the FBI's national crime information computer (NCIC) and then we just wait for the fugitive to stumble into a drunk-driving checkpoint on a Saturday night or get hooked up by the local cops for something else. Sometimes the wife gets fed up with the beatings, calls the cops, and when they arrive for the domestic abuse, she tells them about the federal charge. Bottom line is, nobody spends a helluva lot of time looking for these guys. It's all about priorities.

Although the Weaver case initially fell into this category, he compounded his own problems. After selling the illegal weapons, he had been arrested by the ATF and spent a couple of days in jail. The ATF agents offered him a chance to work his way out of the charge by becoming an informant. If he had, he'd probably have received probation. Instead, he refused to assist them and hid out in the mountains with his family— his wife Vickie, his son Samuel, and his daughters, Sarah, Rachel, and baby Elishaba. That little bit of Old Testament stuff in those names was a clue that wasn't lost on us. Vickie and his mountain neighbors did his shopping in Sandpoint for him, while Weaver refused to come down off the mountain for fear of being locked up again. He'd been down to Richard Butler's Church of Jesus Christ Christian in nearby Hayden Lake for a while but he couldn't quite buy into it. So he packed up his family and moved to the isolated Ruby Ridge area, where he built a primitive cabin at six thousand feet. Weaver didn't need Richard Butler; he had enough crazy ideas for his own religious cult, starting with his family. Unfortunately, Weaver mixed weapons with his religion.

If Weaver had kept to himself everyone would probably have

forgotten about him. Instead, he and members of his family would challenge every stranger and hiker in the area at gunpoint, threatening to shoot anyone on his property. All the family members, including the kids, walked around with weapons strapped on their waists. Weaver also taught them how to shoot all his shoulder weapons. And Weaver had told all his neighbors that if the federal agents showed up on his property he'd "take some with me."

The local media trumpeted the fact that the law enforcement officers knew where Weaver was living but were doing nothing about it. It wasn't long before the sheriff began to feel this unwanted heat from his constituents. The hikers registered complaints with the Boundary County Sheriff, who passed them on to the U.S. Marshal's office since the ATF warrant was a federal warrant. Even though the case was started by the ATF, federal arrest warrants are held by the U.S. Marshal's office, which has the responsibility of executing arrest warrants for all the federal agencies. (FBI agents usually handle their own warrants, though, rather than wait for the overworked marshals.) Aware of the fact that Weaver was armed, and that he had armed his family members, the U.S. Marshals deliberated while trying to find a method to arrest him without starting a shootout. After the shooting, many of the news reports indicated that the marshals had placed Weaver under surveillance for eighteen months, but in reality they had just periodically focused on him during that period.

The marshals formed a six-man Special Operations Group (SOG) to conduct a reconnaissance of the area and to set up an arrest plan. In the early morning darkness of August 21, 1992, the SOG split into two groups; one crept towards the cabin to set up to make the arrest, while the other climbed a nearby mountain overlooking the cabin to set up an observation post. After several hours, the mountain team radioed the group below that they had observed Weaver, his son Sam, his dog Striker, and Harris exit the cabin and begin walking in the direction of the arrest team. Unfortunately, Striker picked up the scent of the marshals, started barking, and headed directly towards them.

The marshals retreated from the cabin in an effort to avoid detection but the dog stayed on them. Weaver and the others thought the dog was onto a deer and they followed him into the deep woods. When the dog confronted the marshals, they shot and killed him in an effort to remain hidden. Sam and Harris, however, eventually came upon the marshals and several shots were fired. Who fired first and the justification for shooting by each has always been in dispute between the surviving marshals and Harris. Only those present know the truth, but Sam and U.S. Marshal Bill Degan were shot and killed. Harris escaped and rejoined Weaver.

The marshals later described periodic shooting from Weaver and Harris during the morning, although both Weaver and Harris insist that only the marshals fired and that they ran back to the cabin to seek refuge. When they retrieved Sam's body and brought it to the cabin remains confusing. Nevertheless, after the shooting that morning, they retreated to the cabin and the barricade began.

The marshals radioed for assistance, and it seemed like every law enforcement officer in northern Idaho responded. By Friday night, the remaining members of the SOG had been rescued, and Boundary County sheriff deputies, U.S. Marshals, and ATF agents had gathered at the base of the mountain. The U.S. Marshals headquarters in Washington had also requested the assistance of the FBI. Regional FBI SWAT teams from Salt Lake City, Portland, Denver, and Seattle were deployed to the scene. The Hostage Rescue Team (HRT) quartered at the FBI Academy was notified and just a few hours later was on their way in two Air Force C-130s designated for their use. As they departed from Andrews Air Force Base in Maryland, they assumed they were heading into an ongoing firefight with an unknown number of suspects who had already killed a federal agent. It sounded like a war. The FBI Rules of Engagement (ROE), the use of deadly force to prevent the killing or grave bodily harm of oneself or another, were about to become extremely controversial.

Back on the hill, the initial law enforcement response focused on rescuing the surviving marshals, recovering Degan's body, apprehending the suspects without further shooting if at all possible, and preventing sympathizers from coming up the mountain and joining forces with Weaver. This was a very large operations order.

Meanwhile, Idaho Governor Cecil Andrus declared Boundary County to be in a state of emergency, proclaiming, "The nature of the disaster is the occurrence and the imminent threat of injury and loss of life and property arising out of the standoff situation in Boundary County."

While Weaver and his family hunkered down in the cabin, fifty members of the FBI HRT arrived in Idaho and set up a command post in the National Guard center in Bonners Ferry. By midday Saturday, HRT members had made their way up the mountain and began setting up a loose perimeter around the cabin. This consisted of several sniper observer positions, but it lacked a tight complete perimeter. Agent Lon Horiuchi was one of the HRT snipers.

Late that afternoon, Horiuchi watched the FBI's light observation helicopter fly lazily over the cabin. Minutes later he observed Weaver and Harris walk out the door of the cabin and head toward a small shed on the property. (Unknown to the FBI, Weaver and Harris had wrapped Sam's body in a sheet and placed it in the shed. The shed was used as a bedroom by the Weaver women during their monthly menstruation as Weaver considered them unclean during this period.) Both men carried shoulder weapons. Once they were outside the cabin, Horiuchi saw both men look up at the helicopter. Thinking they were about to shoot at it, Horiuchi fired a single shot from his telescope-equipped .308 rifle at Weaver. The round went through his bicep and slammed into the side of the shed. Horiuchi stated in later interviews that he didn't know Weaver had been hit, but that he had only seen the bullet impact the shed.

Weaver and Harris immediately ran back toward the cabin. As they approached the door, Vickie, with baby Elishaba in her arms, held it open for them. Weaver made it back inside, but as Harris reached the doorway, Horiuchi fired a second shot that hit Harris in the arm and then penetrated his side. Unknown to

Horiuchi was the fact that the round had first hit Vickie in the head before exiting and hitting Harris. Both Harris and Vickie collapsed out of sight just inside the door on the floor of the kitchen. Harris was seriously injured and Vickie died almost immediately. Horiuchi notified his supervisors that he had fired at Harris but did not know if he had been hit. Within seconds the Weaver homestead had been turned into a house of death.

CIRG hostage negotiator Fred Lanceley flew out to Idaho with the HRT. After his early morning arrival, he spent Saturday developing intelligence on the Weaver family and attempting to put together the chain of events. By Saturday night, Lanceley and the rest of the FBI had this basic set of facts:

> Weaver was wanted for a failure to appear (FTA) federal warrant based on an ATF weapons charge.
>
> Weaver was an anti-government, racist, survivalist and free spirit.
>
> Weaver's family in the cabin consisted of his wife and four children.
>
> The relationship of Kevin Harris to the Weavers was unclear.
>
> U.S. Marshal Bill Degan had been killed by Weaver, Harris, or Weaver's son, Sam, on Friday morning.
>
> HRT sniper Horiuchi thought he might have wounded Harris late Saturday evening.
>
> No one had initiated communication with anyone in the cabin.

Early Sunday morning I got the call to join Lanceley. When I got on the plane at LAX a few hours later it was no surprise to see FBI Agent John Dolan from the San Diego office already on board. Dolan and I were both members of the FBI's Crisis Incident Negotiation Team (CINT), which was designed to provide negotiators for complex and lengthy hostage/barricade incidents around the world. During the flight up to Spokane we had a lengthy discussion about what awaited us at Ruby Ridge. When we arrived in Spokane late Sunday we were met at the airport by two local FBI agents who drove us into Sandpoint to spend the night. They gave us an excellent briefing on the chain of events and the history of Randy Weaver during the two-hour drive before we crashed for a few hours at a local motel. Early Monday morning we were driven up to the command post just off state highway 95.

The scene was ugly. A roadblock had been set up by the sheriff's department and was manned by deputies and agents from the ATF and the Marshal's Service. About a hundred rough looking skinheads and foul-mouthed mountain people supporting Weaver were clustered around the roadblock yelling at the federal agents. As we pulled through the roadblock they flipped us off and yelled, "Baby killers!" The lower command post manned by the Salt Lake City special agent in charge (SAC) was a camper surrounded by military tents housing the federal agents, paramedics, National Guard, and local officers. Before we headed to the cabin, we were granted an audience with the SAC. Dolan and I crowded into the camper. The SAC was leaning back in the driver's seat like Captain Kirk in the Starship Enterprise, balancing scrambled eggs, bacon, and hash browns on a plastic plate with one hand. He waved us in with his fork in the other. He had egg stuck on the stubble on his chin that he didn't seem to notice—or care. We introduced ourselves and he waved us silent. We eagerly awaited his words of wisdom.

"Gentlemen," he said pausing. "What we need here is a solution without further bloodshed."

Dolan and I looked at each other. Wow—now there's an idea. We waited a while longer while he chewed thoughtfully. After a few minutes it became apparent that he had lost interest in us and exhausted his pithy comments on the situation. I don't think he noticed as we left him staring at his plastic plate, trying to decide which piece of bacon to devour next.

The ride up the mountain in a military Jeep reminded me again of Vietnam. The thick, lush, dense foliage could be hiding a platoon of armed men, in this case neo-Nazis. And it got colder as we went up. We hung on to the braces of the canvas top to keep from falling out. Bumpy and uncomfortable. A real kidney shaker. Our driver, an HRT member with an attitude, seemed to enjoy our discomfort.

After about forty-five minutes, we reached the HRT forward command post. John and I hopped out of the Jeep and were met by Lanceley and MacArthur "Ed" Burke, a CINT member from Spokane. They comprised the entire negotiation team at the cabin. Two other negotiators, Wilson Lema and Mark Thunder Cloud, were running leads and logistics for us at the lower command post down by the highway. I was astounded by how dramatically understaffed we were for an incident of this magnitude. It also suggested that FBI headquarters had not seriously considered a negotiated solution. They continued to think in terms of aggressive SWAT action only.

Lanceley related that earlier on Sunday HRT had sent a bomb robot forward to the cabin and attempted unsuccessfully to initiate a dialogue with Weaver. A few days later we learned that the HRT guys had failed to remove the shotgun from the front of the robot, which certainly would explain Weaver's hesitation to talk to the robot. When HRT members had searched the shed and discovered Sam's body, they backed off their earlier aggressive stance and became more conciliatory towards the negotiation effort. We spent Monday and Tuesday with HRT in the protection of an armored personnel carrier (APC) in front of the cabin, but Weaver refused to respond to our loudspeaker pleas for a dialogue.

Over the week we rotated nights in the Sandpoint motel but mostly stayed in the tents at the bottom of the hill with the HRT agents so as to be available if anything happened. We usually suspended our efforts to contact Weaver at night as they hadn't been successful, and it offered HRT the opportunity to do some snooping around the cabin during the darkness. With their night vision goggles they were able to move directly up to the cabin and install exterior listening devices. We were also using a thermal imaging device to locate the people inside the cabin. All this was in preparation for HRT to make a dynamic entry into the cabin. If they had to go in they would know exactly where the occupants were located. Fortunately they never had to carry out this plan. Without question more lives would have been lost.

One of the enterprising HRT operators had dug an outdoor privy that consisted of a couple of two-by-fours over a slit trench high up on the side of the mountain. It lacked a lot of privacy but offered a stunning view of Mt. Casey. We showered off the back of Weaver's flatbed truck with a small hose about the size used by a pest exterminator. Primitive, but it worked. We had long ago left our modesty down at the highway. Way up on a mountain in Idaho, we were more worried about the bears, snakes, skunks, and red ants.

Midmorning Wednesday, Lanceley went forward with the HRT in the APC and bullhorned a message into the cabin. He told Weaver that he would be bringing the hostage phone to the robot and that the robot would then drive up to the cabin and attempt to push the phone through a window to establish communications. This would eliminate the need for Weaver or one of the children to come outside to get the phone. Since he had not responded to the loudspeaker on the robot we thought that we needed a better means of communication.

For the first time Weaver responded and his answer was pretty clear: "Get the fuck outta here!" So much for that idea. HRT immediately canceled the plan.

What we didn't know at the time was that the original plan put together by HRT Commander Dick Rogers and the Salt Lake City Special Agent in Charge, Gene Glenn, called for a forward assault to the cabin with an armored personnel carrier borrowed from the Idaho National Guard. If final bullhorned instructions to surrender were ignored, the HRT would begin to demolish the cabin while inserting gas into it. HRT personnel would then make entry and take the occupants into custody. Fortunately, cooler heads prevailed at the FBI headquarters Strategic Information and Operations Center (SIOC), (affectionately nicknamed "the submarine" because of its claustrophobic affect on the occupants after a few hours), and the negotiations component was called into action.

Several days into the incident, the behavioral profilers back the FBI Academy in Quantico, Virginia, forwarded the following assessment to the negotiation team:

The Weavers will not trust anyone representing the government.

Randy will become stronger if he can talk to local supporters.

Family members could be expected to use firearms against HRT personnel if an entry were made into the cabin.

Vickie could become homicidal towards her children and suicidal if it appeared the government was going to drive them out of their home.

The family could initiate a suicidal attack against the HRT agents outside the cabin.

Neutral third-party negotiators were going to have to be used to negotiate surrender.

Our search for someone with credibility led us to his sister, Marnis Joy. However, she wasn't expected to arrive until late Wednesday. In the meantime, Lanceley continued bull-horning his verbal statement at the cabin with no response from the occupants, and HRT tightened up the perimeter. So far the only intelligence we had gathered via the listening devices on the outside of the cabin was Weaver reading the Bible to his children.

HRT also made it very clear to us that a dynamic entry into the cabin really wasn't a serious option, as they would need to climb either the steps or a ladder and the important element of surprise would be lost. This action would surely result in a shootout with three children present. The importance of the negotiations gradually increased and we found ourselves beginning to be treated like royalty in the crowd of law enforcement officers. When we came down from the mountain we were immediately surrounded by other agents asking how the negotiations were going. It was a heady feeling. The weight of this responsibility was not lost on us, however. The sense of impending violence was strong and we continually fought off the growing negativity we were feeling.

On Thursday morning, Marnis Joy arrived with her bearded biker boyfriend. He did a lot of standing around trying to look intimidating, but she was as receptive as we could have hoped for. Lanceley and I sat down on a log with her and explained the situation. Although deeply supportive of her brother, she readily agreed that she felt that he had made a mistake and that the best thing he could do for himself and his family would be to surrender. She was engaging, likeable, and most importantly she was willing to talk to Weaver. As we hiked up to the cabin, she laughed off her nerves by claiming to be an "old biker gal" who could pee in the bushes. Once we got up to the ravine overlooking the cabin, I grabbed the back of her belt. I was afraid she'd make a break for the cabin, join Weaver, and increase the stakes for us. Marnis laughed it off and promised she'd cooperate, but I didn't let go of her until we had returned to the HRT command post. Using the loudspeaker Marnis tried unsuccessfully to connect with Weaver. After a couple hours, we returned to the command post and treated her to one of our military MREs (meals ready to eat). Although nutritionally designed, these plastic packed meals were also called "meals rejected by everyone" since after a couple days they all taste the same. Marnis was a champ and remained with us as long as we felt she could be useful. We tried for several hours again that afternoon, but Weaver refused to respond so we sent her back to Sandpoint with her boyfriend for the night.

We repeated our efforts again on Friday morning, but again Weaver refused to talk to her. We later learned that our strategy was flawed. Marnis started her pitch by telling Weaver that the FBI was sincere in their desire to help him and his family. What we didn't know, of course, was that Weaver held the FBI responsible for the death of his wife, and wounding him and Harris. Trust these guys? Bullshit! So he wrote off Marnis after the first five minutes she started talking to him.

When Marnis left the mountain that day we had an emotional goodbye with her. She had desperately attempted to save her brother's life and she felt that she had failed. She was also afraid that Weaver was going to die on the mountain. What about the girls, she cried? We promised her we wouldn't let anything happen to them, but we wondered ourselves. We also promised to call her when it was all over. I regret that I never did. So many things happened before this one was over, and afterwards, that it no longer seemed important. I do hope that she and Weaver have since gotten together and have taken the time to explain their misunderstandings.

There had been another issue brewing over the last few days. Randy Weaver had been a member of the Green Berets, the Army's Special Forces unit. Another former Green Beret, Bo Gritz, had heard of the barricade while in Arizona and traveled to the Sandpoint area to ostentatiously offer his services. Not by coincidence, he was also running for president as the Populist Party candidate, with the campaign slogan "God, Guns, and Gritz." Gritz turned out to be one helluva guy.

Lt. Col. James "Bo" Gritz, USA (Ret.), was a highly decorated Vietnam veteran who had gained national attention (and had become of investigative interest to the FBI) after staging a couple commando style raids into Southeast Asia to attempt a rescue of the American POWs he was convinced were still being held in jungle camps. Although no POWs were located, Gritz became more famous as a "conspiracy theorist" suggesting that the American government was involved in various cover-ups. He seemed to be a little paranoid and crazy, but he also had incredible charisma, a Clintonesque ability to walk into a room or up to a group of people and within minutes capture the attention of everyone. Gritz had developed an anti-government attitude and a paramilitary following of racist survivalists connected with the Christian Identity religious movement. He was headquartered in Nevada but had encouraged others to relocate to Idaho to join him in the development of a religious compound. In addition to being a former Green Beret, Randy Weaver was also a member of the Christian Identity religious movement. He and Bo had much in common.

For several days, Gritz had begged the FBI to let him talk to Weaver, claiming that their Green Beret military history and association with the Christian Identity movement would provide him the credibility Weaver needed to hear. We had resisted Gritz's offer, as our assessment of his personality suggested that he would be completely uncontrollable. It's also very difficult to withdraw a third party from the negotiations once they are inserted. Nevertheless, we were starting to run out of options and we were still searching for a credible third-party negotiator. Gritz had been holding daily press conferences down at the bottom of the mountain and had boasted to the media and Weaver's mountain neighbors that he could convince Weaver to surrender. He had become closely aligned with the anti-government mountain people supporting the Weavers who had been camping down at the roadblock like a lost tribe.

Crowds of onlookers can cause problems at hostage incidents. Often we have to deal with relatives who appear at a scene, claiming they can talk a suspect into surrendering. However, they are difficult to control and difficult to withdraw from the negotiations once inserted, their motives are suspect, they are not trained in hostage negotiations, and they are emotionally invested. Rule of thumb: keep the relatives out of it—especially the wives. However, if your negotiations fail, the media will question why the police didn't use these volunteers and you're faced with explaining why you didn't use this option. It's a losing scenario faced often by negotiators.

Having discussed all that with headquarters, on Friday afternoon the command post called and stated that they were sending Gritz up the mountain. We were surprised because Dick Rogers, the HRT commander with no interest or apparent confidence in negotiators, had been calling the shots on this one. His initial plan ignored negotiations and he continually talked a tactical resolution. Most of his conversations with the SACs were held without the negotiators present or being invited. In private, the other HRT operators told us they were praying for a negotiated solution. We prepared for the worst.

Gritz arrived shortly after noon on Friday at the HRT command post in his jungle jacket. Stocky, muscular, blazing blue eyes, confident, and very suspicious of getting close to the FBI. Instead of being difficult, though, Gritz was all ears.

Lanceley, Burke, and I crouched inside a tent and gave him the short course on hostage negotiations. He was a quick learner. "No promises," we emphasized. "Just listen. Remember: no promises."

With that, Gritz struggled into a ballistic vest thrown him by one of the HRT agents and he followed Rogers into the APC. We watched as the APC disappeared around the trail up to the cabin. Rogers had refused to allow any of the negotiators accompany Gritz. "There's no room in the APC," he claimed. We shook our heads in disbelief. Obviously he wasn't interested in a negotiated solution. He had pissed off Lanceley earlier shortly after their arrival at the armory when he said to him, "This isn't going to be a long siege." Lanceley couldn't believe it. We also suddenly realized that we hadn't wired Gritz so we had no idea how things we going. We would have to wait until he returned with Rogers. Shaking our heads, we watched the APC grind its way up the path to the cabin.

Once they reached the cabin, Gritz tried to talk to Weaver using the robot speaker and then from a bullhorn in the track. Gritz finally turned to Rogers.

"Fuck this!" he bellowed in frustration. "He's not talkin' because he can't hear me." With that Gritz jumped out of the track, walked up to the front of the APC and began shouting.

And Weaver answered. For the first time in days. It was the first break in negotiations and a watershed.

After an hour the APC returned from the cabin to the forward CP and Gritz hopped out of the rear of the track. "Vickie's dead," he said. "You guys killed her last Saturday night. And Randy and Kevin are both wounded. Shot to shit. The girls are scared to death."

We were incredulous. We had no idea. All we knew was that Horiuchi had thought he may have hit Harris running back into the cabin. Holy shit! All Lanceley's attempts to communicate had talked about Vickie, or were attempts to talk directly to her, and now we find out she had been dead for a week. (Later interviews with Weaver and the children disclosed that they grew to hate Lanceley for his remarks about Vickie as they assumed he knew she had been killed.) Burke, the most cynical of the three of us, wondered aloud if it was really true. Did Gritz see her? Or was Weaver just trying to hold off an assault? Damn. This was bad. Our credibility was shot. This was going to be even more difficult.

Gritz was absolutely convinced Weaver had told him the truth. "He gave me his word as a Green Beret," Gritz said, as if he had just notarized the statement. Well damn, what more could we ask for than the Green Beret code of honor? We remained skeptical.

We didn't like what Gritz was saying. But he said Weaver had agreed to talk to him again tomorrow and he had talked to no one else for a week. We had to take it. We went back to the tent with Gritz and the three of us went over his conversation with Weaver in detail. It didn't change much. Vickie had been shot in the head the same time Harris had been wounded. He had been hit in the arm and the bullet lodged in his chest. Weaver had taken an in-and-out wound in his bicep but he was healing well. The girls were scared, but strong and doing well. Rogers joined us but didn't interfere in a silent demonstration of respect for Gritz. This wasn't lost on any of the negotiators as later we all commented on it. Rogers never took off his helmet or loosened his chinstrap. He always looked like a paratrooper ready to go out the door of the plane.

Gritz continued his description of Weaver's anger. Weaver blamed it all on the FBI. No mention was made of ATF or the federal marshals.

After prepping Gritz for continuing negotiations the next day, he was taken down the mountain for the night. We begged him not to go to the media, but that lasted until he hit the roadblock. He immediately held a news conference and told the world that the FBI had killed half the Weaver family. It really fueled the Weaver supporters at the roadblock.

Frustrated, but undeterred, the four of us sat in the tent putting a negotiation strategy together for Gritz the next day. We had to stress that we didn't know Vickie had been killed. And we had to walk a fine line with Gritz—to ensure that he followed our instructions and didn't turn into a cowboy—while also convincing Weaver that Gritz's efforts on our behalf were genuine and that he could safely surrender to him. We still had our doubts about Gritz, though.

Saturday morning Gritz returned with his "adjutant," a former Phoenix police officer named Jack McLamb. This time we wired him up to allow us to record and monitor the negotiations. He bitched about this, though, saying he couldn't believe he was becoming a snitch for the FBI. Burke, the ultimate cynic, laughed at him and said, "It's amazing what a presidential candidate will do for a vote." Gritz smirked a reply, knowing he was right. Gritz had also brought along one of Weaver's neighbors, Jackie Brown, and a local preacher. Brown had been one of the "baby killer" screamers down at the roadblock, and we didn't like the looks of her at all. She was one hostile woman. They were carrying water and grapes for the family. Although we as negotiators completely opposed the introduction of these two unknown factors to the equation, the command staff never made a clear decision and they all walked up to the cabin behind the HRT track. Sometimes indecision becomes a decision itself. We stood in disbelief as the group disappeared around the trail.

It was mid-Saturday morning. Once forward, Gritz walked alone to the bottom of the stairs of the cabin. For the next couple hours, he and Weaver talked. They talked about Special Forces, Jesus Christ Yahweh, government abuses, white supremacism, and the lying government. And he prayed with Weaver, making the connection and establishing the trust. Slow, monotonous, but necessary and positive. But Gritz made the connection.

Gritz came down to take a break for lunch and said he thought Harris was seriously injured and wanted to surrender. He also suggested that he offer to remove Vickie's body from the cabin. This raised several issues. Although it would provide considerable intelligence, and build on his relationship with Weaver, we weren't sure that Gritz wouldn't go into the cabin and we'd lose complete control. Gritz could become a hostage or another adversary. We constantly worried about losing control of him.

Removing Vickie's body also required that HRT choreograph an exchange to ensure everyone's safety. They suggested Weaver bring the body out to the stairs. Gritz insisted Weaver would never show himself and that Gritz would have to go in. We remained unconvinced. Gritz didn't. He was convinced he could persuade Weaver to allow him to enter and leave safely. He returned that afternoon and the negotiations continued. By late Saturday, Harris was listening to Gritz suggest that he surrender. They had also again discussed removing Vickie's body. Although Gritz had deviated from our instructions, it was a huge break in the stalemate. We were starting to think that we had found our credible third party.

Later that afternoon, Park Dietz, the famous psychiatrist and criminal profiler from Southern California, arrived at the HRT command post. FBI headquarters had sent him to conduct a psychological profile of Weaver and offer suggestions to the negotiators. We sat down in the tent with Dietz and Gritz. Dietz looked around at the motley crew. He looked very collegiate and out of place dressed in Bermuda shorts and carrying a briefcase.

"So which daughter do you think Randy is diddling?" he asked.

We looked at each other. Weaver screwing his daughters? What the hell is this? This guy is the best criminal profiler in the world and he wants to know which daughter he's doing?

Gritz stared at Dietz. "What the fuck are you talking about?" he asked, insulted on behalf of Weaver.

Realizing that he had just thrown a match at a can of gas, Dietz brushed it aside. "Okay, bring me up to date." The match died out.

Dietz sat back and listened silently while we took turns relating the events of the last week. When it came to his intervention, Gritz took over and gave a demonstration of how to conduct a briefing. His years in the military had made him an expert. Dietz listened, made a couple notes, offered no suggestions, got up, walked out and caught the next Jeep down the mountain. No "thank you" or "good luck." Not even a "fuck you." Although I assume he provided an assessment to the suits at the lower command post, we never saw anything on the mountain. And no, we didn't ask FBI headquarters to send him back either.

On Sunday, Jackie Brown showed up again with Gritz and Jack McLamb. Brown said she had some food for the kids. For some reason no one saw a problem with this—except the negotiators. The whole cabin was a crime scene. People had been shot and killed. While I frantically searched for Robin Montgomery, the SAC in charge on the mountain, Rogers and HRT agents brought Gritz, McLamb, and Brown back up to the cabin. We were astounded. It was like no one had ever heard of protecting a crime scene. An hour later, Jackie and Jack returned. She said the kids were okay but scared to death. We shook our heads in disbelief and embarrassment. She was dressed like a pioneer woman wearing an ankle length skirt and had never been searched. I wondered how much evidence she had destroyed, how much she was leaving with, or if she had smuggled additional weapons or ammunition into the cabin.

By mid Sunday Gritz was still talking with Weaver. He had advanced to the theories of Richard Butler and the New World Order. Gritz had convinced Weaver that in the very near future all Americans would have their identity bar-coded on their foreheads and the government would be cloning its warriors. He had taken a position at the bottom of the stairs and was talking to Weaver through the walls of the cabin. Although we had trouble hearing Weaver, we didn't think he was breaking down. But he had mentioned several times that Kevin Harris was hurting.

We seized on this and encouraged Gritz to stress the availability of medical treatment for Harris. This turned out to be successful. By mid afternoon, Gritz and McLamb had climbed the steps of the cabin, carried Harris down the steps and brought him over to the HRT APC. He appeared to be seriously injured. Besides his chest wound, his arm wound had blackened and appeared gangrenous. We gathered around his stretcher when they returned to the CP, but he refused to say anything. The

HRT paramedics rapidly prepped him for travel with an IV and in a few minutes he was down the mountain and being flown to the hospital. Jack McLamb went along to ensure that he was not mistreated, a condition demanded by Weaver and something that offended all of us.

Late that afternoon, Weaver agreed to surrender his wife's body for removal. After returning to the CP to confer with Montgomery, Gritz and Jackie Brown again returned to the cabin with a body bag and retrieved Vickie's body from inside the cabin. The HRT operators immediately returned to the CP and then drove the body down the mountain. Brown returned to the cabin with more water to clean the kitchen of Vickie's blood. By now she had established easy and unrestrained access to the cabin. Our pleas to prevent this were ignored. Rogers had smelled a resolution and he refused to slow down the events to take stock of the risks.

Our group of negotiators huddled Sunday night with Gritz. We had accomplished a great deal. We thought we now understood the chain of events, we had one suspect in custody, we had removed the body of Vickie, and we had connected with Weaver through Gritz. And he had turned out to be a tremendous aid. Whatever he did before and after Ruby Ridge, Gritz was a man of his word for us when he was there. We felt good Sunday night.

Monday morning we sent Gritz back up the hill to talk to Weaver. Overnight, the listening devices had picked up the conversation inside the cabin. Surprisingly, Weaver had talked about coming out, but was dissuaded by his sixteen-year-old daughter Sarah, who reminded her father of all the death and destruction the government had brought down on their family. She was convinced the government planned to kill all of them. Apparently convinced, Weaver backed off and went back to Bible school with the girls.

At one point between negotiations, Gritz and Rogers really got into it when Rogers continued to suggest an assault on the cabin if Weaver didn't surrender shortly. Gritz told him he was crazy and responded with the suggestion that he and McLamb could overpower Weaver and the girls while they were in the house. The two of them countered the argument of the other like the field generals they were. Neither suggestion sounded feasible but it made for good theatre for the rest of us. Gritz had also gained the confidence to take on the FBI management team. He was an old and experienced commander and fighting for superiority came naturally to him.

Later in the day, Gritz continued his negotiations with Weaver. At some point, Gritz had offered the legal services of Gerry Spence to Weaver. Spence was a famous country lawyer from Wyoming known for a voice like Johnny Cash, his fringed buckskin jacket and a huge cowboy hat, and his homespun manner of convincing juries that his client was innocent. Gritz had asked us if we would pay for Spence to represent Weaver. Of course, we said—we'll even give it to him in writing if he'll surrender. Weaver also told Gritz that he wanted the opportunity to explain to the media and the Boundary County grand jury his account of what happened. He considered it very important for him to get his story out to the media. We immediately agreed to allow him to do so. A concession like this, made under duress, has a well-established legal history in hostage negotiations and we weren't concerned about its validity. Robin Montgomery, the agent in charge on top of the mountain, didn't hesitate to provide the written agreement for Weaver. Gritz brought it in. The HRT members around the cabin anxiously waited. After about forty-five minutes, Gritz exited the cabin.

"You gotta get that goddamn robot out of here," he growled. "Randy ain't coming out until that robot goes."

Rogers radioed for the HRT robot operator to immediately start up the robot. We were forced to wait several painful minutes while the operator bent over the console, carefully backing the robot away from the cabin. This took considerable expertise since the operator was watching the robot on a computer screen and he had to negotiate it down a dirt path covered with stones and logs without toppling it over. As the minutes ticked by, we were afraid Weaver would change his mind.

Several minutes later, though, Gritz, Weaver and the girls

came out of the cabin and walked down the mountain to the HRT CP. It was anti-climatic after eleven long, tense days.

Preceded by Gritz, Weaver held his head high and defiant with baby Elishaba in his arms, and Sara and Rachel on either side, each wearing long skirts. The pioneer family Weaver. Weaver had a buzz haircut and looked like a POW. A skinny little shit, pale and weak looking, his skin stretched so tight he looked like he had been shrink-wrapped. Beady eyes. None of them had been searched, although Gritz claimed later that he had patted them down. They walked into a cluster of HRT agents who carefully searched them. It was over. Three people killed, two seriously injured, and countless lives broken—all because this pathetic little man couldn't accept the authority of the United States government.

Lanceley, Burke, Dolan, and I watched HRT and the forensic team enter the cabin to begin to pick up where Jackie Brown had left off cleaning the crime scene. Instead of a quick walk-through the crime scene, as is custom, we just packed our gear and caught a ride down the mountain. All the excitement and activity was focused on the family when they arrived down below. The U.S. Marshal personally took custody of Weaver and he was flown off to booking in Sandpoint. We watched it all with a great sense of satisfaction. After a few minutes we found Burke's vehicle, threw our gear in the trunk, and drove back to Spokane where we checked into the hotel.

After a long hot shower I joined the others in the hotel restaurant for our first hot meal in a week. We toasted our success and dug into dinner like hungry hunters. We were euphoric about what we had accomplished. In spite of the death and destruction that we had walked into, Weaver, his girls, and his protégé had surrendered and no other shots had been fired. We had met an incredible challenge. Yet in the aftermath, no one ever said thank you. No commendations. No incentive awards. No attaboys. Nothing. It was as if the negotiators were never present at Randy Weaver's cabin. We had become nonexistent. And to this day, FBI headquarters has never provided any of the negotiators with any recognition whatsoever of their efforts in the Randy Weaver case. Unknown to us at the time, however, was that the FBI's crisis management leadership had begun to hemorrhage internally as if its aorta had ruptured.

Because of the second shot fired by HRT sniper Lon Horiuchi that killed Vickie Weaver, the entire incident and the FBI's crisis management policy and response would suffer intense scrutiny and a firestorm of criticism by congressional committees, the media, and the public for months to come.

A series of congressional hearings never really answered the controversial questions and the FBI testimony was never convincing that things would be different the next time. The lives of many of those involved were changed forever. Several high-ranking FBI officials would be placed on administrative leave and suffer from an internal investigation that dragged on for two years while Louis Freeh, the FBI director, wished he could amputate the Randy Weaver case from the history of the FBI. One would be indicted, charged with obstruction of justice and go to jail for destroying a written critique of the Ruby Ridge events. HRT sniper Horiuchi would be castigated and indicted for manslaughter for what he believed was appropriate action, although the charge would be later dismissed. Promising executive careers screeched to a halt and then veered into oblivion.

Three months after Weaver came down off the mountain, as promised, Gritz sent me his six-hundred-page autobiography, *Called to Serve*. Inside the flyleaf he wrote:

"Jim, God graced us as Amer-I-Cans. Together we'll win. Forever your brother. B.G. 8 Sep 92. Good job on Weaver mtn. Thanks from one of your fans."

In 1996, Gritz attempted to insert himself into the negotiations during the Montana Freemen standoff in Montana, but his efforts were rebuffed by both the Freemen and the FBI. In 1998 he recruited several volunteers in an attempt to locate Eric Rudolph, wanted by the FBI for the bombing in the Atlanta Centennial Park in 1996. Gritz and his volunteer militia scoured the Smoky Mountains of North Carolina for a week but quietly disappeared when the search came up empty. And then in a strange turn of events, several years later Gritz allegedly shot himself in the chest in an apparent suicide attempt over marital problems. Never one to pass up an opportunity for media sunshine, Gritz, along with other religious pro-lifers, tried to deliver water to a dying Terri Schiavo, caught up in a national right to die controversy in Florida in the spring of 2005.

Kevin Harris recovered from his gunshot wounds and was charged with murder, which was later dismissed. He then filed a $10 million civil suit against several of the government agents insisting that the marshals "shot first" and that he was only defending himself when he returned fire and killed U.S. Marshal Bill Degan. He later settled with the government for $380,000.

HRT sniper Lon Horiuchi has retired from the FBI and lives daily with the weight of the life he took and how it affected so many others.

Randy Weaver went to trial represented by Gerry Spence as we had promised. He was acquitted of the most serious charges, found guilty only of failing to appear for the first charge, and sentenced to time already served. The government awarded him and his daughters $3.1 million in damages for the death of his wife. After the TV cameras shut down, he drifted into relative obscurity hawking his autobiography on the gun show circuit.

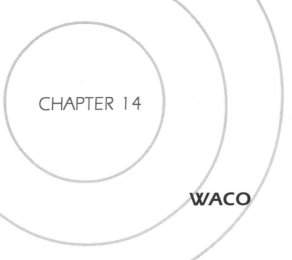

CHAPTER 14

WACO

"So where you guys been eating dinner?" David Koresh asked.

There weren't a whole lot of choices in Waco, Texas, and after a while we had started hanging out at all the same places.

"Last night we went to the Whataburger," the FBI negotiator answered.

Koresh laughed. "You know what, guys? If I find out I really am Jesus Christ, I'll tell you what they put in those Whataburgers."

We all laughed, including Koresh, the Bible teacher on steroids.

It was day ten, and we had been talking to Koresh non-stop.

It had all started on a Sunday morning, February 28, 1993, when a hundred ATF (Alcohol, Tobacco & Firearms) SWAT agents converged on a seventy-seven acre compound outside Waco that was occupied by 125 religious cult members known as the Branch Davidians. Their purpose was to serve a search warrant on the compound in an effort to find evidence relating to the unlawful possession of fully automatic machine guns and grenades. They also had an arrest warrant for Koresh—the CEO of this outfit—previously known as Vernon Lee Howell.

As the ATF agents jumped out of their assault vehicles and began to take positions around the huge building, shots were fired. Each group claimed that the other started firing first. But it didn't matter when it was over. Four ATF agents were dead and fifteen were wounded, several Branch Davidians were killed and up to twenty had been wounded. A Waco police lieutenant had arranged a shaky ceasefire when Koresh surprisingly called 911 asking for the police to intervene. It also allowed the ATF agents to drag off their dead and wounded. Within minutes, the deputy director of ATF in Washington had called the FBI requesting for hostage negotiators to help resolve what appeared to be developing into a very complex situation. A few minutes later Doug Gow, the FBI's associate deputy director in Washington, pulled the trigger on the negotiators from the Crisis Incident Negotiation Team (CINT) and my home telephone rang. Get down to Waco!

The Branch Davidians were an interesting group that had been under investigation by the ATF for over a year after they received information that Koresh was buying automatic guns and grenades. During the investigation, the ATF had also learned that Koresh was apparently engaging in sexual relations with a large number of the women in the compound, some as young as twelve, and that he had supposedly fathered at least fifteen children. These allegations drew the interest of the Texas Department of Child Services, which initiated its own investigation, but eventually stalled due to insufficient evidence to prove physical or sexual abuse. Koresh's Branch Davidians demonstrated many of the typical characteristics of a religious cult: a charismatic leader, a basis in religious thought, brain washing with long repetitive biblical lectures by the leader, a low protein diet, self imposed deprivation of luxuries, development of a siege mentality, peer pressure on less committed members, intimidation and harassment of critics, an "us against them" attitude, and resistance to governmental control. As with other historical religious cults, their stockpiling of weapons was curious and inconsistent with their religious teachings.

Koresh, who had been an ardent Bible reader since he was twelve, believed that he was the reincarnation of both King

David and King Cyrus of Persia and that he had been appointed by God to rebuild Babylon. At various times, Koresh claimed to be Jesus Christ.

By late Sunday the FBI had swarmed into Waco like the Barnum and Bailey circus coming to town. It featured SWAT agents, hostage negotiators, investigators, psychological profilers, aircraft pilots, electronic technicians and radiomen, surveillance teams, media representatives, computer technicians, managers, clerks, moneymen, purchasing agents, and of course lawyers. Jeff Jamar, the special agent in charge (SAC) of the San Antonio Division, was dispatched to Waco as the on-site commander since it was within his geographical area of responsibility. Byron Sage, the agent in charge of the Austin office of the FBI and an experienced CINT member, was sent to take over the negotiations and hold the fort until the rest of the CINT members arrived. The FBI Hostage Rescue Team (HRT) at the FBI Academy in Quantico was deployed with enough weapons and equipment to make the 82nd Airborne Division jealous. Within a few days, thirty-two Texas Rangers had been assigned to Waco, in addition to officers from the Waco police department and the McLennan County sheriff's office. The FBI code name for the incident was "WACMUR," which stood for "Waco Murders."

By 5 PM Sunday, the FBI had established a fully functioning command post, consolidated all the negotiations, and established tactical control of the area surrounding the compound. According to the official U.S. Department of Justice report, during the next fifty-one days, the FBI committed 668 personnel to the standoff and averaged 217 agents and forty-one support personnel on duty each day. Twenty-five CINT negotiators conducted 117 conversations with Koresh for sixty hours, 459 conversations with Koresh lieutenant Steve Schneider over ninety-six hours, and 215 hours of conversations with fifty-four other occupants in the compound. On any given day of the standoff, a minimum of 719 law enforcement personnel were committed on-site.

On that first Sunday, Koresh allowed four children to exit

the compound. ATF supervisor Jim Cavanaugh had established a relationship with Koresh in the first few hours and was instrumental in the release of the first children, although we were to later learn that none of Koresh's own children were ever released. Recently promoted and under transfer orders to the ATF headquarters in Washington, D.C., Cavanaugh had to pull out and turn the negotiations over to others. He was a good guy, and we missed him. Incoming FBI negotiators had to pick up where Cavanaugh left off with Koresh.

I arrived in Dallas early Monday afternoon and rented a car for the drive down to Waco. On the way I listened to the news on the radio, which was nothing but the Waco shootout. The first figures on the dead and wounded were exaggerated as the media struggled to gain access to the situation. When I finally arrived I found the FBI negotiation command post in a nearby airport hanger. I was amazed at the organization already up and operating. The negotiation team, made up of police officers, sheriff's deputies, ATF agents, local FBI agents, and Byron Sage, was humming. Gary Noesner, from the Crisis Management Unit (CMU) at the FBI Academy, had arrived with the HRT and was in charge of the negotiations.

"Good to see you, Jim," Byron called from inside the CP. "You're going to love this one." Byron came over and we warmly shook hands. "Gary is here, but he's in with the boss right now. This one is really going to be a challenge. We've got over a hundred people in there and this guy, Koresh, has been running guns and explosives into this cult for a year. He may even have a .50 caliber sniper rifle. Four ATF agents were killed and fifteen wounded Sunday morning. We're not sure how many were killed or injured inside. We think several. This one is going to take awhile to get sorted out."

As founding members of the CINT, Byron and I had become good friends. We both had considerable field experience as negotiators and respected the ability of the other. Silver haired and Hollywood handsome, Byron was smart, articulate, experienced, organized, and diplomatic. He also wasn't intimidated by the suits and was comfortable around rank.

Moreover, he knew all the cops in the county and was well respected. The negotiation team couldn't have a better leader, I thought.

Gary Noesner walked into the room revved up to red-line at about 7000 RPMs. "Jim, glad you could make it. We got four kids out yesterday and ten today. We've been able to cut the outside lines and we're talking to Koresh directly. CNN and A Current Affair got through to him earlier but we've stopped that now. HRT's set up and I want you to take the supervision of the night shift. We're going to run twelve-hour shifts, six to six. Your shift starts in about two hours. You've got some good negotiators to work with. Byron got them up and running. Let me introduce you around." He was so stoked I wondered if his diet had been anything more than Red Bull and coffee beans since his arrival. I could hardly keep up with his machine-gun briefing.

Nothing like jumping right in. I grinned at Gary's enthusiasm, which was always contagious. We had met back in 1982 in Albuquerque at a huge "coming out party" (practical exercise) for the new Hostage Rescue Team prior to the 1984 Olympics in LA and had been close friends ever since. He had been in charge of the negotiation team of the Washington Field Office and had worked extensively with the local police negotiators who get a lot of work in Washington, D.C., with all the wackos coming to the White House wanting to talk to the president. He had also been involved in several of the international terrorist incidents, including the bombing of Pan Am 73 in Lockerbie and the hijacking of TWA 847 in Beirut. He was comfortable around royalty in the White House and the attorney general's office in Justice. He had testified before congressional committees. In other words, he sported a large headquarters profile. We thought the same way and often called each other about various hostage/barricade incidents going on around the world. I knew I was at the top of his list when the phone rang for these call-outs. I wondered what other CINT members were coming in but I didn't have a chance to ask.

The introductions consisted of meeting SAC Jeff Jamar and didn't take long. Jamar wasn't long on small talk and too busy to be cordial. We shook hands and he turned away to others. He had the tanned athletic build of a Texas football coach with a few middle-aged pounds, the kind of guy you'd see on the 9th hole with a grin and a cigar.

Gary and I found a quiet corner in the CP and we sat down to arrange the handoff for my shift, which was coming at me like a freight train. Gary hadn't slept since Saturday night and he was beginning to fall apart. My negotiation team consisted of an FBI team leader and FBI agents as the primary and secondary negotiators. A police officer from Austin and a McLennan County sheriff's deputy also sat at the table maintaining the log and manning the tape recorder as well as an FBI scribe who took notes of the conversations. An HRT representative joined the team to listen for tactical information and man the status boards. The ATF also provided an agent to monitor the negotiations and to provide any historical intelligence that could be helpful to the negotiators. In addition, we had FBI agents from the Behavioral Science Unit (BSU) at the FBI Academy with us most of the time and a police psychologist on occasion. The shrinks loved this stuff. In all, the negotiation team was composed of approximately 10–12 individuals with varying talents and experience.

Any worries I had about experience, professional rivalry, and turf battles evaporated as I met the people on the team. This multi-agency group came together immediately. We all shared the same objective: to secure the release and surrender of all the occupants of the compound as soon as possible with no further violence. And they turned out to be the best negotiators I have ever had the pleasure of working with—genuine, committed, flexible, patient, smart, tireless, compassionate, professional experts.

The basic strategy was to attempt a negotiated settlement, gradually tighten the perimeter, reduce the living space of the occupants, deny them anything that would make it more comfortable for them to remain inside, and to use force or conduct an assault only as a last resort. The negotiators also wanted to build strong parental responsibilities and obligations in those parents with children inside with them to encourage them to come out together as a family.

Monday night was my introduction to Koresh and set the stage for the negotiations for the next fifty days, a series of seemingly endless and repetitious conversations with him and Schneider. What began to develop late that night was Koresh's demand to release a tape recording to the news media along with his insistence on "Bible study" for the negotiators. Henry Garcia, an FBI agent from Dallas, was the primary negotiator that night. He was a reserved, soft-spoken guy with a constant smile. Nothing upset him and everyone liked him. He was also a very experienced and successful negotiator. Henry deserved an award for the length of time he spent in David Koresh's Bible class that first week. He never tired of working on Koresh.

Another troubling situation was that Koresh had been wounded in the left side and left hand (with possibly the same round) when he opened the front door of the house. He complained about the injury and we eventually sent in a suture kit for him to sew up the wound. It was a long night and the first of many. The day shift would spend much of its time with Steve Schneider while the night shift talked to Koresh most of the time. Usually he would tire of his lectures and begin to wear down about 4 AM. That left me a few hours to catch up my other tasks before the shift change.

As the night shift negotiation coordinator, I had to stay abreast of the issues being discussed by the night shift of negotiators, maintain communication with the HRT out in the field if anything would affect their operations (like a request to come out to feed their flock of ducks in front of the compound), keep the night shift boss informed of developments, set out requests for investigation and review returning investigative results for pertinent information for the negotiators. I also prepared the news briefing for the boss the next morning at 10:30 AM. This briefing became an extremely important function as we realized early on that we could communicate with Koresh and the others in the compound through the briefing, when he refused to negotiate with us. We often thought Koresh and

Schneider were not passing on our messages to the other people in the compound and that the other members of the sect had no awareness of the ongoing negotiations. It also became apparent fairly soon that no one was going to leave the compound without Koresh's approval. Schneider would carry out minor tasks for us and respond to our requests for the most part, but it was a waste of time to attempt to negotiate a surrender with anyone but Koresh. We needed him, and when he refused to talk to us we were stonewalled. So in an effort to prod Koresh, we asked Bob Ricks, the SAC who handled the media, to announce in his morning briefing that "we believe Koresh has died and that Steve Schneider is now in charge and arranging a surrender of all the occupants of the compound." Five minutes later Koresh called the negotiators to remind them that he was still, in fact, alive and kicking.

The first briefing I witnessed on Tuesday morning was conducted by SAC Jeff Jamar. Blunt and unsophisticated, Jamar appeared to be angered by all the questions from a confrontational international media. He also appeared frustrated by the FBI taking the blame for another ATF fuck-up. We were still trying to get over the Randy Weaver Ruby Ridge incident also ignited by the ATF the year before. And some members of the media and the public never separated the FBI from the ATF— to them we were all incompetent federal government killers. The news conference didn't go well for Jamar. Consequently, on the second day, Bob Ricks, another SAC from Oklahoma City, came in to conduct the news briefings and Jamar went back to running the overall operation. It was a good decision. Ricks was much better at handling an international media that was aggressive, demanding, critical, and disrespectful.

When Gary walked in later that morning, the highlight of discussion was the audiotape Koresh had made. Koresh had promised to surrender after it was played on the radio, but we still had some reservations. It seemed too easy. About an hour long, it was typical meaningless Koresh Bible-babble. We had laid the groundwork for broadcasting the tape, but insisted that it be played only on the Christian Broadcasting Network (CBN).

And he agreed to that. We had also insisted that it include a statement that he intended to surrender the occupants of the compound after it was played. After listening to the tape, we sent it back to Koresh because he had failed to add his surrender statement. We wondered if that was intentional and worried that this could become an issue. But an hour later HRT called and advised the tape was coming back to us. Koresh had fixed it by adding: "I, David Koresh, agree upon the broadcast of this tape to come out peacefully with all the people immediately."

We liked it. It had kind of a Moses ring to it. We also thought it would work. We sent it over to Craig Smith of the CBN and it was played on the radio for about an hour. While it played Koresh continued to talk to the negotiators rather than listening to it. We thought that was strange. We thought he'd want to hear every word of it. Nevertheless we remained cautiously optimistic.

We figured this was the end of it. They were coming out. This thing was coming to a close. We made arrangements for buses, emergency medical workers, crime scene technicians, DCS caseworkers, and arrest teams. By 3 PM we were ready. The negotiators were now talking to Schneider who related the activities inside: "David is giving a last sermon to the people, the children have loaded their backpacks, and the people are coming out any time now. They're lining up and getting ready. We're coming out." We were ecstatic. It was happening.

The negotiators insisted on talking to Koresh to keep him hooked, to push the surrender and keep him on point, but Schneider refused to bring him to the phone, saying that he was busy. Then Schneider also disappeared and the line stayed open. For hours. We kept ringing but no one picked it up inside. We started to get edgy and frustrated. What's the holdup? A surrender is a very volatile action. It's difficult to give up the gun and the power of holding a hostage, of forcing a government to listen to you. Yet he had given us his word and we had kept ours. What the hell was going on?

At 5:58 PM Schneider came back on the line. "David told me

that God had spoken to him and told him to wait. David is now in deep thought and meditation. He can't come to the phone. He wanted to come out but he has to wait for the word of God."

We looked at each other in total disbelief. God—now there's an admirable adversary. We could fight David Koresh, but we certainly couldn't fight God. Had we ever been snookered! Although we were all frustrated and angry, Jamar was livid. He was the one who had to explain this to FBI headquarters.

All of our expectations, planning, and anticipation of resolving this confrontation—halted by God. We should have seen this coming. We were dealing with a cunning, egotistical, manipulative psychopath who was enjoying his performance on the world stage. We took our frustrations out on Schneider but he remained philosophical about it. "Whatever David says," he would say so often over those fifty-one days. We thought about all those inside who were now sentenced by Koresh to waiting for God to act.

I was beginning to realize how just how unique and enormous this event had become. The number of people and agencies involved complicated decision-making. The numerous deaths and injuries on both sides were sobering and the continuing potential for more violence was frightening. The cult leader's preoccupation with apocalyptic scriptures heightened the possibility of mass suicide, and the large number of children inside the compound who could become innocent victims played on the emotions of all of us. And of course, the personal involvement of very high-ranking government officials, the unusually high interest of the international media, and the acute awareness of the consequences of an error in judgment by the command staff, created an incredibly difficult situation. We couldn't make a mistake and we all knew it.

Early on the morning of March 5, nine-year-old Heather Jones was released from the compound. Cute, polite, and articulate, she impressed us. But pinned to her shirt was an ominous note written by her mother to Heather's aunt. It said goodbye and that by the time the aunt received the note, she would be dead. Although both Koresh and Schneider had consistently insisted that they had no plans for suicide, we were beginning to get Jonestown flashbacks. In the early 1970s another religious leader, Jim Jones, formed a cult named the Peoples Temple in the San Francisco area. Seeking a refuge for his people, Jones relocated the flock to a place in Guyana that he named Jonestown. When a delegation of California officials and concerned relatives of the cult members arrived in November 1978 to check allegations of abuse, members of the cult attacked the delegation killing five and injuring several. In the wake of the attack, Jones convinced his followers drink kool-aid flavored cyanide and over nine hundred men, women and children died. It has been called the largest mass suicide in over 1,900 years. We certainly considered a similar suicide by Koresh a strong possibility and we didn't want to play into his hand and create an Apocalypse by pointing a gun at him.

When the children were released from the compound those first few days, we brought them into the negotiators' command post and allowed them to speak to their parents inside the compound using our hostage phone. We wanted to verify to their parents that the children were well and in the safekeeping of the Department of Children's Services (DCS). During one of these conversations, as one of the mothers said goodbye, she told her daughter that she would "see her on the other side." We considered this terribly ominous and confirmed that at least some of the Branch Davidians were certainly thinking this would end in an attack by the government or suicide. This made it difficult for the negotiators. The kids were clean, respectful, and apparently well taken care of, and now they were being separated from their parents because of this religious nut. Many of them bravely fought back tears in the presence of all these strangers. We resented Koresh for having made these innocent kids pawns in this deadly game and it motivated us to intensify our efforts to push Koresh to release more children; but he refused. He realized what a protective shield they formed for him. In a display of understanding and compassion, the DCS workers arranged for a large foster home in an effort to keep the children together to reduce their anxiety and fears from being separated from their parents.

Because of the effect of the kids, we decided to send a videotape to Koresh and Schneider of all the hostage negotiators giving short speeches about themselves and their own families. We wanted to put a face on the voices of the negotiators and show us to be caring parents ourselves, hoping that it might encourage parental concern for the rest of the children and result in their release. But the plan backfired. In response to our tape, which he must have found entertaining, Koresh sent out to the negotiators his own video introducing several of his wives and twelve of his children. It was pathetically manipulative and disgusting. There he was, lying on the floor in a wife-beater t-shirt, laughing as he showed us the wound in his side. One by one he called several of the young wives to his side, many appearing to be 14–16 years old, who would cuddle with him and proclaim that they wanted to remain inside the compound with him. He would then hold up the young children he had fathered with them to show to us. He couldn't even remember the names of two of the children and had to ask the mother. By the end of the tape, we were convinced that the allegations of sexual abuse of the young women were true. Seeing all the young children who could die also had a huge emotional impact on the negotiators.

Koresh also had a practice of taking the wives of other members to become his "sexual partner." We found this astonishing. Even Steve Schneider's wife Judy had fallen prey to Koresh. When we questioned Schneider about this in an effort to drive a wedge between the two, he said that it was a "gift" to Judy that Koresh had selected her. He seemed totally accepting of this and remained subservient until the end. We desperately tried to build some leadership in Schneider in the hope of encouraging him to take the initiative to release some of the people on his own. But although he would coordinate things inside and carry out minor tasks for the negotiators, like verifying the identity of someone inside the compound for a family member outside, he refused to attempt to arrange any releases. He referred those decisions to Koresh. Eventually he became whiny, annoying, and useless.

After it became apparent that Koresh was not seriously thinking of coming out until he received "word from God," we focused on his theory of the Seven Seals in Revelations. Koresh had said that if we could prove his interpretation of the Seven Seals wrong, he would surrender. The Seven Seals is a concept from the Book of Revelation which suggests that at the end of the world and the coming of Christ, the Seven Seals will be opened for understanding. The Seals are represented by symbols commonly interpreted as death, wars, famine, earthquakes, and the anti-Christ. Koresh was convinced that only he could adequately explain and interpret the Seals for his followers. He had been refining this religious delusion since he was twelve years old, and no one could match his familiarity with Biblical passages as he went from one book and one verse of the Bible to another. He could talk for hours in a circular method of argument that was difficult to follow, and he was unwilling to compromise his well-developed and delusional beliefs. He ensured that no one could really understand what he was saying to prove him wrong, because if they had, he would lose his unqualified leadership of the cult. It was designed to be incomprehensible for a selfish purpose.

Nevertheless, thinking that an understanding may end the standoff, our attempt to understand and open the Seven Seals fell to Henry Garcia, Koresh's favorite Bible student. And he got into it. Henry would sit at the negotiators' table in the command post with the Bible on one knee, and the Koran on the other, scribbled notes and diagrams in front of him. Koresh would go back and forth from one to the other, from Genesis to Revelations with Henry desperately trying to keep up with him. Henry is a patient and considerate man, and he refused to give up those long nighttime sessions with Koresh. He kept hoping to understand the seals and break the impasse. But when one of the women released after several days advised us that Koresh was just enjoying himself running Henry around in biblical circles, even Henry had finally had enough.

"That's it, David," said Henry. "No more Bible school. Class is out. It's over."

And that was it. Henry closed the Bible and went back to the here and now. Gradually, he pulled Koresh along. At times Koresh became very concerned about going to jail and being thrown in a cell "with some bubba." He was very worried that he would be considered a child molester (having fathered several children with underage girls), and he knew child molesters don't do well in prison. So in spite of his historical religiosity, David Koresh also had the ability to become very contemporary.

When we cut their telephone to prevent CNN from interviewing Koresh during the first couple days, the Branch Davidians were furious and hung a banner outside the tower of the compound that read, "God help us, we want the press." The news media, which had set up and encamped in "Satellite City," responded by putting up a sign that read, "God help us, we are the press." Two days into the siege some guy showed up with t-shirts made up for the siege confirming that Waco had turned into an international event. And David Koresh loved it. He had finally captured the world stage.

At another point in the siege, Schneider mentioned that Koresh was listening to the popular radio announcer Paul Harvey, who had described a shooting star called the "Guitar Nebula." It was a neutron star formed by a supernova explosion flying through space at over one thousand miles per second leaving a wake in the shape of a guitar. Experts have estimated it to be 6.5 light years away. We thought we had certainly found our "word from God." Within minutes we had researched the Guitar Nebula and began to create a biblical significance for Schneider and Koresh. We all turned into instant astrologists. This offered Koresh an extraordinary opportunity to claim this unique galactic experience as his own. How could he pass this up? Minutes passed and we held our breath. Then Schneider returned.

"David says it didn't travel fast enough to be a message from God."

Dammit! And we thought we had the perfect solution. Beaten

by God once again.

Late one night during a lull in the negotiations we tried to put together the reasons for the initial shooting. The ATF had expected to surprise the Davidians early Sunday morning. Yet, they walked into a hail of bullets as soon as they arrived. What had failed? How was the raid compromised? The ATF had requested paramedics follow them into the compound as they executed the raid. We had heard that one of the medical personnel allegedly leaked the news to a TV station, which immediately sent a crew out to the compound to record the raid. While in the area, a mailman drove up and asked what they were all doing. And of course they told him. Very unfortunately, the mailman was connected to a Davidian inside the compound and he immediately telephoned him.

There was also an ATF informant or agent (we never did find out which he was—and there is a huge difference) named Bobby Rodriguez inside the compound with Koresh when they learned of the impending raid. Rodriguez said that he thought Koresh had suspected his true identity and surprisingly told him it was time for him to leave right after receiving the phone call. After he left, the agent immediately notified the ATF commanders that the surprise of the raid had been compromised. Koresh knew they were coming. Nevertheless, because of the large number of committed personnel, the months spent in training, and other reasons known only to them, the AFT commanders decided to go ahead. It was a decision they would regret the rest of their lives.

Everything we sent into the compound—water, milk, suture kit, medicine, vitamins, videotapes and camera, blankets, food— had a transmitter in it. And Koresh knew it. He would often ask us where we had hidden the bug and we'd laugh and tell him he had to find it. One night we had sent in some milk in a bugged container, which ended up in Koresh's bedroom. For once the transmission was as clear as a bell. We listened intently, hoping to overhear him discussing some strategy—but instead we listened to Koresh's biblical lecture to his wife and his moaning when he painfully turned over. Mercifully it was finally stopped for us when the dog got a hold of it and ripped it up with loud growling and snorting.

Working nights, the days had begun to run together, and I began to become sleep-deprived. The human body just isn't designed to be nocturnal. I'd leave right after the morning news conference, grab breakfast on the way back to the motel, and then crash for a few hours. We all lived on the excitement and hope that the standoff could end at any moment, and we all wanted to be a part of it. After a couple days though, I began skipping the morning news conference at 10:30, which had only allowed for 3–4 hours sleep. Although my shift ended at 6 AM I had to wait until 7:30 or 8 for SAC Ricks to come in to brief him for his 10:30 news conference. After discussing the issues to be covered in the conference, I'd run right back to the hotel. There were times when I was so tired I slept on top of the bed in my clothes. Up at 3:30 PM and eat through the drive-in on the way in for my shift starting at 6 PM. There were times during the late nights that I thought I was actually hallucinating. Dozing in the negotiations command post, listening to Koresh's hoarse voice droning on about the same thing, I kept seeing The Red Horse of the Second Seal, with a faceless rider, coming from the heavens, circling me and then consumed in a nightmarish whirlwind of black and red dust. When I woke up Koresh was still talking about the Seven Seals. Nothing changed. His repetitious and monotonous lectures and the vivid descriptions of Revelations were brainwashing me too.

Routinely I'd come into the command post about 4 PM to read the hourly intelligence reports and status boards in the main CP, then review the negotiation investigative responses from our Rapid Start computer program (any requests we made were sent around the world for investigation and usually responded to within twenty-four hours), check on the current issues the negotiation team was dealing with, and then sit down with Jeff Jamar and Gary for a half-hour chat before the night shift negotiation team took their places. At 6 PM we were online, picking up where the day crew left off and trying to stay on track with the current negotiation issues. The primary negotiator's hot seat didn't cool off for fifty-one days. We lived on adrenaline and hope—adrenaline from participation in this enormously critical worldwide incident and hope that we could talk our way out of this thing and get everyone out of there, especially the children—those who had no choice or voice.

Throughout the days and nights, we talked to many people inside the compound besides Koresh and Schneider. One night John Dolan, an FBI negotiator from San Diego, spent two hours on the line talking to a "Cita." For two hours she hovered on the edge of coming out. She had sent two of her three children out the first day, and her husband had been wounded in the shootout. But she just couldn't make that move. At one point she left to find Koresh and to tell him she was leaving. But after talking to him, she lost her drive, and gradually shut down. When she finally left the phone, she tearfully thanked Dolan for his sincere efforts to encourage her to come out. She told him that he was a good man, and that she trusted him, but that she had decided to stay. We had all huddled around Dolan and the speakerphone during that time as we felt she was extremely close to coming out. When she hung up Dolan pushed back his chair, put his head in his hands and wept silently. A few weeks after the end of the siege, I opened a copy of *Newsweek* to see a photo of a smiling Floricita Sonobe with her daughter Angelica. Cita had perished in the fire with her daughter, two poor souls killed by David Koresh.

On March 12, Janet Reno, the cigar-smoking judge from Florida, was sworn in as the attorney general of the United States. Reno looked like a female prison warden. Although it was only rumored that she wrestled alligators, Reno was large enough to do so and dwarfed Louie Freeh, the later director of the FBI who was somewhat short and mild looking. In all the pictures of the two of them standing together he always looked like her sad little nephew. Reno eventually approved the plan to introduce gas into the compound and has been criticized ever since. But despite the criticism, Reno hung tough and insisted that based on the facts she was given, her decision was the right one. And in so doing, she took all the heat off President Clinton, who had also approved the plan. We had a lot of respect for Janet Reno.

Over the next few days we continued talking to Koresh and Schneider but had few successes. Between March 5 and March 12 only one child and two adults came out of the compound. We also fought our own internal battles. There were constant breakdowns in communication between the negotiators and the HRT tactical guys on the perimeter. While we were attempting to establish an honest and respectful dialogue with the Koresh and the others, Schneider reported that the guys on the perimeter mooned them and flipped them off. Schneider also complained that the SWAT guys drove their tanks over Koresh's motorcycle just to piss him off. When we complained to the HRT supervisor, he put on his bullshit face and claimed it had been done for tactical reasons. This kind of irresponsible action undercut the serious efforts of the negotiators.

At some point, one of the FBI leaders decided to play various audiotapes over a loud speaker to the compound to keep the occupants awake and to irritate them. Apparently he forgot or didn't care about the children inside. Religious chants, patriotic and rock music, and even the cries of a dying rabbit. This had no negotiation value and later became an embarrassment to the FBI during the congressional hearings. In retaliation, Koresh ordered tapes of his own electric guitar to be played on his own loudspeakers. It was awful and pissed off the tactical guys on the perimeter. Privately, the negotiators cheered Koresh's chutzpah.

On another occasion, Jamar ordered the power to the compound turned off after touring the perimeter with HRT. This came on the heels of an earlier release of two women. So in effect, their reward was more deprivation. We protested, saying that our good faith negotiations were being undermined. But Jamar refused to relent, claiming that the Branch Davidians needed to know who was in charge. Jeff got that way sometimes, usually after touring the perimeter with the SWAT guys. It got so that when he walked into the negotiator command post, the first thing we checked was his boots. Mud on his boots meant that he'd been out walking the perimeter and talking to SWAT and was ready to muscle up to the Davidians. No more Mr. Nice Guy. The trouble was, it always seemed to happen when the negotiators needed it least.

To be fair, the stress on Jamar was immense. Not only were the headquarters suits back in Washington critiquing his every move, the whole world was watching this incident play out. He really wasn't a bad guy. He just took all the criticism for the FBI. One night after a particular rancorous discussion among the negotiators and the tactical guys, Jeff cornered me in the hall. He grabbed my shoulder and turned me around. I thought he was going to choke me out.

"Sorry, Jim. This thing is getting through to me. I transferred down here to San Antonio thinking all I had to worry about was being able to afford a golf membership. I never heard of David Koresh or the Branch Davidians. And now I'll be in court the rest of my life." He sucked in a deep breath that sounded life saving. Then he grinned. We both laughed and shook hands. Leave it to those damn Branch Davidians to fuck up a perfectly good retirement job.

On another night Schneider called us and asked for permission to send out two Davidians to feed the ducks. I considered this an opportunity to develop some intelligence from the two, and also an opportunity to give them something of value to build trust and good faith. I called the HRT commander, Dick Rogers, and advised him of the request. I told him I thought we ought to allow it.

"Absolutely not, Jim," Rogers snarled. "Anyone coming out of that compound for any reason other than to surrender will be considered a threat and subject to deadly force."

I couldn't believe it. They had a tight perimeter, it was under control, and the Branch Davidians had notified us what they planned to do. They were going to walk into the front yard, unarmed, in full view of all the tactical guys and just feed the damn ducks. The ducks had no tactical significance and constituted no threat. But Rogers was insistent. There would be no duck feeding on his watch—no way. I explained the negotiators' position and potential benefits. Nope. It ain't gonna happen. His refusal reminded me of his stubbornness during the Randy Weaver barricade in Idaho a year earlier. Rogers had no use for us pussy negotiators. He was all about submachine guns, explosives, and kicking in doors. HRT muscles and panther piss.

We called Schneider back and told him his request was rejected. He reacted with surprise and then anger. He too realized what an insignificant request this was. But instead the SWAT guys had to remind him that we still had the big guns. It was another lost opportunity for the negotiators. The FBI had succumbed to the common failure of hostage/barricade crisis management when SWAT drives the decision-making. If the only thing in your hand is a hammer, you start looking around for something to hit. And a SWAT team is an enormous and deadly blunt instrument. By the end of Waco and after the congressional hearings, the FBI finally agreed that it had better start controlling its tactical option, and to make better use of its hostage negotiators.

At one point early in the negotiations, Jack Harwell, the McLennan County sheriff, came into the negotiation command post to say hello. Jack was impressive—a classic sheriff, right out of a Louis L'Amour novel. Tall, lean, cowboy hat and boots, he was the real deal. He was quiet, friendly, and warm, and somewhat embarrassed that this incident had occurred in his county, like he had somehow failed. He had known Koresh from prior minor contacts and he offered to speak to him. We hesitated to insert the sheriff into the negotiations. When you go to the top you have no insulation or time delay for decision-making. As the county sheriff, he was considered by most to be the chief law enforcement official in the county. We thought Koresh would expect Jack to be able to make immediate decisions without the FBI, and we didn't want to put him into that difficult position.

However, Jamar liked the idea and Jack did talk to Koresh for a few minutes. Still, it had no appreciable effect. A close personal friend of Byron Sage, Jack accompanied Byron during two volatile face-to-face meetings several days later just outside the compound with Schneider and Wayne Martin, a Branch Davidian attorney from inside the compound. The meetings failed to bring the occupants out and Jack wept with the others when the fire destroyed the compound and the children failed to escape. They aren't many left like Jack Harwell.

Late one night, Agent Jim Duffy called me from the SIOC (Strategic Information Operations Center) at FBI headquarters in Washington. It was about 2 AM.

"Jim, Director [William] Sessions has offered to make a personal appeal to Koresh in an effort to convince him to surrender."

I laughed. Duffy was a good friend and fellow CINT member from the Baltimore office who was doing his time in the SIOC as the negotiation team representative.

"Duff, you gotta be kidding. The director?"

"No, seriously, he really is thinking about this, and he wanted the opinion of the negotiators on the scene."

"Duff, tell him that's an insane thought. No, tell him he is fucking crazy. No way are we going to insert the director of the FBI into this thing."

"Okay, that's all I needed. I'll tell him. I hope you don't mind if I quote you. Although he may ship your ass to a Montana Indian reservation by tomorrow." We both laughed. Hoover was dead. The FBI didn't do that anymore. Or did they?

But that was it. I never heard another thing. Months later Duffy told me he personally relayed my message to Sessions, somewhat more diplomatically of course, and that he accepted my decision without protest. Sessions had turned out to be a bumpkin in Washington who would pull open his suit coat and display an FBI badge pinned on his lapel when he was introduced to someone as the director of the FBI. He and his wife later became an embarrassment to the FBI and we were glad to see him go.

On March 15, Robbin called me with a family emergency back in LA It always seemed to happen when I was gone, another crisis at home. "Get back here. Now." Reluctantly, I left Waco the same day and flew back to LA. Although I had pulled out of the trenches, I continued to follow the activities every day with calls back to the negotiators. Clint Van Zandt, a negotiator and profiler from the Behavioral Science Unit at the FBI Academy, and Dwayne Fuselier from the FBI office in Denver replaced Gary and me as the supervisors of the negotiation team. Clint was a born-again Christian who tried to match Bible wits with Koresh, but Koresh ran circles around him like he was a young child in Sunday school. After awhile Clint refocused on the current issues.

On March 26 a guy who went by the name Jesse Amen embarrassed the HRT by sneaking through the HRT perimeter and entering the compound. Amen came out a week later but after a lengthy interview the FBI investigators concluded that this goofball could provide little intelligence on what was going on inside. No wonder Koresh let him leave the compound.

On April 14, Koresh advised that he was writing an explanation of the Seven Seals for the FBI negotiators. Just what they needed. On April 16 Schneider advised that Koresh had finished the first Seal. At this rate, there would be eighteen days left. No way. We considered this ridiculous.

As the siege continued, Koresh's wounds healed, Schneider frustrated the negotiators, promises to surrender were broken, and two local attorneys became involved. Dick DeGuerin and Jack Zimmerman offered their services and despite the strong protests of Jamar, who was overruled by FBIHQ, they eventually met with Koresh on several occasions over several days.

Introducing attorneys into a hostage/barricade situation forces the police negotiations into neutral. The attorneys will always claim that they are developing a positive relationship and that the subject(s) is probably going to surrender. "He just needs a little more time," they say. But once they're involved, it's difficult to withdraw them. And if they are withdrawn and prohibited from further contact and the suspect is later injured or killed, your decision will be challenged. The attorneys will always say that they could have convinced him to come out. They just needed more time, but the government was impatient. And the lack of patience resulted in the loss of life. That's difficult to explain, and to justify. Waco was no different. The government was forced to suspend active negotiations, which had now been usurped by the attorneys. It was a total loss of control. Jamar realized this; FBI headquarters didn't. Once the lawyers became involved in the negotiations, the FBI negotiators became mere spectators.

Nonetheless, the negotiators had been discussing a tactical option for days with the HRT supervisors and Jamar. Not an assault into the compound, but the insertion of CS gas following the destruction of part of the compound itself. The negotiators concurred with this suggestion as a psychological method of coercion—using the military vehicles to destroy portions of the compound after the occupants have been warned. Reduce their living space, crowd them together, increase their claustrophobia, and then insert gas after warning them. We never planned an entry. Just insert the gas, and wait it out. It could take a day or two. We desperately hoped parental instincts would force the families out, or at least result in the release of the children.

I called Clint from LA on the morning of April 18 for an update. "Tomorrow's the day," he said. "We're going to put in the gas tomorrow. Reno approved it."

Behind the scenes, FBI officials from Waco had flown back to Washington and presented the plan to Attorney General Reno on the 17th. Reno called the president after the briefing and advised that the FBI planned to use gas, but that it would be delivered incrementally and that the Branch Davidians may well take two to three days to surrender. Clinton concurred.

All day long the HRT agents began to remove vehicles from the sides of the compound in preparation for the insertion of gas the next day. Although the negotiators tried to reassure the Davidians by claiming this was being done for safety reasons, Koresh didn't buy it. "If you don't stop what you're doing, this could be the worst day in law enforcement history," he said prophetically. Nevertheless the HRT continued its removal of the Branch Davidian vehicles.

April 19. About 11 AM. Ron Iden, the agent in charge of the criminal division in Los Angeles, called me. "Jim, come up to my office. Waco is burning down."

I couldn't believe it. Burning down? It was supposed to be just gas insertion. I ran upstairs to find Ron mesmerized in front of his TV. The compound was a red fiery mass. Thick black smoke billowed out of the compound.

I called Clint in Waco. "What the hell happened?"

They're not coming out," Clint said somberly. "The kids are still inside. Maybe they're in the bus. The Davidians started the fires inside."

HRT had moved two military CEVs (Combat Engineering Vehicles—M60 tanks with attached booms) up to the compound to penetrate the walls and to deliver tear gas. Nine Bradley vehicles were deployed, four to deliver more gas, four for other tactical purposes, and one for medical evacuation and rescue of fleeing occupants. This was preceded by negotiator Byron Sage advising Steve Schneider of the plan for the insertion of gas. "We are not going to make an entry," he told Schneider over and over. Schneider's response was to throw the hostage phone out the front door. Sage then advanced with the HRT agents and repeatedly bullhorned the same message to the compound occupants from a Bradley vehicle nearby:

"We are in the process of placing tear gas into the building. This is not an assault. We are not entering the building. This is not an assault. Do not fire your weapons. If you fire, fire will be returned. Do not shoot. This is not an assault. The gas you smell is a non-lethal tear gas. This gas will temporarily render the building uninhabitable. Exit the compound now and follow instructions."

"You are not to have anyone in the tower. The tower is off limits. No one is to be in the tower. Anyone observed to be in the tower will be considered an act of aggression and will be dealt with accordingly. If you come out now, you will not be harmed. Follow all instructions. Come out with your hands up. Carry nothing. Come out of the building and walk up the driveway toward the Double E Ranch Road. Walk toward the large Red Cross Flag."

"Follow all instructions of the FBI agents in the Bradleys.

Follow all instructions.

"You are under arrest. The standoff is over.

"We do not want anyone hurt. Follow all instructions. This is not an assault. Do not fire any weapons. We do not want anyone hurt.

"Gas will continue to be delivered until everyone is out of the building."

Sage repeated this message for hours as the CEVs continued to pour gas into the compound from 6 AM until 11:40 AM. The CEV vehicles used to insert the gas were fitted with a Mark-V liquid injection system that dispensed a stream of liquid tear gas propelled by non-combustible carbon dioxide approximately fifty feet for fifteen seconds duration. As the CEVs ground back and forth in front of the compound like huge steel insects in a sci-fi movie, automatic weapons fire from the compound occupants banged off the vehicles like a hailstorm. Jamar ordered the Bradleys forward and they began firing M-79 Ferret tear gas rounds into the openings created by the CEVs.

At 10 AM, Washington, D.C., time, Attorney General Reno, who had been watching the events in the FBI SIOC in Washington, left for a speaking engagement at a judicial conference in Baltimore. The fires hadn't started yet.

Down in Waco a strong wind started blowing, which dissipated much of the gas that HRT had delivered over the last six hours. For a long time no one came out.

Until the fires started.

The first indication that the Branch Davidians had started fires within the building came from the FBI aircraft flying overhead. Shortly after noon its FLIR (forward-looking infrared) device picked up infrared readings of fire in three locations. Several HRT tactical agents on the perimeter also reported seeing individuals start fires in several locations inside. And several listening devices, which had been introduced into the compound during the standoff, picked up voices talking about "starting the fires." Graeme Craddock, a Branch Davidian who escaped, reported hearing others inside talking about starting the fires and Clive Doyle, another surviving Davidian, told the Texas

Rangers that the fires were started inside by the Branch Davidians with Coleman lamp fuel.

Within minutes the compound became a raging inferno. Nine Davidians exited the compound during the fire and were taken into custody by the HRT agents watching in shock and disbelief. Where were the kids? Davidian Ruth Riddle jumped off the roof and then turned around and started back into the burning building. An HRT agent jumped from his Bradley, exposing himself to the Davidians still shooting at the Bradleys, and pulled her to safety. As he dragged her back to the Bradley to save her life, she struggled to break free and run back into the burning building.

Around 12:30 PM the HRT agents on the perimeter heard systematic gunshots suggesting methodical suicide, rather than ammunition "cooking off" (which occurred later). And the subsequent search of the compound disclosed that many of the Davidians did die from gunshot wounds. Autopsies disclosed that many of the children died from blunt force trauma (probably from the crumbling building) and gunshots. Eventually the bodies of David Koresh and Steve Schneider were found and identified. Koresh's skull had a bullet hole in the middle of the forehead.

Intelligence had been developed that the Davidians had buried a school bus as a kind of "bomb shelter" for the children in the event that Koresh's prediction of an apocalypse came true. As soon as the fire slowed down, HRT agents entered the compound to search for it. The agents located the bus, but they found no children.

The children were still inside the raging inferno, which was collapsing the building. No one could believe it. What parent would allow their child to die so senselessly? The HRT Bradleys drove around the compound frantically waiting for more occupants to run out of the inferno but it didn't happen.

Iden and I watched the smoldering ruins on his TV. I thought of all the kids inside, of Cita who had been close to coming out that night, and of Koresh, that Bible-reading wacko who had truly stolen the hearts and minds of all those innocent souls who were searching for some meaning in life. Cult members are always searching for something. They were easy prey. But the children!

For fifty-one days, the FBI had desperately tried to avoid a mass suicide. And now it had happened. We later learned that the best estimates were that seventy-five people perished in the fire. After-action reports and testimony before congressional committees confirmed that during the entire fifty-one-day standoff, the FBI did not fire a single shot, including on the last day. Yet, the FBI has been called "baby killers" ever since by those who were convinced that the FBI started the fires inside the compound. It's a frustration and a disappointment that those agents—who were so dedicated to trying to save those lives— live with daily.

Adding possible injury to insult, three months later FBI headquarters advised that tuberculosis had been discovered in the remains of the compound and that all FBI employees who had been assigned to the Waco standoff needed to be tested. I tested negative, but unfortunately two of the crime scene technicians reacted positive and had to be treated for a few months.

Two years later, on April 19, 1995, Timothy James McVeigh, a twenty-seven-year-old Army veteran of the Gulf War, backed a yellow Ryder rental van loaded with four thousand pounds of explosives up against the front of the Alfred P. Murrah Federal Building in downtown Oklahoma City. He shut off the ignition, hopped out, and casually walked away. Two minutes later the bomb in the van detonated, killing 168 innocent people. A day later when he was pulled over by a highway patrolman on a routine traffic stop and arrested for carrying a concealed weapon, his identity as the bomber had been established. McVeigh later told FBI agents that the bombing was to avenge the deaths of the Branch Davidians allegedly killed by agents of the United States government.

That kind of vengeance has kept those of us committed to preventing domestic terrorism awake at night worrying. How many other monsters spawned by Waco are still out there? Ticking quietly.

The *Los Angeles Times*, in September 2004, reported that Donald Feldpausch, a car wash owner from San Antonio, bought the 1968 Camaro owned by David Koresh for thirty-seven thousand dollars at an auction in Fredericksburg, Texas.

"What a great piece of American history!" the auctioneer had crowed.

"I'll bring it out for things like parades," said Feldpausch.

CHAPTER 15

THE BAKER OF RANCHO CUCAMONGA

Charlene was a mocha-colored, honey-voiced survivor of South Central Los Angeles and the "heard it all before" nightshift telephone receptionist at the FBI office in Los Angeles. She had listened to every nut in LA for years at 3 AM and knew all of their delusions. Since the FBI was open 24/7 (including holidays), these people knew they could always find someone to talk to during those dark hours when the voices in their heads started up again and no one else would listen.

The nuts always fascinated me. I would listen to them if I had the time during my shift in "the barrel," sitting at the complaint desk answering the phone and interviewing walk-ins. It's amazing what the human mind can create. Most of them were paranoid schizophrenics who had delusions of persecution—often claiming that the FBI or the CIA was following them or that someone was trying to kill them. Some had delusions of grandeur—that they were Jesus Christ or Elvis Presley. One guy claimed that he was Richard Nixon and called to constantly proclaim that he was "not a crook." Some were hospitalized, most just wandered the streets. Harmonica Joe would call from a pay phone a couple times a week and treat Charlene to a few minutes of music before he thanked her for listening and then wandered off. Here in Hollywood we had some of the best. When they graduated from other places they came to LA. Some were neighbors of the FBI living a stone's throw away in a gated community on the other side of the 405 freeway—at the Brentwood V.A. hospital psych ward.

One of the classic legends in the office was that an old guy wearing a tired fedora and walking with a cane had rubbed two quarters together to take the bus up from Long Beach one day and reported in to the FBI complaint duty agent. He identified himself as an "FBI special operative" and asked the agent for his next undercover assignment. The agent, recognizing a rare opportunity and without missing a beat, told him that the LA office didn't have anything for him right now, but suggested that he go to New York and check in with the FBI office there for his next secret assignment. The guy agreed and left, a happy man on a mission. About three months later he came back to the LA office and asked for the same agent he had spoken to previously. When the agent came into the reception room, he instantly recognized the old duffer and remembered that he had sent him to New York.

"How's it going?" he asked.

"Okay," the old man answered, "but I'm disappointed. New York didn't have anything for me either."

Although we all laughed, I hoped the story wasn't true. Jerking these mental misfits around wasn't my style. They were really sad, and they were an incredible emotional, financial, and physical drain on their families—if they had one. Unfortunately, paranoia often brought the mentally disturbed knocking on our door.

While I was fascinated with these people, most of the agents just hung up on them, put them on hold or ignored them. Sometimes Charlene listened; when she was busy she'd put them on hold, and then check in with them every few minutes. Most never missed a beat. Sometimes she sent the call into a new agent for training or to the night duty agent for entertainment. But everyone agreed, Charlene was a sweetheart and she could handle anything.

So it was Charlene then who called me at home one night at 4 AM. The telephone rang on Robbin's side of the bed. She handed me the phone without waking up, something she had become very adept at over the years.

"Jim," Charlene said sounding somewhat bored, "I've got a guy on the line who says he's got a bunch of hostages in a bakery in Rancho Cucamonga and he wants to talk to the FBI."

I shouldn't have been surprised about the call after all the years of being on duty round the clock for the FBI. My only real escape was to flee the state. If you were around, they found you. And you went when they called. That was the thing about the FBI. It sucked the life out of you. The FBI was number one. The family was second. And there was a price to pay. For some of the guys, the house was empty when they got back.

"So shall I connect you?" Charlene asked. She knew I was the chief hostage negotiator in the LA office.

"Go ahead," I said, shaking Robbin awake.

A male voice on the line came alive. "Hello, hello, FBI?" Sounded white, middle age.

"Yes, hi, what's going on?" I asked.

The voice continued. "Listen, I got some people here in the bakery and I've got a message for the president."

Here we go again. Another wacko. A few minutes later Robbin was on a cell phone back to Charlene at the FBI office. Writing furiously on a pad, I gave her instructions for Charlene to call the San Bernardino Sheriff's office. A small community east of Los Angeles County, Rancho Cucamonga was in their jurisdiction and they needed to know what was happening. They may not know this incident was occurring. I continued talking to him.

During the course of what seemed to be hours, while I got dressed with one hand and Robbin brought me a cup of coffee, the hostage taker's diatribe changed constantly. To this day I still really don't know what he wanted. He made vague threats and only occasionally referred to the hostages, which he referred to as "people." This was a good sign. It suggested that he considered them humans and not merely pawns to be bargained for. For some reason he had found this bakery and wandered in thinking it would give him the leverage to obtain what he needed. It was my job to find out what that was. And then to make him think I would give it to him.

Determining motivation is critical. The first question a negotiator asks is, "Why is this happening?" A mistaken assumption can cost you in any number of ways. Several years ago a gunman entered a bank in Redondo Beach in the South Bay and shot a teller. The arriving police officers and negotiators assumed that they were dealing with a failed bank robbery. In actuality, the shooter had entered the bank to kill his girlfriend who had aborted his baby without his agreement. After toying with the negotiator for awhile, he walked out of the bank with a gun taped to the head of a hostage, at which point a sniper shot and killed him. A subsequent search of his apartment disclosed a suicide note and clothes laid out for his funeral. After killing his girlfriend, he obviously begged the cops to take his life. It was suicide by cop.

Sometimes these guys can't remember why they took a hostage and they need a little help with their demands, so we'd try to create a demand that was acceptable to them, and that would work for us. Sometimes you need to poke at them with a stick every now and then to get them to focus. Sometimes it just requires patiently listening to them for hours. Most hostage takers feel that they just haven't been heard, and they need to take a hostage to get your attention. So you listen. And you try to convince them that you care and you try to make that connection. And once that connection is made with the negotiator and the trust is established, they begin to listen to you and follow instructions, and you pull them along to surrender. Often they insist on surrendering personally to the negotiator because of the trust established. Those are big wins for the negotiator and sometimes piss off the SWAT guys who want to handle the surrender their own way. But it just means the negotiator has to work with the SWAT team to choreograph the surrender. And it's really a win for everyone, including the bad guy. Any avoidance of the use of force is a good thing.

The Baker of Rancho Cucamonga was no exception. At one point he allowed one of the hostages to talk to me, during which he confirmed that "The Baker" had a gun. He hadn't harmed anyone, but he really seemed "somewhat confused," which we considered code for "a nut." When he put The Baker back on the line, he started off on Vietnam and everything it had done to him and how the government was failing to take care of its veterans. As a Vietnam vet myself I began to focus on that but it rapidly became apparent that he hadn't been within ten thousand miles of Vietnam. He was crazy but not stupid, and he gradually backed off the subject of Vietnam when he realized he was talking to an actual Vietnam vet.

One of the best ways to determine military experience is to ask about his MOS, which is military occupational specialty. Every job in the military has an assigned MOS designation, from truck driver to cook to artillery. Many of the Vietnam Army vets were 11B, or "Eleven Bravos," which means "Light Weapons, Infantry," the throwaway grunts of the war. If a hostage taker claiming military service in the Army was confused by MOS, or he didn't know what an "11 Bravo" was, he probably wasn't a combat veteran. The Baker failed the test.

When I asked The Baker why he was holding these people and why he had selected this particular bakery, his answer was vague. He said he just needed people, which was pretty common. Many times a hostage situation is created simply to force others to listen. The hostages became currency. Sometimes the hostages are nothing more than just a bus ride. A vehicle. Once you get downtown you don't need the bus (or the hostages) anymore.

His answer to the second question—that the bakery had lights on at night while they were baking that he could see from the street—provided a rough description of its location. For the cops who worked the area, it then became a simple task to locate the right donut factory. Robbin gave me a note saying Charlene had contacted the sheriff's office and that the SWAT team had zeroed in on the location.

Now the challenge was to affect a smooth handoff to a sheriff's negotiator at the scene in Rancho Cucamonga. It was tricky because I also had to hand off the fragile rapport that The

Baker and I had developed without losing him. An interruption in negotiations can be dangerous. If left without a contact, a hostage taker may become frustrated and violent or back up on an agreement to surrender or release a hostage. Even though I had a cell phone and another negotiator was at the scene, I knew things can break down when you turn over communication from one negotiator to another at a different location. I explained to The Baker that to continue our conversation I needed to be closer to him and suggested that I come to the scene. And while I was en route, my "good buddy" (a sheriff's negotiator) would be talking to him until I got out there. With little hesitation he accepted this explanation. After confirming with Robbin that the sheriff's guys were ready I said goodbye to The Baker and hung up.

Charlene quickly connected me to the sheriff's command post and I provided an update to the negotiation team. Then I kissed Robbin goodbye and hauled ass to Rancho Cucamonga, convinced that The Baker would be in cuffs before I could get there. Like LAPD, the San Bernardino Sheriffs' Department didn't have a reputation for patience. Those desert rats did things their own way.

At 5 AM it took about an hour and a half to drive east to Rancho Cucamonga. Other than its funky name, the town was known for nothing. When I got to the scene the negotiators had set up a command post in a nearby office building and were still going strong with The Baker. Mike Mascetti, one of my old buddies, had become the primary negotiator. I had been teaching hostage negotiation for years and knew most of the police negotiators in Southern California. The Baker had released a couple of the hostages after the handoff and Mike's negotiations posture had become increasingly more confident and aggressive. Mike continued while we ordered breakfast. We settled in and tried to enjoy our Egg McMuffins without thinking about what we were eating. In the absence of threats to the hostages, and without deadlines, we were beginning to enjoy ourselves.

Another hour passed and The Baker announced that he had to pee. But that he was afraid to leave his hostages.

"Why not just let them leave, then you can pee alone, in private?" suggested Mike.

Amazing. The Baker hadn't thought of that.

"Okay," he answered. And out came the hostages, all four of them. A few minutes later he came back on the line.

"So, where can I pee?"

"Why not just use the restroom in the bakery?" suggested Mike, since the hostages had left the building.

"No," he said. "I'm afraid the SWAT guys will come in and beat me with their flashlights." This guy sounded like he had some prior experience with SWAT.

We could feel his hesitation. We waited a minute and he came back on the line.

"How about I just pee in my shoe?"

We looked at each other in total disbelief. This idiot had just released all the hostages, he had the entire bakery to himself, including a restroom, and he wanted to pee in his own shoe?

"Hey, man, whatever. It's your shoe," said Mike, smothering a laugh. "This is America."

"Okay, give me a minute."

We waited a few minutes and The Baker came back on the line.

"Okay, I'm ready to come out. Do you want me to take my clothes off?"

This guy obviously knew the routine.

"That's a great idea," Mike quickly responded. "That will show the SWAT guys that you're not armed."

"Okay," he agreed.

I looked at Mike. Could this be it? The surrender for a hostage taker is difficult. It's hard to give up the power. I've often likened it to giving birth. There's a lot of false labor, it starts and stops, it's painful. Sometimes there is screaming, and it takes time. But it feels good when it's over, or so I've heard, and everyone is happy.

Minutes later The Baker walked out the back door of the bakery—totally nude.

Now it's common to ask a hostage taker when surrendering

to take off his shirt to show that he's not armed, and they often do strange things at the denouement of an incident. But totally nude! He could have spared himself the derogatory comments from the SWAT guys about being "hung like a bird." But he seemed unfazed and was more concerned with complying with our instructions for surrender, which he did without hesitation. Minutes later, in custody, bug-eyed, with a shaved head, a blanket around his shoulders, and slumped in the rear seat of a black-and-white, The Baker of Rancho Cucamonga looked more like a little kid who had been abandoned by his parents in the bus station than an armed and dangerous hostage taker.

After promising to join him for his booking at the jail, we waved goodbye and then walked into the bakery. We usually toured the crime scene after the surrender to get a feel for it and to close the book on the incident. Many times the story was incomplete until the last "walk through." We walked into the bakery, and then into the office where he had held the hostages—and there it was.

The shoe. The goddamn shoe!

We all stood around and looked at the sneaker like it was O.J.'s bloody glove. We couldn't fucking believe it. Finally, one of the officers poked at it with his baton like a half-dead rattlesnake. Yep, it smelled like piss. He really did it. He pissed in his shoe.

With all the R&D that Nike had conducted on this shoe, this was one test they probably hadn't considered necessary.

CHAPTER 16

THE LAX HOTEL JUMPER

Alanna LaVelle and I leaned out of the fifth-story hotel window and looked over to our left. We almost laughed. Twenty feet away from us, a fifty-ish white female was threatening to jump to her death. She had hiked her skirt up to her knees and had one leg hanging over the ledge. She had also tied pillows to her back and to her stomach. Five floors directly below, a dozen firefighters struggled to hold a large inflated bag billowing in the wind. It looked like a huge brown ottoman with yellow buttons around the outside. The firemen looked pissed—they deserved to be. She had been hanging out of the window for several hours. It was cold and it was getting old.

Just west of Sepulveda, the hotel was on Century Boulevard, the main access leading into LA International airport. A major artery. For the last few hours, however, Century had been closed to all traffic. Fire trucks, ambulances, police cars, and media periscopes were strewn all over the intersection of Century and Sepulveda like pickup sticks. *NYPD Blue* couldn't have staged the scene better.

The hotel manager had called the FBI because the jumper insisted on talking to them. LAPD had responded initially, but she said she didn't trust the LAPD and refused to talk to them. After all, "you were the ones who beat up Rodney King," she said. LAPD just couldn't seem to put Rodney King behind them.

I wasn't surprised that they hadn't bothered to call us and ask for help. We'd been fighting and feuding with them for years. During the federal civil rights investigation of the Rodney King case, the FBI agents had been ordered by the attorney general to interview the LAPD officers in their homes or outside the police station. That pissed off all of them and they refused to provide their home addresses. Chief Daryl Gates and Larry Lawler, the FBI Agent in Charge, got into it over that one. And then their police union gave them a uniform statement of refusal to be interviewed by the FBI so the whole thing became worthless. None of the FBI agents wanted anything to do with the case either. The Rodney King incident was an open sore for both agencies.

I had asked Alanna to join me because she had a mellow personality that worked well for her as a hostage negotiator. She was like the girl next door and everyone's little sister. She also spoke five languages fluently and there was some question about the nationality and language of the jumper. Occasionally Alanna would take a couple weeks off from LA and fly down to Latin America to conduct Spanish-speaking interviews for an overworked legal attaché in Mexico City. Most agents considered a road trip like this punishment. Alanna considered it an adventure. She never complained about anything. Alanna was a great partner.

We parked in the middle of the street behind a hook-and-ladder and walked a couple blocks to the hotel, badging our way through the police lines. The manager was at the front desk eagerly waiting for us to solve his problem. Someone threatening to jump out of a window in his hotel was bad for business.

When he showed us up to the fifth floor, we noticed only patrol officers from the Pacific Division in the hall. LAPD's SWAT team hadn't arrived yet. We walked into the hotel room next door to the jumper's and identified ourselves to a lieutenant standing there. Normally these things were a horse race followed by a title fight with LAPD. This one was different.

"FBI? Okay, you got it," he said. "She won't talk to us. She only wants to talk to the FBI. Fuck it. She's yours." He motioned to the open window looking out on Century Boulevard. Across the street we could see our reflection in the side of the opposing glass walled building. He walked out with another uniformed officer. Alanna and I leaned out the window.

"You FBI?" the woman asked, with a bit of an accent. It was hard for me to understand her, and the wind made it more difficult. It didn't seem to bother Alanna.

"Yes, FBI," Alanna yelled leaning further out the window. It was cold for Los Angeles, and the wind was swirling down Century. This was going to be uncomfortable. The firemen below looked up at us hopefully. I figured they were probably much more uncomfortable than we were.

"You really FBI?" she asked again.

"Yes, what's your name?" Alanna asked.

"Maria, and they're trying to kill me."

"Who's trying to kill you, Maria?"

"The Mafia. They tried to get in my room and gas me. How do I know you're FBI?"

Alanna shuffled through her purse and produced her FBI credentials. These work for most people even though J. Edgar Hoover doesn't sign them anymore. She leaned out the window and showed them to Maria.

"What about him?" she said, pointing at me. I also pulled mine out and pointed them at her.

"How do I know those are real?" she said.

Alanna and I looked at each other. We were in trouble.

"Who's the director of the FBI?"

"William Webster," Alanna answered.

"Who was the director before him?"

What the hell is this, *Jeopardy*?

Alanna looked over her shoulder at me for an answer. I knew she was in trouble. Frankly, after Hoover, we kind of lost count. There was L. Patrick Gray, an old Navy guy who got fired for destroying some FBI documents for Nixon, a guy named Ruckelshaus who came in and sat down for about twenty minutes, and then Clarence "Dick Tracy" Kelly, the former police chief from Kansas City who came in for a couple years before

William Webster. Webster was the one who always insisted that he be addressed as "Judge" rather than "Director," which pissed everybody off. Here this guy becomes the director of the FBI and he still wants to be called "Judge."

"Why are you doing this, Maria?" asked Alanna, meaning threatening to jump, but also wondering what the pillows tied around her had to do with it.

Maria then launched into a confusing explanation of the Mafia because of some secret she knew, of them poisoning her food and trying to gas her in her room, and something about Hawaii. I now understood why the lieutenant had thrown her at us. LAPD never gave us anything good. But I was sure of one thing. Maria wasn't going to jump.

Alanna and I hung out the window and listened to Maria for another hour. Alanna tried the basic suicide prevention stuff—make the personal connection, find out what happened in the last forty-eight hours that triggered the incident, and then find "the hook." Something they cared about enough to keep them from doing it. Nothing worked. She just kept rambling. It was boring. And then it got annoying. I started to hate her thick accent.

Fortunately, LAPD had pushed the crowd back to Sepulveda, which prevented them from seeing the woman and yelling for her to jump, like they do so many times. It's amazing what the public will do for entertainment.

After a while, Sgt. John Christensen, LAPD's crisis negotiation team (CNT) leader, and a couple female negotiators joined us. He also had a couple SWAT guys with him. LAPD uses SWAT officers as well as investigators as hostage negotiators. This has always drawn criticism from our East Coast cousins in the NYPD who feel that SWAT officers are not totally committed to a negotiated solution. Although they have a point, I considered LAPD's negotiators very effective and successful. I think it's just a commitment to which hat you're wearing at the time.

"John, she's never going to jump, and we can't seem to find a hook. She's 5150." Cops refer to this section of the penal code when labeling wackos.

"We've got to find a way to get into her," I told him. Christensen listened thoughtfully. John was a classy guy and we had been friends for years, even traveling back to the FBI Academy together to share a training seminar. We had worked well together by ignoring the upper-level politics of each of our departments.

While Alanna took a break, one of the LAPD female negotiators decided to try her hand at talking to Maria and only totally pissed her off by arguing with her. She had that PMS or "I'm in a bad marriage" kind of attitude. She was just kind of nasty for no reason. She refused to allow Maria to talk to "that FBI girl" and insisted that Maria had to deal with her. No way. Maria still wasn't buying the LAPD. With amusement, I watched LAPD's arrogant female negotiator fail. I also noticed for the first time that Maria had a serious mustache—like a Greek grandmother. She also looked like she'd be more comfortable lying on a couch in a dirty housecoat watching *Oprah* than hanging outside a hotel window on Century Boulevard.

Christensen came back in the room. "Okay, here's the deal. We're going to put the SWAT officer in the room above Maria's, tie him off to a crossbar in the bathroom, and he'll rappel down into Maria on the ledge forcing her into the room. Simultaneously, the fire department in the hallway will make entry with a ram through the door of her room. They'll be followed in by an armed officer in case she has a weapon, although we don't think she has one. Your negotiator has to keep her attention and distracted. I'll call it from here."

"Bitchin'," as the cops say. I liked the plan. It involved the tactical use of the negotiator, which is sometimes necessary. This means that the negotiator suspends legitimate attempts to negotiate surrender and instead uses negotiation techniques to mask the execution of an operation designed to end the barricade or hostage incident tactically. I also really liked the idea of ending this bullshit situation. It had been three hours of nothing but aggravation.

Gradually, we began to implement the plan. We pulled the

LAPD negotiator out and Alanna resumed her position hanging out the window. Maria continued her rambling but she continued to hold her attention. It never failed—everybody always liked Alanna.

I walked into the hall and watched four yellow-jacketed firefighters line up with a twelve-foot ram. They had to open the room door across the hall to line up for the charge. The firefighters shouldered the ram and grinned with anticipation. I should have been a fireman.

I moved back to the window with Alanna and, without looking up, watched the reflection in the glass windows directly across the street. Suddenly the window opened and the SWAT officer appeared on the sixth floor directly above Maria. Cool. Very cool. He backed out on the edge of the window ledge leaning on his rappel line, gradually becoming horizontal to the street, braking with his right hand in the small of his back. Six stories up. Then he paused. I resisted the urge to look up. Instead, I prayed that Maria would keep looking at Alanna and me and fail to notice the impending violence poised up above her.

Christensen stood in the doorway of our room, radio in hand, looking from the firemen in the hallway to me in the room. As Alanna continued to hold Maria's attention, and at a nod from me, he radioed, "GO! GO! GO! GO!"

The SWAT officer backed off the window sill, pushed out from the sixth floor window, swooped out and then dropped down a story crashing into a very surprised Maria, just as the firefighters crashed through the door of Maria's room. Everyone had timed it perfectly. Alanna's distraction, the SWAT officer's action, and the breach by the firefighters came together to resolve a potentially deadly situation.

Alanna and I hugged briefly to congratulate ourselves. It was over.

We listened to the chaos next door for a few minutes. When it subsided we walked out into the hallway just in time to see Maria handcuffed and strapped face down on a gurney being pulled out of the room by the firemen. She still continued to struggle.

"Alanna!" she cried, "They got to you too! Oh my God, now they're going to kill us both!" We tried to reassure her that these people wouldn't hurt her but she didn't believe us. All of us had now become part of her frightening delusion. Maria was still screaming for Alanna as they wheeled her down the hall and into the elevator.

We looked into her room and discovered that Maria had stuffed the vents with pieces of bed sheets. The room was a mess. Everything she had partially eaten or had worn for the last two weeks was strewn around the room. The smell burned my eyes. She had obviously been living there for a while, holed up from the predators she imagined were trying to kill her

We congratulated Christensen and his people. They had done one helluva job. Especially Spiderman, who couldn't stop grinning. I guessed he'd probably have an erection for a week.

Alanna and I walked back to the window and watched the firefighters pack up their gear. They were slowly deflating the bag. The cops were breaking down the police lines. We waved to them and sucked in the sights of the carnival from the window for a few minutes waiting for the adrenaline pump to slow down. The euphoria from a win like this never lasted long enough.

As they wheeled Maria's gurney out of the front entrance of the hotel, the media mob charged at her like she was Michael Jackson arriving for a court appearance. Alanna and I looked at each other and laughed. The media never disappointed us.

CHAPTER 17

THE SOUTH GATE KIDNAPPING
AND THE JUAREZ CARTEL

Terry Kincaide and I stood on the El Paso side of the Rio Grande levee and watched the twinkling lights of Ciudad Juarez—a pulsating sea of humanity crawling over each other like angry insects confined within a hive. Two million souls mingling in poverty, hopelessness, frustration, and violence. Four hundred street gangs. It was 1995 and with over two hundred homicides already recorded, the Mexican border town was on a pace to set a new annual record. It was also overrun with drug traffickers. Which is why I had come to this dump. Somewhere out there the Juarez Cartel, the largest Mexican drug trafficking network, was holding two kidnapping victims from Los Angeles. Its leader, Amado Carillo Fuentes, was nicknamed the "Lord of the Skies" because he used a Boeing 727 aircraft like FedEx to ship cocaine around the world. This was week seven of the kidnapping.

A mid-level LA dealer named Louie had "lost" a five-million-dollar load of Carillo's cocaine and now he had to pay. That's one of the problems with dealing dope. Once received on consignment, someone else still owns it. Sell it, use it, or lose it, you still owe on it. Louie claimed he'd been ripped off. The cartel figured he ran off with it. But whatever—the cartel didn't give a shit what happened. It was still Louie's problem and he still owed them five million. He had bull shitted and stiff-armed them long enough.

So to motivate Louie, the cartel had brazenly kidnapped his aunt and the woman's niece from South Gate, a depressing little city in southeast Los Angeles County policed by the LA County Sheriff's Department. They left a ransom note found by a neighbor in their car left running in the garage. A day later they called Louie with a second ransom demand, giving him a week to produce the five million, which was impossible unless he ripped off another major dealer or robbed the Federal Reserve Bank. When the other relatives got wind of it, they called the LA County Sheriff's Department, and then the FBI. They knew this was serious and they couldn't work this out by themselves. After a brief interview with the cops during which he denied everything, Louie had gone into hiding. And he left us with a whole lot of unanswered questions.

Kidnapping and holding a relative hostage until a dope load was repaid was something the Mexicans had learned from the Colombians—along with brutality. But it was difficult to be sympathetic in these cases when the victims were also suspects in other violent crimes.

Ron Black, the tough-talking captain in charge of the LA Sheriff's Department's Special Investigation Detail (SID), had dedicated the majority of his team to the case but asked us to provide additional investigators. SID handled sensitive, complex and lengthy investigations for the department. Within a couple days we had formed a tight-knit squad working out of the department's new Century Station in the southeastern corner of the county. The sheriff's guys had answered the phone calls from the kidnappers and posed as buddies of Louie trying to reduce the amount of the ransom demanded, or at least to create a repayment schedule. The kidnappers spoke Spanish but also functional English. It would have been easy to keep it going in Spanish and we used native Spanish speaking negotiators, but nevertheless we were determined to keep the negotiations in English. To slide into Spanish would reduce the number of those able to monitor and understand the conversations, be a capitulation to the kidnappers, create transcription problems prior to court (each conversation was recorded, transcribed and reviewed), and complicate a court presentation if we ever got that far. But it was primarily an important issue of control, which is the first thing you need to take away from a kidnapper.

The first few weeks consisted of constant daily calls from the kidnappers to Louie's phone, which had been routed into the sheriff's Century Dtation. Although we could have really used the background information Louie could have provided, he remained "in the wind" (ITW) and was useless. During the first couple weeks, he'd call in to see how things were going, but he refused to come in for an interview. His parole officer, who offered the potential threat to send him back to prison, also had trouble reaching him. But the parole violation process would take months and we had just days. When the kidnappers finally agreed to meet us in El Paso, we sent most of the dheriff's team and two agents down there. Unfortunately, the El Paso office of the FBI had their own problems and didn't have the personnel to assign to our investigation. They had too many dope kidnappings of their own to fix. In addition, once we arrived, the kidnappers backed up and again refused to come into El Paso. They insisted on a Juarez payoff, which we considered too dangerous at the time. After a few days the guys called me and begged to return to LA, so it was back home and back to square one.

After negotiating with the kidnappers for a couple more weeks, we decided that we were going to have to make a second trip to El Paso. This time I led the troops myself, taking fifteen FBI agents and sheriff's deputies. We included several tech agents with state-of-the-art mobile computer equipment to assist us with the cell phone tracing. We had determined that the kidnappers were cloning the electronic serial numbers (ESN) of innocent cell phone users, and then discarding the phones after three to four days. For a few hundred dollars, anyone could buy an electronic instrument that could decode ESNs from a phone in use. A popular location for doing this was LAX, with international travelers unaware that they were sharing their cell phone contracts with others. When we identified the assigned user and located them, they were astounded that Mexican kidnappers were using their cell phone. Our only hope was to triangulate the phones when they were in use, pinpoint the location of the user, swoop in to make the arrest, and then hope they would cough up the victims. But because these were sophisticated drug traffickers, we knew they had likely assigned the debt collection itself to experienced kidnappers. These guys knew what they were doing and were going to be a challenge. They realized that the kidnapping is easy, but the payoff is where you get hurt.

But we couldn't get them to budge to attempt a pickup in El Paso, and we hadn't ventured into Juarez. Yet.

I looked away from the lights of Juarez and over at Terry Kincaid, an FBI supervisor and our El Paso liaison. "We're going to have to go over there, Terry. There's no other way."

He nodded silently, both of us knowing how dangerous it would be to play kidnapping games in Mexico, where you had to balance the bad guys with the State Judicial Police, the federales, and the corrupt political system. Plus Janet Reno, who had just become Clinton's attorney general, would probably take a very dim view of her federal agents screwing around in someone else's country with electronic snooping gear attempting to arrest their citizens. Needless to say, we knew this could turn into an international incident. DEA had already had their share of problems with the Mexican cops. But sometimes it's easier to ask for forgiveness than permission.

We had moved the whole entourage from LA into a motel complex on the east side of El Paso. Sixteen rooms of cops, and another assigned to the negotiators. By now we were also using a new cell phone. We had to assume that the kidnappers would try to trace our calls (just like we were doing), and that they would assume we may be holding some or all of the five million dollars. If they could find us, they would probably attempt to rip off the money in a straight violent robbery. These were guys who had no hesitation about walking into a public restaurant and shooting up the place to kill a rival, so we had to figure they'd be willing to do the same to us. The negotiators were beginning to get nervous and seemed wired all the time. We had to set up our own security perimeter around the negotiator's room to give them some sense of safety. We also were changing phones every couple days just like our criminal counterparts.

It became more tense every day. And every day was the same. We played along with the kidnappers, telling them we had finally got the money, but we were afraid to go into Juarez. They refused to meet us in El Paso. It's much more difficult to buy your way out of an El Paso jail than one in Juarez. Both of us had agreed to use cutouts (neutral third parties hired to make the exchange), but we just couldn't agree on where or how it could be done.

In the meantime, Terry and I met with the DEA agents in El Paso. They had better liaison with the Juarez city police department than the FBI did. All the stories out there about the fighting and feuding between the FBI and DEA are true, and El Paso was no exception. The DEA guys relished the fact that the FBI had to ask for their help and they played it out as long as they could. We heard one lame story from them after another. They would try to contact the Juarez Comandante but he was not a fan of the FBI because they had embarrassed him in another drug case before. The Comandante was out of town. He would be available tomorrow. No, maybe the day after tomorrow. We tired of their games, but we had no recourse. Finally, after waiting three long days, the Juarez Comandante, the Chief of Police, arrived at the DEA office in El Paso.

The DEA chief ushered the chief and two of his compatriots into the office. I couldn't believe we were talking to the right guy. In walked a well-fed Mexican in his late twenties, wearing black jeans, cowboy boots, a leather jacket, and a huge pearl-handled .45 automatic tucked in the small of his back. His deputy chiefs looked like truants from the local high school. He looked like the back door bouncer at a cheap strip joint. This was the police chief of a city of two million?

We were then treated to a completely unintelligible

conversation in Spanish among the DEA agents and the Mexican police, which was finally concluded with giving photos of our victims to the chief. He turned to me.

"I will do my best to find your kidnapping victims," he said in heavily accented English. He then stood up, shook hands with all of us, and clomped out with his entourage.

As I watched them leave, my hopes for their assistance plummeted. I had lost complete confidence in this method of solving our problems. It was further underscored by DEA's assessment.

The DEA agent who had led the conversation in Spanish with the Comandante explained. "In all probability the Comandante is well aware of the kidnapping, the location of the victims, and the current status of the negotiations. You have to understand he bought his position as the chief of police from the drug traffickers, for probably about $250-300,000. And where do you think he got that kind of dinero? Right. Drogas. And he will last until he pisses off someone in the cartel. The last chief was found shot to death, in the trunk of his car with two of his sons. About a year ago. So he's walking a fine line. But rest assured that he will report to the cartel that this matter has certainly gained the attention of American law enforcement— and the FBI."

He laughed as he added "and the FBI." Another DEA put-down.

I looked at Terry. He grimaced and looked down at his boots.

Police corruption in Juarez and the State of Chihuahua was rampant. Juarez city police were paid about $230 per month as new officers, while the state police made about $400. It was estimated that half the city police take bribes from the drug dealers. If our investigative measures failed, the best we could hope for was to beat the political bushes to turn up the heat and force the cartel to give up the victims. But how much pressure would it take to absolve five million dollars?

I walked out of the meeting more frustrated than ever. Terry just shrugged his shoulders. "That's the way it is Jim, it's just the way they do business down here."

When I returned to the conference room in the FBI office where we had been camping, I gave the rest of the troops a briefing on the meeting. It was no surprise that everyone was disappointed. They expected the Mexican police to jump right on it. And the DEA games pissed them off. Plus our suggestions that we get a search warrant for the cell phones were met with pessimism. This just wasn't going to happen in Juarez. It was a challenge to remain optimistic.

Fortunately we had included Lt. Dennis Slocum in our traveling entourage. Denny was in charge of the sheriff's contingent of investigators. Besides being an outstanding investigator, he was our in house comedian. When the frustration level rose, Denny would entertain the troops with X-rated stories from his days working vice and the demented escapades of bored deputies working the night shift in the county jail. His description and then demonstration of how he taught his potbellied pig to eat bacon from his mouth while he laid on the living room floor was worthy of an invitation from Jay Leno for the *Tonight Show*. He was a Caucasian Chris Rock. Insightful, insensitive, politically incorrect, and incredibly funny. When all else failed, Denny always had another story and another laugh.

After waiting two days and hearing nothing from the Comandante or DEA we tried another avenue. Feeling stonewalled, we called our Legal Attache (Legat) in Mexico City and requested that the matter be presented to the Mexican Attorney General. This was a dangerous request because it "back doored" the Juarez Comandante, suggesting we had no confidence in him. If we offended him, he could stop any efforts to help us. But we felt he had left us no choice. When the DEA guys heard we had called for help in Mexico City they went ballistic. What the hell were we thinking? Didn't we know what this would do to their relations with the Comandante? Goddamn FBI fools! I tried to explain our frustration with the lack of results but it was useless. From then on DEA backed away from us and they seemed to be too busy and distracted to provide an update from the Comandante on his efforts. We lost their help completely.

And they were right. A few days after the Legat in Mexico City contacted the attorney general, a flying squad of kidnapping specialists arrived in Juarez. Supposedly they were not connected to any of the corruption or bribery going on in Juarez and would be able to handle the investigation impartially. Right. DEA reported that when the Comandante heard about their arrival (which was probably before they arrived), he informed DEA that he would have nothing further to do with this FBI investigation. And to twist the knife a little more, he reported that he had developed some significant leads, but that now he would not work with the American FBI. We had put all our money on some "out of town" cops who were strangers in Juarez whose efforts would probably be thwarted by the jealous Juarez Comandante.

We began to feel that all was lost and the negotiators were beginning to melt down. They were not only tiring of saying the same thing several times each day to the kidnappers, but they had begun to obsess on the possibility that they had been discovered and that they were being watched in anticipation of a rip-off. They had become more and more paranoid about being watched and followed. Suddenly everyone in the hotel coffee shop looked suspicious. Maybe the maintenance guy working on the hallway air conditioner, the front desk receptionist, and the maids were working for the cartel. The couple lying in the sun out around the pool. It felt like we were in a netherworld. We lost track of time and the days. We were all feeling the pressure.

Terry and I sat in his office morosely watching the sun go down. Fortunately he didn't have a bottle of scotch in his desk. We would have abused it.

"C'mon," he said, "Let's take a drive."

An hour later we were back standing on the levee staring at Ciudad Juarez. Although the tech guys had made a couple hits during the phone calls, they had never been close enough to pinpoint a location from the American side of the border. We were going to have to go into Juarez with the electronic gear and hope for a hit. The alternative was to just sit on our hands and wait for something to happen. Unfortunately, this breakdown of negotiations could typically result in the victim being held for months, and sometimes eventually killed.

Mexico can be a lawless place and the Mexican cops consider due process an American joke. American travelers sometimes assume that if they get into trouble in a foreign country, the State Department will simply bail them out. Not true. Foreigners in Mexico can spend weeks in jail for having been involved in a traffic accident in which they were not at fault. Possession of guns can result in a ten-year jail sentence. They don't even want American cops to have guns. Terry related the story about an El Paso patrol cop pursuing a stolen vehicle that headed for the border. Once across and stopped, he received the same treatment as the car thief. His patrol vehicle and weapon were confiscated, and he was jailed for several hours while they confirmed his identity and police officer status. They eventually released the officer and returned the patrol vehicle the next day, but he never saw his gun again. So here we were planning to send a dozen unarmed American agents into Juarez to arrest Mexican citizens.

When I announced our intention the next day to take the tech vans into Juarez I was met with a rebellion by the troops. "No fucking way. We're not going into Mexico."

Most of the sheriff's guys were anxious and ready to go. They were convinced it was the only alternative other than just walking away from the whole thing and returning to LA. But the agents balked, citing the threat of police corruption and Mexican injustice. I was reminded of the DEA agents kidnapped and tortured by Mexican police in the mid eighties. One, Kiki Camerena, had been killed in 1985 when he became involved in a police corruption case in Guadalajara. The discussion turned nasty, especially when the FBI El Paso Assistant SAC announced that any agent refusing to go into Juarez would be considered a coward and sent back to LA immediately. This offended everyone and several guys blew up. We discussed various scenarios and security for the operation. But the troops had legitimate concerns. Mexico was a dangerous place. And the cops really couldn't be trusted to take care of us—especially those who had flown in from Mexico City. We argued all day. Eventually they relented and finally agreed to the operational plan, but it was ugly. When we later got back to LA, some regretted some of the things that were said during the meeting.

We would take two electronic equipped vans and three vehicles into Juarez in the late afternoon and early evening— the kidnappers calls were the most prevalent from 5–9 PM— accompanied by armed Spanish-speaking federales who were staged in a Juarez hotel. If we were able to lock on to a cell phone and pinpoint the location, the federales would jump out and make the arrest. The American law enforcement officers would never leave the vans or the vehicles. No Americans would drive a vehicle or carry a weapon. The subjects would remain in custody of the federales in Mexico, who would conduct the interrogations. FBI agents would not conduct or be present during the interrogations.

That night we set up the caravan and crept toward the border full of anticipation. The border crossings into Mexico are an incredible sensory experience. Lines and more lines. Lines of cars, lines of pedestrians, lights, uniformed police officers and customs officials, Mexican and American, fences, and barbed wire. Hordes of people. Many who crossed the border daily were employees of the foreign-owned assembly plants in Juarez and were called *maquiladoras*. The U.S. Customs department estimates that over four hundred and fifty thousand pedestrians and three hundred and fifty thousand vehicles cross the El Paso/ Juarez border each month. With all these potential mules, it's no wonder that the dopers can routinely smuggle tons of cocaine over the border every day. Frankly, I found it amazing that the Mexicans could show any interest in what was entering their country. After all, these are the people who accept our illegally dumped toxic waste if the price is right, regardless of the threat to the welfare of its citizens. Ciudad Juarez didn't disappoint me. It was a wasted city. We finally managed to enter after about an hour in line without encountering any problems.

We rendezvoused at the downtown hotel being used by the federales. Once inside we walked into a suite of rooms loaded with lounging Mexican policemen. Most seemed to be in their mid-twenties and were lying around in their underwear. They all seemed to have gunshot wounds, which they proudly displayed to us, laughingly as only survivors of a gunfight can do. There were also guns of every type lying around the rooms, shotguns, Uzis, MP-5's, M16's, large 9mm semi autos, and pearl handled revolvers. These guys were ready for war. One of the federales was pointed out as "The Interrogator." He was a dark-skinned Indian from deep in southern Mexico, who dozed in an easy chair in the corner. Next to his chair was his "tool box," a small silver Samsonite briefcase containing the "equipment" he used to obtain confessions. We didn't ask about the contents. We could imagine. The others laughed about him. They said he was lazy, but very good at his craft. One went over and flicked his finger at his nose to wake him, but he just readjusted himself and continued his nap. We laughed, but only to be polite. Amazing place, Mexico. A federal police "interrogator" could extract confessions through torture but we couldn't get a search warrant for the cell phones used by the kidnappers! God bless America.

After discussing our plans with the team leaders of the federales, we fanned out into the night hoping to get lucky. It was creepy, driving aimlessly around Juarez in the darkness, steering around the street dogs and a million motorcycles, hoping for a hit from the kidnappers, but just as anxious about the confrontation that could follow. We were convinced we wouldn't survive the night without some kind of vehicle accident. The traffic lights seemed to be merely a suggestion for the Mexican drivers. We were also concerned about street crime and a possible carjacking by street thugs. Or an "express kidnapping," where they drag you at gunpoint over to an ATM and force a withdrawal before they whack you and run. I felt very vulnerable venturing out into this strange and frightening world without a weapon.

But the first night in Juarez was dead. No calls. It was like the kidnappers knew we had entered their jungle and they were just watching us from around a corner or behind a building. After several hours we returned to El Paso, more frustrated and pissed than ever. For weeks they had insisted we come to Juarez, and now that we had arrived, they had ignored us. It was like they knew. We also wondered if we were being counter-surveilled by the Comandante's officers. After all, it was their town. We were convinced that they knew we were here and they resented it. We wondered if they would conspire with the kidnappers to turn a ransom payoff into a shootout.

The next day we did the same thing and about 4 PM we got lucky. The kidnappers were on the line to the negotiators back in El Paso. The tech guys jumped on their computers and began to triangulate the call. Minutes passed with them continuing to instruct the drivers. Keep going straight, go left, keep going, slow down, try a right here, stop, wait a minute, Okay, keep going. Within minutes we were outside a small restaurant. Thinking the kidnappers were inside, our federale immediately radioed his leader back at the hotel. He acknowledged the message, but advised that he needed additional officers. Minutes passed. Nothing. Then almost an hour. Where were the reinforcements? The kidnappers had hung up. Dammit. Our guys started to get anxious about staying in the area. Had they been made by the bad guys? Could they see us outside the restaurant? Our federale refused to go into the restaurant alone. He kept talking on his radio, but gave us little explanation.

After another fruitless hour, we gave up and drove back to the hotel. I walked inside and confronted the boss of the federales.

"Where the hell were you? We thought we had them located."

"It was siesta time," he responded. "My officers were resting."

Siesta! From mid to late afternoon it was siesta time, when the federales relax and sleep, read girlie magazines, and watch TV. That's why they didn't respond when we called for them. I couldn't believe it. After all these plans, with the kidnappers possibly cornered, the federales were taking a goddamn siesta!

Crossing back into El Paso later I became more depressed about the way this thing was going. There was no end in sight. It was becoming more and more difficult to keep up the spirits of the guys I had brought over from LA. It was also becoming more difficult for me as the leader of our entourage. They expected me to solve this case—to find the victims. But we couldn't just walk away from this thing. We had two innocent kidnapping victims who had never asked for this. They were out there, somewhere, waiting for someone to come and take them back home.

The next night we drove down into Juarez again and set up near the location where we had been the night before. Shortly before 10 PM we got another hit. The kidnappers were back on the line and the tech guys thought they had them located. But they kept moving. We then started a slow-motion vehicle pursuit that lasted for over an hour but never seemed to really bring us closer to the kidnappers. We knew they were out there, but they remained elusive and seemed to be just one step or a block ahead of us. Eventually they disconnected. We waited another hour for them to call back, but when they didn't we decided to shut it down. Frustrated with failure, we sat in line waiting to cross back into El Paso, watching the border insanity, but too tired to be amused anymore. At least we didn't get the siesta excuse this time.

The next day we met with the El Paso ASAC to review the game plan. He wanted to pull out his personnel. Whatever we had tried wasn't working and we had exhausted his resources. We finally decided to go back to beating the political bushes again from Mexico City. So we placed a call to the Legat in Mexico City and requested that the Mexican Attorney General continue to push the A.G. in the state of Chihuahua, as well as the Comandante in Juarez. Then we sat back to wait. I gave the troops the day off to visit the Laundromat, shop for cowboy boots, and go to a movie.

Two days later I was sitting in Terry Kincaid's office trying to decide on a productive investigative strategy when the phone rang. It was an American Border Patrol officer at the checkpoint.

"I've got an African-American female in my office who says she was kidnapped from South Gate, California. You guys interested in talking to her?"

Terry laughed, "Ah, the pressure of being a government official. Somebody just couldn't stand the heat." We had apparently made it uncomfortable enough for those in charge to force the cartel to release the victims.

Within minutes agents Mark Wilson and Peggy Smith were on their way to the border to take custody of the victim. An hour later, Louie's aunt was telling her story to the rest of us in the FBI office. She said they had promised to release her niece the next day because it was too risky to bring them both to the border together. They had initially been held in a condo in Palm Springs and then taken to El Paso. The kidnappers seemed to know all the intricacies of the border screening and procedures— they had passed through within minutes—and brought them to a ranch in Juarez. No, they hadn't been abused or mistreated, and as a matter of fact, the female who took care of them in Juarez had been very nice. The aunt had even picked up a little Spanish and some Mexican recipes. Oh, and another thing. As she left they told her to remind Louie that he still owed the five million, and that they'd be coming back to LA again to collect from him. I imagined that Louie had changed his name six times by now and moved to Timbuktu. He knew his normal his life cycle was in jeopardy. He had run off with their five million dollars, and more significantly he had disrespected them, and they had been forced to capitulate. They would kill him now, regardless of whether he repaid the debt. Probably slowly and painfully.

A few hours later the Border Patrol called again and confirmed that the young girl was also in their custody. Within hours Mark had made arrangements for them both to be flown back to LA together. We briefly interviewed them in El Paso but neither was able to describe where they had been held in Juarez and their descriptions of the kidnappers were so general they were useless. We would conduct a more detailed briefing for the two victims back in LA. So we quickly shuttled them to the airport with a large squad of agents and officers. It hadn't taken the troops long to check out of the motel. They had probably been packed and ready to leave for days.

I remained in El Paso for another day to settle the administrative and financial matters. It had been a long nine weeks and although it had not culminated in the arrest of the kidnappers, we were convinced that our efforts had finally convinced them to release the victims. We had also crept into the backyard of the cartel and poked at them with a stick, a very dangerous thing to do, and survived. It was an anti-climactic resolution to a long exercise in frustration, but we took it and ran.

Once back in LA, everyone, with the exception of Mark Wilson, quickly returned to their normal investigative assignments and tried to forget Louie, El Paso, the federales, and the infamous Amado Carrillo Fuentes. Mark, though, hung on to it and after a couple years he identified the kidnappers, who had been later arrested by DEA in an unrelated dope deal. As usual someone started talking. More of the details surfaced but really didn't change anything. It was just another dope kidnapping, too difficult and uninteresting to prosecute. Nobody went to jail.

Then in 1997, the cartel took a major hit when, at the age of forty-one, Carrillo died in a Mexico City operating room while undergoing surgery to change his appearance. Despite positive identification of fingerprints by DEA, the rumors persisted that he had survived and his death remained controversial. Everyone had a theory or explanation as to why it really wasn't Carrillo's body. Probably the best confirmation that Carrillo had actually died, however, were the dozens of drug related deaths in Juarez in the weeks following his reported death, as the various players flexed their muscles to replace the Lord of the Skies.

Carrillo was later given a huge funeral in his hometown of Guamuchilito, Sinoloa, where he was considered Robin Hood because of all the gifts he gave to the townspeople, including a local church. In a *Los Angeles Times* article, one of his hometown friends recalled, "He was a simple man who loved baseball and enchiladas stuffed with hot red chile." Joining in with another tribute, a local Chihuahua police officer said, "As far as we know, he has not committed or been a part of any illegal activities here."

CHAPTER 18

THE PSYCHEDELIC SHOWER

It was in one of those shit-box hotels down on Pico Boulevard, just west of downtown Los Angeles—the kind with a drunk sleeping one off in the lobby and "Cash Only" or vouchers for the rooms. The hallways always smelled like piss, the clerk always looked like a pervert, and you took your chances with the elevator. This one also had a notice asking for blood donors taped to the wall by the stairs. A place where people paid cash and kept to themselves. For a guy from Las Vegas wanted for beating the dog shit out of his girlfriend, it was a perfect place to cool off. So it made sense that's where they found Angelo Carrera early that June morning in 1995.

FBI agent Scott Hanley and LAPD Investigator Bob Vanina walked up the ten flights instead of taking a chance on the elevator. Years of experience in the Chicago projects had taught Hanley to never get caught in a dead elevator and leave yourself vulnerable to being shot or someone throwing gas on you and firebombing the thing. By the time they got to ten both were winded. They waited for a couple minutes, catching their breath, getting the lay of the land, and checking for the right room before moving on. Both had pulled their guns by the time they hit the eighth floor.

They stood outside the steel plated door and looked at the key that the dirt bag at the front desk had given them. Their

225

hearts were pumping. You never knew what was on the other side of that door. Maybe nothing. Maybe he was out buying more dope or sticking up another 7-Eleven. Maybe he was passed out on the couch in a drunken stupor or OD'd with a needle hanging out of his arm. Maybe he was rolling around in the sack getting a Lewinsky from a local hooker. And then again, if you didn't move fast enough, maybe the guy inside with the gun would get the drop on you. I had a good friend get shot in the face that way. The asshole beat him to the draw. So it was normal for them to pucker up a bit. Heads you win. Tails you die.

For a moment they listened for any sound. TV. Radio. Snoring. Breathing. A newspaper rattle. Water running. Toilet flush. Anything to confirm the room was occupied. They heard nothing.

Hanley inserted the key into the lock and slowly turned it. The shifting pins clanked like Big Ben, making way too much noise. Immediately realizing they had lost surprise, he spun the key and rotated the door handle. The door moved in, but much too slowly. It was too heavy, maybe blocked by something. As they glanced into the room, they saw Carerra coming off the couch with a large revolver in his right hand.

In an instant, realizing that neither he nor Vanina had a clear shot, Hanley jerked the door shut and spun away from it, expecting to draw fire from inside. They heard Carerra moving around but he hadn't fired. They both backed down the hall while pointing their guns at the door. Hanley yelled the usual "FBI, come out with your hands up" stuff a couple times but received no response from inside. They waited quietly a few minutes. The silence throbbed. Nothing happened.

Leaving Vanina covering the door, Hanley eased himself down a few steps on the stairs and pulled out his cell phone. He turned to the side and called FBI dispatch.

"We need some help down here," he said. "We've got an A&D [armed and dangerous] fugitive wanted for attempted murder barricaded in his hotel room. Call SWAT."

He gave her the address, flipped the phone shut, and rejoined

Vanina leaning against the wall pointing his Beretta 92F 9mm semi-automatic at Carerra's door.

"We fucked up," Vanina whispered. Hanley nodded and smiled grimly. Then they tried to get comfortable while they waited for the cavalry. Hanley kept talking but received little response from Carrera, who told them to just go away. It was a long thirty minutes before the first SWAT agents started to arrive.

By the time I got there, an army had assembled in the street. This included patrol officers and investigators from the Rampart Division of the LAPD as well as FBI SWAT agents and the suits from both agencies. Because an armed suspect had a tenth floor view of Pico Boulevard and could fire down on it, LAPD had closed down the street. They had also offered the services of their SWAT team, which we immediately declined. Fuck LAPD. This one was going to be ours.

The arriving FBI SWAT agents suited up, assembled, and then began to work their way into positions on the tenth floor on either side of Carerra's room. They began to quietly evacuate the floor one apartment at a time. It took an hour before they were ready for the negotiators.

When I finally made it up to the tenth floor I ran into Hanley, who apologized. These are tough situations and he felt they probably should have fired on him instead of pulling out. This kind of second-guessing can gnaw at you. Bottom line, no one had been hurt. Yet.

We didn't know much about Carerra other than he had attempted to kill his girlfriend in Las Vegas. Unfortunately, many times you really don't have much on these guys and you have to just start talking. And hope that he'll give you something or your investigators come up with something you can use. We had time, though, as he was contained and there was no indication of other occupants that could be potential hostages. The SWAT team had finally completed the evacuation of the other apartments on the floor while Hanley kept trying to talk to him, yelling through the door. Hanley was a relatively new negotiator and I thought this was a good opportunity for him so I let him continue attempting to talk to Carrera.

I listened to him for a while, but eventually it became apparent that the conversation wasn't going anywhere. Carrera was argumentative and kept telling Hanley he "hadn't done anything." He admitted his identity but denied the beating, shooting into her house, and insisted that he was innocent. It was all a big misunderstanding. He refused to discuss coming out. It was frustrating, but at least we knew we had the right guy.

After a while Hanley started wearing down and I replaced him with a female negotiator, but when Carerra started referring to his former girlfriend as a "cunt" and capped off two rounds through the side of the door I pulled her out and moved in Hank Orzinski. Hank was an easygoing, round-faced guy who always had the worried look of a young kid hoping for approval from his older brother. I figured if anyone could bring this guy out, Hank could.

The negotiators worked while huddled right next to the SWAT team, and they were forced to yell through the door. Although extremely dangerous, there was no other way to do it. The room had no telephone and there was no access point to throw in a hostage phone. We thought about lowering one from the floor above but figured Carerra would be afraid to open the window and face the snipers. After he fired into the hallway we backed off a bit, though. It was more tiring for the negotiators to be yelling from a distance but much safer. Orzinski wasn't having any more luck than Hanley. Carrera just wouldn't budge. There were long periods of no response.

Hours passed and he continued to refuse to discuss coming out. Carerra offered no indication of what he wanted to do, and made no threats or demands. He had resisted providing any personal information. Our negotiation assessment was that nothing positive had been accomplished other than he was still talking to us periodically. But we hadn't progressed to anything to suggest that he was going to give it up. He hadn't talked about suicide, but since he hadn't asked for anything we had to figure he was probably considering it. He had very few options and escape was not one of them. He could just play this out for a while but we weren't going to go away. Eventually he had to accept that fact. Walk out. Or do himself in. We tried to minimize his Vegas crime and stressed a positive outcome. But he wouldn't have any part of it. He was just pissed that the FBI had found him and that he was now jammed.

About four hours and three negotiators into this thing with no positive results, I huddled with Hanley, SWAT team leader Bob Rattelman and the suits. Our consensus was that negotiations were not productive and that Carerra deserved a little stimulation. Eventually we all concurred with Rat's recommendation to insert pepper spray into the apartment.

Pepper spray is some mean shit. Also called "OC" (from Oleoresin Capsicum), the main ingredient is capsaicin derived from chilies. It's classified as a non-lethal chemical weapon, which means the Marines can't use it in Baghdad, but it's okay for all the cops in America (as well as in a diluted form available to soccer moms at the Arco minimart.) The U.S. Postal Service was the first agency to use it in the 1980s as a dog repellant. Law enforcement and correctional agencies rapidly adopted it for use in subduing unarmed but violent suspects. Law enforcement grade OC can be three hundred times as strong as a jalapeño pepper. A good hit makes your eyes snap shut instantly, your face burns like it has been firebombed, your throat clogs up, and your breathing becomes difficult. Your lungs burn and lots of runny stuff starts coming out of your nose. Psychologically it produces confusion, claustrophobia, and panic—usually followed by compliance. Like I say, it's some mean shit.

SWAT took a large pressurized container of OC similar to a fire extinguisher and snaked the small hose under the door. As soon as he heard the hissing, however, Carerra packed wet towels under the door, minimizing the amount he received. It also backed up the gas into the hallway with the SWAT team and negotiators, chasing the suits out of the hallway and into the stairwell down a couple floors. Huddled against the wall, the negotiators had all masked up with the SWAT guys, but this significantly reduced our communication. It's pretty hard to carry on a conversation when your voice sounds like you're talking through a sweat sock. By now we had concluded that the "make nice" stage of the negotiations were over. He had become much less responsive with long periods of silence but we didn't know whether it was the gas or his attitude. I pulled the negotiators back and we watched the SWAT team from the head of the stairs.

This is a bad time. When the suspect stops talking, he's usually putting together his plan of action. He may shoot (or simulate shooting) a hostage to get your attention or force you to give him something. He may come out shooting, or he may commit suicide. He may be waiting for the SWAT guys to come in after him. Or he may just be sitting inside trying to figure out how the hell to get out of this thing and save face. A lot of these guys start something without an exit plan. Sometimes they'll let you help them out of the situation, so you try offering them something you really can give them. Saving face is huge; sometimes just promising a private surrender will do. Sometimes you just have to wait.

We waited.

Another hour crept by. Finally SWAT decided to breach the door to introduce more concentrated OC. Using shotgun delivered impact rounds designed for high impact but low penetration, two SWAT agents fired at the door hinges while others kicked open the door. Although Carerra had barricaded furniture against the door, they forced it open and fired more OC into the room. The entry team lined up along the wall and waited for the pepper spray to work.

The rank smell of violence billowed out of the apartment like thick smoke. We all choked on it. This one was going to go down hard.

More minutes passed with no movement. The SWAT team waited. Then we all heard a single muffled shot.

Still, everyone waited patiently. There was no need to hurry now.

After a few minutes, one of the SWAT guys crawled up to the door and slowly scanned the room with a small periscope. Without backing out, he shook his head slowly.

The entry team edged closer to the door.

Suddenly the SWAT agents tossed a flash-bang diversion device into the room. Immediately after the explosion the entry team rushed into the apartment.

A minute later one of the SWAT guys poked his head out of the apartment and motioned to me. Still masked I walked cautiously into the contaminated apartment and then into the bathroom.

Carerra was slumped down on his heels in the shower. He had put a .357 caliber revolver in his mouth and pulled the trigger. Skull, hair, and brains had been blown into the ceiling and ricocheted onto all four walls of the shower. It was a stunning, bright red graphic. And amazingly symmetrical. Psychedelic. One hand held the gun loosely on his chest. He looked about thirty, maybe thirty-five. Inside the shower it felt wet, blood still misting in the air.

I backed out and looked around the sparsely furnished room. He hadn't left much. Two handguns, two containers of gasoline (we never did figure that out), a little over seven thousand dollars in cash, and a short suicide note instructing Hanley to give his personal effects to Goodwill, or to his family if he could find them. It ended with a "thanks" and his signature.

Another short life.

I walked outside into the hallway. Fortunately the gas was still strong enough to keep the suits away for a while longer.

The huge exhaust fans set up by the fire department soon went to work, and after the gas dissipated a bit, the officer-involved shooting (OIS) teams from the FBI and the LAPD arrived and surveyed the scene.

They immediately got into it. Like always.

Rich Noyes, the agent in charge of the FBI's shooting investigation team, walked into the apartment, took one look in the shower, and walked back out.

"It's LAPD's," he declared.

Noyes was an old-time Hoover agent born and raised in the Big Sky country of Montana—where the rubber meets the road, the men are men, and the sheep are nervous, as he always said.

He wore wire rimmed glasses and an outdated comb over, but he had a set of hammers and was as strong as an ox. He was our own Dick Butkus. Pretty much everything was black and white to Noyes. He was a real no-bullshit guy, and if you hesitated crashing through a door for a fugitive, he'd run over your back. He never really seemed to be afraid of anything, although he did admit to being cautious around grizzly bears. Nobody intimidated him, especially LAPD's big guns from the robbery-homicide division who handled the officer-involved shootings. He loved butting heads with LAPD.

Noyes refused to assume responsibility, stating that the FBI had not fired a weapon at the suspect. As far as he was concerned it was just another piece-of-shit suicide in the City of Angels, making it LAPD's jurisdiction. The crime scene and the body were theirs—along with the crime scene clean up and a lengthy death investigation. Angelo Carrera was just another out of state fugitive and statistic.

The senior homicide detective from LAPD's Rampart Division responded with a "fuck you, FBI" and insisted that the whole operation from the get-go had been an FBI caper and that it was our responsibility to conduct the entire investigation.

I watched the argument with amusement. Occasionally they took a break and let their partners continue the argument like a tag team match. They snorted, postured, and tried to intimidate each other like two welterweights getting instructions from the referee before the fight. Sorting out who was going to do what at an OIS scene was always a turf battle. It involved important investigative decisions, and each agency had to protect its interests and liability. And of course it could be very important to the officers involved if a case eventually went to court. And they all do.

By the time the coroner's people arrived and pulled the gurney into the apartment, Noyes and the LAPD detective had finally decided who was going to do what and had shaken hands in agreement. Like always. Until the next one.

I was disappointed that we had lost this guy. An in-your-face death like this always made me think about what's really important, what's worth doing in my own life. I had recently become eligible for retirement and I found myself looking back over the years. There comes a time in every man's life when he realizes he won't get drafted by the Dallas Cowboys, he isn't going to be president, and he's never going to become a millionaire. It's a sobering realization. Is this as good as it's going to get? Maybe it was time to try something else, something really simple. Maybe go up to Oregon and grow Christmas trees. Or build a cabin in northern Michigan and hire out as an Orvis fishing guide. Something without guns.

I walked slowly down the stairs alone, seriously thinking it may be time to pull the pin and throw in my papers. I knew Robbin would certainly be receptive and supportive. She had never been able to push aside the worry about all the shit that could happen out there in the streets. Maybe it was finally time to walk away from all this emotional debris before I completely lost my mind.

CONCLUSION

I walked outside the restaurant into the rain and watched them happily say their goodbyes before driving off. I'd just attended the annual holiday luncheon of the Los Angeles FBI's crisis negotiation team in the crowded back room of a little Italian place on the north side of the city. Except for the presence of a couple dozen agents, it was the kind of place Tony Soprano would have been comfortable in. It was packed with all the new people and a few of the old-timers. I noticed there were more female agents and fewer of Mr. Hoover's "regular white guys" than in my day. In fact, the team these days looked like the United Nations. I thought that was a good thing. A lot of things had changed since I walked out of the FBI twelve years ago.

We had shared a lot of laughter and war stories during lunch along with the pasta, garlic bread, and tomato sauce. Surrounded by the new kids periodically texting into their Blackberrys, I felt old—really old. I remembered the early days when I'd sometimes driven all over LA looking for a public phone that wasn't trashed and how it took me days to master my first cell phone. I looked around the room at the retired elders. Sonny Benavidez, still recovering American hostages held around the world, but now for a large private security corporation instead of the FBI. Scott Hanley, who had been one of my SWAT partners, had gone on to become a local prosecutor in the D.A.'s office. And Kevin Kelly, the man who had provided the organization and structure for the hostage team in LA in its formative years, still working in law enforcement. I was proud of how this revolutionary concept and this team of talented people had evolved since we struggled to put it together in the late '70s.

Meeting the rookies bursting with enthusiasm and commitment was invigorating. Some were eagerly awaiting the opportunity to test their negotiation skills in an actual incident and were unscarred by the traumas of this profession, this business of saving lives. I resisted the urge to tell them my war stories, to share with them my emotional scars. Instead I listened to what they had to say about the Bureau, the new priorities and technology, their career expectations, the counterterrorism challenges, and above all, the lifetime friendships that were forming. I found them inspiring, but I also sadly realized that their innocence and naiveté wouldn't last. Not in this business. There was too much tragedy and heartbreak.

The FBI had given me a passport to invade the personal lives of many over the years. I'd become involved with religious megalomaniacs, misguided skyjackers, end-of-the-road losers, racist bigots and white separatists, desperate and violent prison inmates, failed bank robbers, vicious kidnappers, societal misfits, and run of the mill scoundrels. Their lives were tales of failure and survival, pathos and hysteria.

David Koresh took six dozen innocents with him to a fiery grave in Waco. The life of Luis, a prison hostage, was spared for reasons unknown to him or to me. Patty Hearst recovered from the violent brainwashing of a militant group, married her bodyguard, and became an author, an actor, and a happy mother. Rodney King won the lottery but squandered it away in a life of desperation. Robert Mathews died a fiery death along with his evil dreams for an Aryan nation. Randy Weaver lost his wife, his son, and his dog because he was too stubborn to accept the authority of the United States government. The cherished toddler of a young couple was returned to them unharmed after a week with his kidnapper. The families of FBI agents Jack Coler and Ron Williams killed in South Dakota during the uprising at

Wounded Knee still grieve for them just as the family of Buddy Lamont, the American Indian also killed there, grieves for him. Leonard Peltier, convicted of killing the two agents, remains in federal prison while his supporters and his detractors continue their bitter argument about his guilt or innocence. The Mexican drug cartels continue their vicious violence against anyone who challenges their existence and criminal activities. And the FBI's Crisis Incident Negotiation Team perseveres in its mission of saving American lives around the world.

The FBI, or "the Bureau" as those inside call it, rumbles through our lives like a late-night train on its way to who knows where. Seeing the opportunity, we scramble aboard and take the ride for a while. And then, somewhere down the line, when our time is over and we step down, the train continues on with others who take our place. Hopefully, we've used this opportunity to improve the lives of others. My twenty-five-year ride was the thrill of my life.

ABOUT THE AUTHOR

Jim Botting was born and raised in Grand Rapids, Michigan. He received a Bachelors Degree in psychology from Calvin College, a Masters Degree in police administration from Michigan State University, and another Masters Degree in counseling psychology from California State University at Northridge. After serving in the U.S. Army as a platoon leader in Vietnam, he became an investigator for the U.S. Treasury Department in Cincinnati. He transferred to the FBI in 1971 and was assigned briefly to offices in Mississippi before moving to the Los Angeles office, where he spent most of his career in its Violent Crimes and Major Offenders Program. He also served twelve years in the LA office's SWAT program and seventeen years as a hostage negotiator. Botting received numerous awards for valor and meritorious service from the director of the FBI and from the special agent in charge of the FBI in Los Angeles.

Following the end of his FBI service in 1995, Botting became the vice president of corporate security for MGM Studios in Los Angeles and then the chief of police of the Ventura County Community College District. He has published articles on kidnapping/hostage negotiation and workplace violence, as well as consulted with business, industry, and government about the prevention and management of threats and violence in the workplace. In 2007 he was inducted into the Wall of Fame at the

School of Police Administration and Criminal Justice at Michigan State University.

Botting remains involved in policing, conducting investigations of cold homicide cases for the local county sheriff's office. He is married with three adult children and resides with his wife, Robbin, in Southern California. Whenever possible, although never often enough, he can be found fly-fishing on a trout stream in the high Sierras of Northern California.